W9-BFB-135

COMPACT
CITY

COMPACT CITY

CITY

A PLAN FOR A LIVEABLE URBAN ENVIRONMENT

George B. Dantzig   Thomas L. Saaty

W. H. FREEMAN AND COMPANY
SAN FRANCISCO

Cover Photo

David Powers/Jeroboam Inc.

Copyright © 1973 by W. H. Freeman and Company

No part of this book may be reproduced by any mechanical,
photographic, or electronic process, or in the form of a
phonographic recording, nor may it be stored in a retrieval
system, transmitted, or otherwise copied for public or
private use without written permission from the publisher.

Printed in the United States of America

Library of Congress Catalog Card Number: 73–8679
International Standard Book Number: 0–7167–0784–5 (cloth)
0–7167–0794–2 (paper)

9   8   7   6   5   4   3   2   1

PREFACE

Compact City is about finding better ways to develop urban areas. Our presentation is purposely introductory, and we have included many illustrations, in the hope that such a presentation will influence as many people as possible of the need for change in the way cities are built. The book begins with a warning that if we continue to expand cities or to rebuild them along conventional lines, we can expect that various urban crises will continue to plague us. Among these are shortages of energy, growth of slums, and increased congestion and pollution. The problem is of international as well as national concern, for citizens of this country are faced with a question: Can the United States preserve and extend a high and spacious standard of living in a world where populations are ever increasing, and where all seek to match our standards by taking more and more of their fair share of the world's nonrenewable resources?

After sounding the warning, we review some of the solutions notable urban planners have proposed for controlling city growth, and point out that computers can be expected to help in future planning because they can be applied to socioeconomic as well as physical aspects of complex urban systems. Our studies show that many urban improvements can be achieved by making more effective use of both the vertical dimension and—through around-the-clock use of urban facilities—the time dimension. To illustrate the feasibility and the advantages of making cities more "four-dimensional," we make a specific proposal based on present-day technology. We will show that through implementation of this proposal, many urban problems that currently plague us could be bypassed.

Our book is the outgrowth of efforts by the authors to understand an altogether strange institution: the human settlement. In 1968 we decided to gain as much knowledge as we could about city planning methods; our previous experience had been with the planning methods of large organizations. To learn firsthand about urban problems, one of us went to work temporarily for a group whose main concern was with socioeconomic aspects of the city, including its underprivileged residents and its slum neighborhoods. We made dozens of contacts with people who are knowledgeable about every aspect of city operations, ranging from distinguished architects to air-conditioning experts, from cement industry people to elevator and transportation engineers, economists, social workers, sociologists, city planners, seismologists, waste-removal engineers, environmental conservationists, and indoor plant experts.

While writing the book, we actively sought out individuals who could serve as devil's advocates; we debated with them and learned from their criticisms, going back to the drawing board many times to revise and to redevelop our ideas.

We hope that the many controversial ideas presented in this book will be a starting point for debate. America has a history of accepting challenges and has the means to improve its cities.

George B. Dantzig and Thomas L. Saaty

September 1973

ACKNOWLEDGMENTS

The criticisms, reactions, and ideas of many people molded this book. For the following assistance, we are particularly grateful to the people mentioned here:

Drawings:

John Lange (architect), Barbara Alexander, Tom Nakaiye, Daniele Nedzela, Donna Salmon, Kelly Solis-Navarro, Robin Chiang

Critical reading:

Alan Manne, Frank and Irma Adelman, Olaf Helmer, Charis Taylor, Oliver Yu, Jane Bavelas, Malcolm Levin

Secretarial assistance:

Gail Lemmond, Marilyn Dalick, Junne Rock, Carollyn Kufis, Sheila Hill

General reading:

Eric Anschutz, Richard Brumberg, Robert Dowling, I. Heller, Shui Ho, Michel Nedzela, Rozann W. Saaty, Francisco Sagasti, Gabor Strasser, Kenneth Webb

Suggestions on construction and systems:

John W. Fondahl, William P. Scott, Sidney Shore, David A. Wallace

Suggestions on recycling:

Nathan Buras, Timothy Corcoran, C. Roger Glassey, Robert B. Gordon, James W. Sawyer, Judith L. Sloss, Fred Smith, John T. Winneberger

Suggestions on health care:

Morris F. Collen, Sidney R. Garfield, John R. Goldsmith, Charles Flagle, Arlin Torbett

Suggestions on transportation:

Robert Ratner, Howard I. Simkowitz, Rudeger Ventker

Suggestions on ghettos, indoor plants, finance, energy, respectively:

Paul Bradford, K. L. Goldsberry, Nelson Lipshutz, Michael P. Tinkleman

CONTENTS

Part One

THE
PROPOSAL

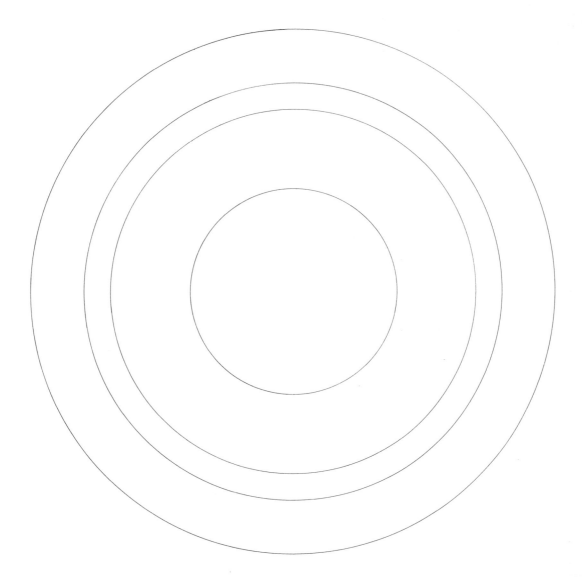

The need to redesign urban areas arises out of the dynamics of change in today's cities. Change is taking place rapidly, but is it change for the better? In Chapter 1, Why Compact City?, we discuss the nature and consequences — good and bad — of overgrowth, and we develop some of the challenges and objectives to strive for in deciding what form future cities should take. In Chapter 2, we proceed to give a short review of solutions to uncontrolled urban growth that have been proposed by well-known urban planners. Here we also introduce two principles which form the central theme for this book — namely, that cities should be designed to make more effective use of the third dimension (vertical space) and the time dimension (around-the-clock use of urban facilities).

Utilizing these two principles, we outline a general structural plan for a proposed city in Chapter 3 and a plan for its transportation system in Chapter 4. In Chapter 5, It's a Bargain, we estimate some dollar costs in the new city and compare these with costs of facilities in today's cities. We then point out, in Chapter 6, the advantages of a compact city of the kind we have outlined. We believe that it is possible to have a spacious, low-density city that is more convenient for its residents and safer for its children — and at lower costs — than are today's cities: a city which, at the same time, causes little disruption of the ecosystem and minimizes use of natural resources. Even access to nature would be made easier for residents of the city we envision than it is in cities today.

In Chapter 7, Where Do We Go from Here?, we outline some of the tasks involved toward implementation of the proposed new city.

WHY
COMPACT CITY?

The past is our heritage.
The present, our responsibility.
The future, our challenge.

David de Sola Pool

Generally speaking, the interiors of the dwellings, shops, work facilities and schools within cities are becoming more pleasant places to be, not less so. But several aspects of city life have become dangerous, time consuming, inconvenient, expensive, and unpleasant. Everyone wants to be free of the urban pollution he can directly sense: the smog, smoke, grime, litter, odors, city heat, din, poor water, and the slum conditions. But the environmental degradation associated with urban development can also be measured in terms of disrupted ecosystems and wasteful use of green space and natural resources. Our purpose will be directed towards a redesign of the urban environment so as to be rid of these negative aspects and to preserve and to enhance the qualities of urban life that we (and most of the world) have come to accept as desirable. We want to arrange the city so that it works better — so that neighborhoods become more lively, safe, and relevant for children; and so that the city itself becomes a more exciting center for personal interactions in today's fast-moving world.

1.1 Orchards in Bloom

Let us begin by taking a look at how the dynamic forces have been at work within the past two decades. Touring California's Santa Clara Valley in 1950 was a wonderful experience. Orchards were in bloom. To the east and west rose the coastal mountain ranges, sharp and clear. The valley's business center, San Jose, nestled at the foot of San Francisco Bay, was then a lush farm community of 95,000. But twenty years later, "the mountains are still there but you cannot see them for taco stands and smog."[1] In twenty years San Jose's population has increased to a half a million and is now part of a vast metropolitan belt of over four million people that sweeps for 60 miles up both sides of San Francisco Bay. Passing San Francisco on the west side of the Bay and Oakland on the east side, this metropolitan area extends into the vineyard country to the north and reaches like tentacles towards California's great Central Valley to the east.[2]

Four hundred miles south of the San Francisco Bay Area, a far greater sprawl continues to spread in typical conurbic patterns around Los Angeles. And on the Eastern Seaboard of the United States, from south of Washington, D.C., to north of Boston, sprawls one single megalopolis four hundred miles long and one hundred or so miles wide. See Figure 1-1.

This story of exploding urban areas is a familiar one that is unfolding throughout the United States. Sir Patrick Geddes uses the term *conurbation* to describe the process whereby first unorganized settlements spot themselves along a main highway at some distance from a city; then, between the radiating highways, real estate interests develop a fine grid of "endless rows of little boxes or of larger boxes with picture windows,"[3] and finally there is the back flow of developments which close the gap between the suburbs and the city. Meanwhile the central city, weakened by the flow of its vitality to the suburbs, rots and turns to slums.

All the evidence points to continuation of this exponential growth of urban areas with the possibility that it will not slow down and stabilize until around the year 2000. At that time the ratio of older people to young people will be greater than it is today, perhaps great enough for the mortality of the old to catch up finally with the births of the young. The U.S. Bureau of Census, using conservative assumptions, estimates the U.S. population was 203 million in 1970 and will be 282 million by the year 2000. Less conservative assumptions estimate that population for the year 2000 will run as high as 361 million.[4] Based on these estimates the size of urban areas will increase by at least 40 percent in the period from 1970 to 2000.[5] But population is only one of the causes of urban growth.

Here is a list of a few of the socioeconomic pressures that work to accelerate urban sprawl:

1. Overall increase in population.
2. Movement from the farms to the city.
3. Density of the inner city.
4. Decay of residences around the city core.

---

1. Throughout the book, notes and references appear at the ends of chapters.

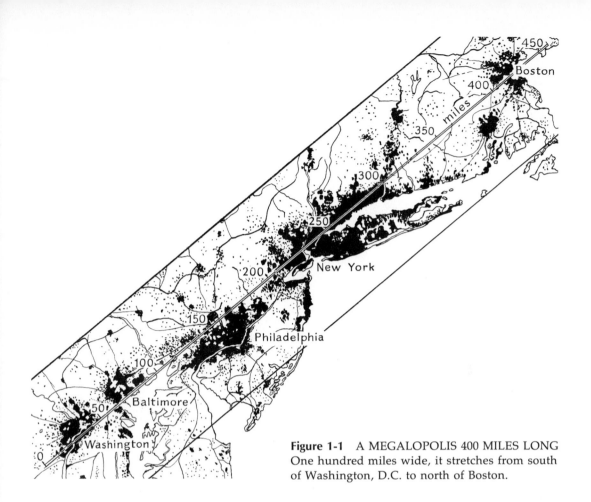

Figure 1-1 A MEGALOPOLIS 400 MILES LONG
One hundred miles wide, it stretches from south
of Washington, D.C. to north of Boston.

5. Rising economic means permitting residents in the inner city to move to suburbs and residents in suburbs to move to larger homes on larger lots.
6. Development of extensive highway systems.
7. The relocation of industry
8. The development of the multicar family.
9. Rising urban transportation problems.

These trends are, of course, interdependent, but once established, they seem to have a life of their own. Thus, possessing more than one car has become a family need beyond the family's need for basic transportation. Not only has the automobile become a symbol of freedom for the young but also for the housewife trapped in her nice suburban home. Another example is the "self-perpetuating spiral" resulting from the policy of using gasoline taxes primarily for highway construction. This makes it feasible to build new tracts of homes farther away from metropolitan centers. This, in turn, leads to greater use of cars and more gasoline taxes to construct more roads, more homes, and so on, in an ever increasing spiral spurred on by population and the other pressures listed above.[6]

Let us now examine some of the consequences of *urban sprawl*. Later we will see how a total-system approach to urban planning might enhance some of the good features of bigness and avoid some of the negative aspects.

1.2 Consequences of Urban Sprawl—Good and Bad

Granted that vast urban sprawls exist and will undoubtedly continue to spread unabated, so what? For many, a suburban ticky-tacky home or apartment is a very comfortable place to be. To those who have recently escaped from the inner city the suburbs are wonderful places indeed! According to Alvin Toffler, author of *Future Shock*, "The working masses in the high-technology societies are totally indifferent to the call for a political revolution aimed at exchanging one form of property ownership for another. For most people the rise in affluence has meant a better, not a worse, existence, and they look upon their much despised 'suburban middle-class lives' as fulfillment rather than deprivation."[7]

But the "fulfillment" Toffler refers to is not free of inconveniences. Some of these inconveniences have come about so gradually that many people have grown to accept them. Take the daily commute. Portal to portal time (the total time a worker spends away from home for employment) varies. Based on an informal spot survey by the authors, moderate income professional workers in the Greater New York metropolitan area now spend three hours a day (on the average) commuting. Typically for the larger cities, about an hour to an hour and a half of the principal wage earner's day is spent in portal-to-portal travel.[8] Mothers spend a good part of each day chauffeuring their children because streets are unsafe, distances have become too far to walk, and because public transportation is too infrequent or is nonexistent. Suburbanites often drive two miles for a pack of cigarettes or a loaf of bread. The decision as to where to shop is often based on the convenience of driving and parking. No one wants to shop (or go to a theater) downtown in big cities any more if it involves the use of an automobile. It's not worth the time and effort to fight the traffic and the parking is too inconvenient and expensive.

Streets are dangerous places. In a metropolitan area with a population of two million there are over 500 traffic deaths and 6,000 injuries per year. Highway accidents have become just another abstract statistic. (For those who measure deaths and serious injuries in dollars, the average losses, including lost future earnings, were estimated in 1970 at about $5,900 per accident. Since there are over one-half million fatalities and serious injuries per year in the U.S., the total economic loss exceeds $3 billion per year.[9]) On the other hand, Americans *are* concerned about battle death statistics. One President concluded he could not be reelected in a year in which battle deaths in Vietnam rose to one third the number of traffic deaths on our highways. (Battle deaths in 1968, the peak year of the Vietnam War, were nearly 15,000, while auto deaths were over 50,000.)

On quiet streets in the suburbs, much time and effort is spent organizing activities to keep small children from getting run over by cars. Often gardens and homes are fenced in for this reason. It is well to reflect on the psychological effect that all this shepherding and isolation must have on the growing child.

The relation of smog to urban sprawl is well known. The more sprawl there is and the more the residential, commercial, recreational, and shopping functions are zoned apart from each other, the greater will be the energy expended in getting people and materials back and forth between them, and so, the greater will be their contribution to air pollution. Everything is interrelated. The question is: What effect do population trends, patterns of urban growth, zoning, and improved exhaust devices or fuel have on air quality? One thing is certain: if there is to be an improvement in air quality under the present governmental approach, it will have to come about by equipping factories with expensive antipollution devices, by modifying the design of cars, by using smaller vehicles and different types of fuels, by curtailing the use of cars and by developing mass transit, and so on. All have a price tag and it means that direct and indirect costs of transportation will be even higher. The direct cost of transportation now runs about 10 percent of the budget of a moderate income family.[10] Later, we will show that alternative designs for urban areas could make more effective use of time and space, and that these would be economically feasible because of the resultant savings in transportation alone.

Most people seem to derive pleasure out of their ability to control an automobile and to drive long distances cheaply and comfortably. To them, the automobile is nothing short of wonderful. It gives freedom to go where and when one chooses. With a car one can live in the most remote of areas. One can go for a ride with a girl friend and park in privacy where there is a lovely view. If people are unhappy, it is not with the automobile per se but with the inconvenience and cost incurred when it needs repair, with the tension of driving on high-speed crowded freeways, with the bumper-to-bumper traffic jams, and with the problems of finding a parking place. Indeed we have become so enamored with the auto that we have gone to great lengths in its behalf. Lewis Mumford,[11] the well-known social philosopher and authority on cities, describes the passion this way:

> The current American way of life is founded not just on motor transportation but on the religion of the motorcar, and the sacrifices that people are prepared to make for this religion stand outside the realm of rational criticism. Perhaps the only thing that could bring Americans to their

senses would be a clear demonstration of the fact that their highway program will, eventually, wipe out the very area of freedom that the private motorcar promised to retain for them.[12]

What Mumford laments is the patchwork planning that allows an auto-based transportation system to displace all other transportation forms. In his book *The Highway and the City* he tries to warn the British not to follow in American footsteps. He cites Oxford, England as an example of a city that has "suffered incredible devastation" from the overuse of the automobile. Mumford predicts that soon the entire British Isles will become a greater Oxford, with an ever increasing number of

> car owners vainly seeking to escape, at a high speed that turns into a crawl, into a countryside that no longer exists. . . . Cities, in turn, will be transformed into extravagant parking lots; and before you awaken from this nightmare you may, if you ignore the experience of Los Angeles, Detroit, Boston, and a hundred other American centers, dismantle the one kind of transportation that would, if properly organized, rescue you from this fate: the railroad.[13]

Morris Neiburger, an expert on air pollution, states it a little differently:

> I don't believe controls can be devised that will adequately reduce the poisons given off by automobiles and other machines that burn fossil fuels (such as gas and oil). All civilization will pass away, not from a sudden cataclysm like a nuclear war, but from gradual suffocation in its own wastes.[14]

The consequence of the uncontrolled use of the automobile in a rapidly growing urban area leads eventually to an impossible transportation problem at the urban center. One after-the-damage-is-done solution is mass transit. In the San Francisco Bay Area, the $1.38 billion BART System[15] began operation in 1972. This is basically an improved (costly) version of the old Key System (of electric interurban trains) that was still operating in the 1940s but was displaced by the automobile. Another mass transit system, the $2.98 billion METRO System for the Washington, D.C. metropolitan area is scheduled for completion in 1974.[16] Many planners feel, however, that the best way to eliminate chaotic transportation habits within cities is to construct satellite cities, in which people can live in a satellite community that is close to the part of the city in which they work. Others feel that the answer lies in rebuilding the inner city, using superblock apartments, each superblock surrounded by green space, with good transportation from these to the city center. We will discuss these and other planning solutions later.

The central city has suffered from the flight of its citizens to suburbia. With their departure went their tax dollars and their interest in civic affairs. As the vitality of the city was sapped, slum conditions were aggravated. But there are other consequences. The replacement of a slum with a superblock project looks beautiful on paper. In practice, these projects have profoundly altered the structure of community life and not always for the better. For example, street life, which some planners consider "unwholesome" and which disappears when superblocks are built, has, in its hustle and bustle and unstructured supervision, something which helps to raise kids successfully, according to Jane Jacobs.[17] Community life in the suburbs has also been found wanting. The practice of fencing in homes and gardens (for privacy and protection) and the practice of using the car for every errand have the effect of isolating the family from personal encounters with those who live in the neighborhood. To overcome this runs the risk of becoming overly friendly with one's next door neighbors and losing one's privacy. Apparently there is no happy in-between and so one usually ends up staying isolated. Again this raises questions: Is this a good environment to be in? Is it really secure against crime? Is it good for raising children?

Concern about pollution, about the preservation of wildlife, about man's effect on the ecosystem, and about the kind of world left for future generations have become, in the decade of the seventies, national issues. Some people, on the personal level, try to collect cans, bottles, and newspapers for recycling. Others become smoke spotters or show up at meetings to protest the location of a new atomic power plant or the proposed site for Disney's latest wonderland. Most people feel that something must be done to undo man's negative impact on nature, but the accelerative thrust of fast-moving world societies has left everyone with a feeling of utter helplessness. The key question is always: If we stop the "progress" that harms the environment in one place, do we only make it worse somewhere else?

Clearly, many of the problems connected with urban sprawl could be avoided by *total-system planning*. The problems of urban development are too crucial to the future to be left to real estate developers and urban planning authorities who recommend more freeways, multilevel parking facilities, and other patchwork cures. For example, the *Report of the Governor's Task Force on Transportation for the State of California* (November 1968, page 11) recommends expenditures of $50 billion through 1985. For this much money, as we will see, it could be possible to build a completely new city for 2 million people, give them their homes and work facilities mortgage free, and still have money left over.

The *total-system approach* is a term that refers to methods for evaluating the effects of a proposed design on as many aspects of the urban system as possible—in particular, operations research, mathematical models, and computers can all be used to simulate and analyze the total system. We discuss details of this in Part Two. An observant reader will soon note that while we point out the need for a total-system approach, there are many aspects of the city, such as the form of its government, its economic and educational systems, or the way it handles race relations, that we only touch upon. These are important areas that should be studied in the context of a compact city. However, in the interest of keeping the book short, we have placed the emphasis on those aspects which, in our opinion, would be substantially affected by our proposal to make more effective use of space and time, the vertical and the time dimensions.

1.3 Our Objectives

It seems to us that there are a number of reasonable goals that constitute a better quality of life. Primarily, urban areas should be designed to provide

A good life but not at the expense of future generations
A viable center for business, culture, sports, and government
A new start for the disadvantaged

They should also provide

Ample sized homes
Private gardens (for those who desire them)
Work and shopping within walking distance from home
Clean air, water, and a pollution-free environment
Easy access to natural recreation areas, and to top cultural and shopping centers
Major activity centers that are close to each other
Freedom from frustrating delays
A safe environment for children
Low density
Flexibility

James W. Rouse, the architect who designed Columbia, Maryland, expresses his goals for new towns a little differently:

The elimination of all slum and blight.

A job for everyone who needs and wants work.

Good housing for everyone at rents and prices he can afford.

Education designed to meet the people—youth and adults—at their point of need, and to help them grow as individuals.

Health facilities to build health, prevent illness, provide best possible care at lowest possible cost.

Recreation facilities close to home, appropriate to the various age groups, from tiny kids to old people.

A police system that works scientifically and resourcefully to rid the city of organized crime and works humanely and sympathetically at the neighborhood level to develop respect for law and order and assist the deviant to learn and grow.

A communications system that makes it easy for people to know about one another, to be informed about life and activity in their neighborhood as well as in the larger community.

A transportation system that allows people to move easily, pleasantly, and inexpensively throughout the city without dependence upon the private automobiles.

Parks, playgrounds, green areas threading through the city to bring nature, beauty, repose, and space close to all people; also, to assist in breaking up the city into neighborhoods that will be in a scale with people; capable of being identified, embraced, managed by the people who live there.

Arrangement of housing, schools, churches, stores, health and recreation facilities, in such relationship to one another within a neighborhood that people will have easy, natural opportunity to know one another and their teachers, ministers, merchants, doctors, public officials; share joys, sorrows, and common problems; reshape systems and institutions that don't work properly; build new ones to provide answers to their needs and yearnings; know that they have the opportunity to influence their destiny.[18]

We have chosen to discuss ways to achieve such goals in terms of certain principles and to illustrate them by painting a picture of a possible city that could be built in the 1970s. We could have chosen to discuss simultaneously many possible designs for new cities and to compare them with each other and to more conventional cities. We believe that such a form of presentation would yield at best a blurred image of the various possibilities. Our hope is that by focusing on one possible *new city*, it will become more real in your imagination. If it should turn out to be not entirely to your taste, it can serve as a base for your own thinking about urban change.

The new, Compact City we will endeavor to explore with you would be economically inexpensive to build and maintain, yet spacious; it would have private gardens for those who want them, and public parks. Only a few minutes of travel time would separate homes from schools or work, and residents would be able to choose to walk, bicycle, or ride public transit. We will consider the advantages of having stores, restaurants, delivery service, health facilities, and all other routine services fully available, without delay, day or night, Monday or Sunday, winter or summer. In the Compact City we wish to establish there would, of course, be no suburban sprawl, freeways, traffic, smog, or other forms of urban blight. The amount of land needed for building Compact City would be negligible. Moreover, construction could be made flexible so that it would be easy to remodel, renew, and rearrange parts of the city, and thus avoid the process of urban decay that eventually results in slums.

Compact City could be arranged so that the allotment of space per person is the same as that of a thinly populated conventional city.

It could be designed to expand into a large city, yet always remain a simple, convenient place to live. To test the economic feasibility of a low density arrangement such as this, we will make the space availability per person overly generous. For example, we will plan to make Compact City effectively less densely settled than the general area around San Francisco, a location beloved for its spaciousness, natural settings, and beautiful surroundings. Space could be provided within Compact City for community squares, parks, meeting places, and recreational areas. Residents of the city should be able to reach the rural environs of the city within a few minutes from any point in the city.

Compact City would be a four-dimensional city. Thinking of time as a dimension, we believe that Compact City would be the well-planned four-dimensional counterpart of our present-day predominantly two-dimensional cities, which are constantly being partially patched up to solve urban problems. The downtowns of large cities today are gradually utilizing more and more of their vertical dimension as buildings are torn down to be replaced by ever taller skyscrapers. The difference between today's cities and what we hope will characterize future cities is that this expansion into full use of the vertical dimension today (through the technique of tearing down and rebuilding) results in cities that are many times more expensive, more inefficient and inflexible, less attractive, and less exciting than Compact City.

We appreciate the inherent and salutary diversity in human nature. Different people want different things and prefer to live where there is a choice of environmental settings. We believe there would be a framework for greater diversity in Compact City.

Ordinarily, man seeks change on a gradual basis. It would seem desirable to plan for such gradual change, but things are happening too fast. For a better insight into this point, read Toffler's *Future Shock*, "a book about what happens to people overwhelmed by change . . . a current so powerful today that it overturns institutions, shifts our values, and shrivels our roots."[19] Because in the past mankind did not plan ahead, we are now off on the wrong foot. Society invests in freeways, a self-perpetuating mistake. As we have already seen, these invite greater urban sprawl, pollution, destruction of the countryside, and appalling death on the highways. They create a suburbia that has the unfortunate side effects of draining the money and the richness of life from the inner city. Suburbia, in turn, fosters long-distance travel to work, with corresponding waste of time at commuting. And this creates the need for more and more extensive and expensive mass transit systems. Traditional patchwork approaches of repairing and expanding present-day cities can only aggravate these trends, for they do not alleviate the pressures of an increasing population, rising expectations, inner-city decay, and industrial movement; all of which add up to a probable doubling of the area covered by the urban spread by the year 2000.

The objective then is to design a city that can grow, yet remain a convenient, simple, and exciting place to live. If possible we wish to design a city that preserves and enhances the good aspects of modern living, yet alleviates the population crisis, postpones the deterioration of the environment, and conserves the environment for the day when measures designed to control population become a reality. We will show that much can be done to improve cities. Compact City, as presented here, could be used as a yardstick of what might be expected if the patchwork approach is replaced by the total-system approach. What we think is remarkable is that Compact City, with all its spacious accommodations and accessibility, could be built largely by saving the cost of what is now wasted on transportation. In brief, Compact City should be a model city that demonstrates the feasibility of constructing new cities which would meet our needs and could be financed realistically.

1.4 Challenges

The city is the gathering place where man creates and competes, works and plays. It is the web, the matrix that interlocks man with his fellow man. Modern man and his city are inseparable. His successes and failures take shape within its arena. It provides the source of motivation for those who wish to achieve. In the city man has been able to maintain a modicum of individuality and still be a member of a group with which he communicates and works. It is the citadel of stability and continuity for social institutions. But the city is also the stage for political unrest when the social and economic institutions fail to catch up with the rapid pace of changes in population and scientific progress, or when they fail to respond to the aspirations of its people.

All of society appears to be in an ever increasing state of flux. People change jobs more and more often. They are constantly moving from one home or apartment to another. Marriage partners are permuted and children of fractured families are redistributed. Businesses start up, shut down, expand, contract, and relocate. Schools consolidate and children are bussed to classes. A new tract of homes goes up, an old cherry orchard disappears. Life becomes a game of "musical chairs."

The first challenge is to find a way of constructing the city so that it serves as a "platform" for flexibly changing and rearranging internal structures. Our current cities do not have the flexibility to meet the needs of a fast, turbulent, growing, trans-industrial society. The downtowns of cities try to adapt. They are an odd mix of the new and the ancient — they are forever in a state of demolition, jackhammering, and rebuilding. Unfortunately, once a building goes up, economics dictates that it remains until it rots. If the industrial or commercial area where we work is no longer suitable, the city's inflexible construction usually forces a major uprooting.

If the decision is to relocate, the move leaves behind those who could not or would not adapt. A change to a new job in another part of town means enduring a frustrating commute, or else uprooting the family and forcing its members to find new neighbors, friends, teachers, and places to shop.

The second challenge concerns political organization. Present city administration is faced with a dilemma. It must create opportunity for its poor and renew its slums, programs which require tax money. But city politicians no longer have the backing of wealthy communities that identify with the city's hopes and aspirations. The city has its poor, it has its commuters who do not pay taxes, and it has businesses which are only too ready to move. Essentially, the problem becomes one of political jurisdiction, for the technical and financial means to revitalize city life exist in the combined city and its surrounding sprawl, i.e., in the megalopolis as a whole. The challenge is to restructure the design of the city so that the exploding pressures that drove families to the suburbs will become an implosion bringing them back to the city.

The third challenge has to do with conservation. The encroachment of creeping suburbia on the countryside has destroyed valuable farm land that may be needed one day to provide food to meet the population crisis. It has destroyed the ability of urban man to have easy access to unspoiled nature; this is, in effect, a kind of destruction of man's soul. More important, vast ecological problems have been created that can only be alleviated by the effective redesign of the city to conserve land, water, energy, and waste. Cities consume enormous quantities of water, electricity, and petroleum and other fuels, but reprocess little of their waste products. A major technological challenge is to redesign the city in such a way as to make it possible to share facilities, to conserve resources, and to contribute positively to the environment and to the future.

In the end the challenges merge and become one with our objectives — namely, to try to make our cities into convenient, simple, exciting places to live; to make them more flexible to changing needs, more compact in order to curtail sprawl, and to be less destructive of the natural environment, with the hope that population growth will be curbed before the countryside disappears.

The means exist to meet these challenges. Our technological society is able and well equipped to prepare a better world for all our children and the children of our children; and yet, only the most meager of technical ideas are pursued for the benefit of the billions who will live in tomorrow's cities. Instead, material resources and energy are dissipated negatively in the pursuit of nationalism, war, and power.

In the chapters that follow we shall try to outline an approach, which we shall call the total-system interactive approach, for redesigning cities. But first let us see how some of the well-known contributors to urban development view the problems we have just outlined, and let us take a look at some of their proposed solutions.

1. "Boom Town," *Newsweek*, Sept. 14, 1970, page 68.

2. Stanford Environmental Law Society, *San Jose: Sprawling City*, Stanford University Press (Stanford, Calif., 1971), 109 pages. Also, Editors of *Fortune* magazine, *The Exploding Metropolis*, Doubleday (Garden City, N.Y., 1958), 177 pages.

3. Paul and Percival Goodman, *Communitas*, Vintage Press-Random House (New York, 1960), page 28.

4. *American Almanac 1970*, "Statistical Abstract of U.S., Table 5 (Series D)," Grosset and Dunlap (New York, 1970), page 7.

5. For an interesting discussion of population structure and projection see Chapter 3 of Paul R. and Anne H. Ehrlich, *Population, Resources, Environment*, Second Edition, W. H. Freeman and Co. (San Francisco, 1972).

6. For a good survey of the evolution of our cities, their current problems, and future prospects see the special issue of the *Scientific American* entitled *Cities*, Vol. 213, No. 3, September 1965.

7. Alvin Toffler, *Future Shock*, Bantam Books (New York, 1971), page 475.

8. Stanford Research Institute, *Future Urban Transportation Systems, Final Report*, I, Stanford Research Institute (Menlo Park, Calif., March 1968), pages 51–63.

9. U.S. Department of Transportation, *Economic Consequences of Automobile Accident Injuries*, U.S. Government Printing Office (Washington, D.C., 1970), 1.17:AO 2, 1970. 2 vols. and supplement.

10. *American Almanac, op. cit.*, page 347.

11. Lewis Mumford, an American sociologist, is perhaps best known for his popular books *The Culture of Cities*, Harcourt, Brace and Co. (New York, 1938) and *The City in History*, Harcourt, Brace and World, Inc. (New York, 1961).

12. Lewis Mumford, *The Highway and the City*, Secker and Warburg (London, 1963), and Harcourt Brace Jovanovich, Inc. (New York, 1963).

13. *Ibid.*

14. Morris Neiburger, quoted in *San Francisco Chronicle*, August 9, 1965, page 12.

15. Bay Area Rapid Transit District, "Fact Sheet II, Engineering Details of the General Bay Area Rapid Transit District," BART (Oakland, Calif.), July 19, 1971.

16. Washington Metropolitan Area Transit Authority, "Metro News Release," Wash. Metro. Area Transit Auth. (950 L'Enfant Plaza South, S.W., Washington, D.C.), December 31, 1970.

17. Jane Jacobs, *The Death and Life of Great American Cities*, Random House (New York, 1961).

18. James W. Rouse, "Cities that Work for Man—Victory Ahead," address at University of Puerto Rico symposium on "The City of the Future," Oct. 18, 1967.

19. Alvin Toffler, *op. cit.*, page 1.

2

SOLUTIONS

2.1 Some Basic Needs

A city must be a place with which one can make a true acquaintance, in the sense of Albert Camus, who said, "Perhaps the easiest way of making a town's acquaintance is to ascertain how people in it work, how they live, and how they die." This, in turn, raises some questions about what man is, how he thinks and feels, how he relates himself to other men and to his environment, how he works and moves about in this environment, and what knowledge and technology do to change his views and estimates. Thus, to understand how man relates to the city is to understand all of life. The best anyone of us can do, operationally, is to adopt a point of view that helps to evelute alternative plans for urban development. The plan that we, as authors, will present has been tempered (we admit) by social acceptability, economic feasibility, and the socioeconomic trends that we feel will be characteristic of our society in the years before 2000. It is not necessary for the reader, however, to accept our approach to urban planning—we have found that others, with quite different interpretations of what the future has in store, seem to arrive at about the same conclusions.

There are a number of architects, sociologists, engineers, conservationists, and professional writers like Camillo Sitte, Frank Lloyd Wright, Le Corbusier, Buckminster Fuller, Eliel Saarinen, Lawrence Halprin, J. L. Sert, Moshe Safdie, Paolo Soleri, Lewis Mumford,

Stewart Udall, Paul and Percival Goodman, Jane Jacobs, Hans Blumenfeld, Paul Geddes, Victor Gruen, E. A. Gutkind, and C. A. Doxiadis, all of whom have expressed their thoughts about cities—some in books that are now classics. We will say more about their ideas presently.[1]

Before doing so let us note some of the basic needs that a proposed solution must satisfy. At the most elementary level a city should be so structured and organized that it meets:

1. *Man's Physical Needs.* Among these are food, air, water, shelter, sanitation, waste disposal, electricity, gas, transportation, and places for work, entertainment, exercise, and some degree of privacy.

2. *Man's Love of Nature.* This embraces love of sunshine, fresh air, trees, parks, and beaches. If possible, a city should be located so that it is surrounded by hills or mountains, or located on the side of a mountain overlooking an ocean, or a lake, or rolling forests.

3. *Man's Need for Social Life and Social Care.* This is the need that dictates that urban design should be tasteful. Civic wealth should be adequately distributed so that poverty does not exist. City facilities will need to include educational, health, and work institutions. The city will need to accommodate the old, the crippled, and to rehabilitate the displaced worker; to have family care services (such as day care for children of working mothers); to control juvenile delinquency and crime; and to maintain adequate health and safety standards (such as the control of pests and pollution). A man needs a home and a job he can take pride in. He needs to send his children to school. He also needs health and leisure.

4. *Man's Need for Growth.* He must replace—in a planned and flexible way—obsolete facilities, complexes, and institutions.

Moshe Safdie, architect of Montreal's Habitat, who has developed a design for modular units that can be stacked together to form a community, goes beyond these basic needs and asks the key question: What makes a city tick? Safdie says:

> I prefer San Francisco to Los Angeles. I prefer New York to Philadelphia. Why? The kind of concentration that is achieved in them creates certain choices, an openness of society that is not possible in the lower-density environments. I want my children to be able to meet and play and communicate with many other children on their own, not only when they are driven somewhere. I want them to grow up in an environment that is not just a place where people sleep but where people work . . . and where people enjoy themselves, or as the Goodmans say in *Communitas:* "The city must be the integration of work, love and knowledge." . . . We want two extremes. We want the intensive meeting place, the urban environment, the place where everybody is together, and we want the secluded open space where we are alone in the country with nature.

We need and want both. . . . This is the contradictory desire in our utopia. . . . We want to live in a small community with which we can identify and yet we want all the facilities of the city of millions of people. We want to have very intense urban experiences and yet we want the open space right next to us.[2]

2.2 Garden City

Modern city planning began around 1898 when the English planner Ebenezer Howard proposed the building of new towns to attract residents away from London.[3] Howard's Garden Cities would have their own industries, and those who worked in them could live close by. Each new small city would have various sections zoned for commerce, culture, and schools, but most important, there would be generous expanses of green areas. Each town would be encircled by its own agricultural belt so that all residents would be in close proximity to green countryside. Howard's goals were to open up the urban setting, to screen off ugly work areas, to bring people and green space together, and to eliminate the need for long-distance transportation.

There was, in the original Garden City concept, an implied assumption that as population grew, there would be plenty of open land in which to locate new towns in the rural countryside at the various node points of a connecting network of highways. There are, for example, vast areas of open land in the United States and Canada which would permit such a development. See Figure 2-1.

Garden City proponents also assumed (a) that the replication of many small towns, each averaging a population of about 30,000, would be a stable arrangement, i.e., that most residents would settle for long periods of time in their Garden City and find work there too; (b) that rather than living in large cities people would

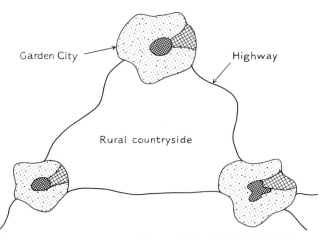

Figure 2-1 EBENEZER HOWARD'S GARDEN CITIES
Patterns represent various land uses.

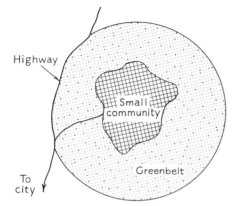

Figure 2-2 A GREENBELT COMMUNITY

really prefer to live in a small town close to green countryside; (c) that a decentralized social order made up of more or less self-sufficient repetitive units would be intrinsically better than that of a big, centralized city in which many kinds of specialized life-pursuits are possible.

Ebenezer Howard succeeded in establishing one Garden City— Letchworth in England—but his hope that Garden Cities would proliferate never materialized. Nevertheless, the concept of Garden Cities influenced all subsequent urban planning. Various planners have given the Garden City assumptions various names, but all are basically similar. Let us briefly examine three outstanding realizations of the Garden City approach.

Greenbelts

A watered-down version of the Garden City is the greenbelt community. See Figure 2-2. These consist of rigidly zoned neighborhoods each surrounded by a "belt" of undeveloped land. Examples in the United States are Greenbelt (in Maryland), Baldwin Hills (near Los Angeles), Radburn (in New Jersey), and Fresh Meadows (in New York). All are attractive, carefully planned bedroom communities, but they do not replace the city in the lives of residents. The household breadwinner commutes over considerable distances to some far off place for work. The Goodmans describe the greenbelt culture in *Communitas*: "the women are neighborly, they spend ten hours a week playing cards." Dependent as they are on the central city, greenbelt communities are a form of leapfrog suburbia and, as such, unfortunately serve to augment the sprawl.[4]

Decentralized Cities

In 1934 Frank Lloyd Wright displayed a model of a decentralized Garden City which he called *Broadacres*. His chief argument for decentralization was this: "The traffic problem, if tied up with

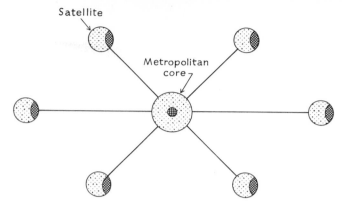

Satellite

Metropolitan
core

Figure 2-3 SATELLITE CITIES
In an ideal plan, industrial areas would be located
downwind from residential areas.

the skyscraper, is insolvable by any busy city." Wright's goal was
to open up the city and bring farm values to it. In his book *The
Living City,* he proposed allotting "no less than an acre to each
individual. . . . If he can work on his ground, he should do it . . .
barring disability he should not eat if he does not work . . . except
when he can fairly trade . . ."[5] So thoroughly did Wright believe
in the importance of urban man's need to be close to the soil that
he concluded *The Living City* with an excerpt from Ralph Waldo
Emerson's *Essay on Farming.*

Satellite Cities

Another variation on Garden City often advocated by planners is
the concept of satellite cities, which consist of a number of Garden
Cities (each different from the other in some way) located around
a larger central city. The central city would function as a general-
purpose commercial and cultural center, fulfilling certain administrative and commercial functions that would otherwise be unnecessarily
duplicated in the satellite cities. People would live and work in the
same satellite. To preserve the greatest amount of green space around
the central city, urban growth would take place only in newly formed
satellites. Reston (in Virginia) and Columbia (in Maryland) are examples of towns planned and built to serve as satellites. They are
located near Washington, D.C. College campuses and their neighborhoods are also examples of communities that function as though
they were satellites.[6] See Figure 2-3.

The analogy of satellite cities to living cells is, of course, inescap-
able. If not too specialized, living cells (for example, cells at an early
embryonic stage), when separated from the parent body, will replicate the parent. Compatible living cells, when clustered, become

interdependent and specialize their functions (e.g., some become nerve-cells, muscle-cells, or eye-cells).

Victor Gruen, the well known city planner, says: "I can visualize a metropolitan organism in which cells, each one consisting of a nucleus and protoplasm are combined into clusters to form specialized organs like towns which, in turn, are meaningfully grouped together to form cities and finally, in a still more highly developed organism, the metropolis of tomorrow." The latter he envisions as a cluster of ten cities surrounding a metropolitan core.[7] To which we might add that the cell analogy becomes even more striking and potentially significant when cities—like biological organisms—are considered as bodies existing in three dimensions.

Architect Eliel Saarinen, a proponent of satellite planning, envisaged the "organic decentralization" of the big city by the gradual transfer of its people and industry to satellite towns each more or less self-contained and restricted in size. To facilitate the transfer he recommended that the town designer play the role of an "enlightening master-butcher" and suggested "transference of property rights from one location to another."[8] Saarinen advocated decentralization because he saw no other way for oversized cities to maintain good physical order. Nevertheless, he felt "the greater the number of those having opportunity to become culturally influenced in the city's atmosphere, the stronger and the more lasting the social order will be." Others have echoed Saarinen's advocacy of decentralization through the formation of satellite cities. Wolf von Eckardt, an architectural critic, has stated that he believes new satellite towns are the best answer to the problems of inorganic, uncontrolled megalopolises.[9] And Hans Blumenfeld also believes the satellite town's appeal to some people is its organic unity. But he questions its practicality. "It is rooted in a conscious or unconscious desire to escape from the complexities of our rapidly changing times into a simpler and stabler world . . . that probably never existed and certainly cannot exist today."[10] Blumenfeld quotes English town planners, for whom the term New Town serves to describe satellite planning, who say "the special problem of a New Town is how to get the process under way and keep it going. The New Town in the end becomes a dormitory because of rapidly shifting industrial needs. Industry prefers to locate where there is a potentially large employment pool to select from." There is simply not enough flexibility in the satellite for it to remain viable in a fast-changing world.

2.3 Le Corbusier's "Glorious City"

The French architect Le Corbusier is probably most famous as a leader of modern, or functionalist, architecture. His passion, however, was urban planning. In the 1920s he exhibited his plan for a city to house three million people and published his first book,

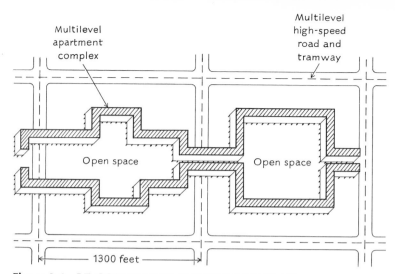

Figure 2-4 LE CORBUSIER'S SUPERBLOCK PLAN

Urbanisme (The City of Tomorrow). His second book, *La Ville Radieuse* (The Radiant City) appeared in 1933.[11] Indeed, he was constantly exhibiting or writing about plans for new cities and redesigns for old cities. He presented these ideas to the International Congresses of Modern Architecture (C.I.A.M.). In this way he succeeded in implanting, in the minds of architects and city planning authorities, an image of what he thought cities ought to look like, an image which, for better or worse, underlies much contemporary design. A biographer, Norma Evenson, commenting on the plan of Brasilia, which was influenced by his ideas even though it was not designed by him, states:

> The most thoroughgoing adaptation of Le Corbusier's urban design conceptions may be seen in the capital of Brazil, begun in 1956. This new city, Brasilia, comprises a cross-axial plan in which a sweeping motor freeway punctuates its intersection with a classically ordered government axis by means of a multilevel transport center. Bordering the freeway are residential superblocks containing standardized apartment blocks set amid open space, while the business center near the hub is designed for unified high-rise building.[12]

The theme of Le Corbusier's plans was to bring *"soleil, espace, verdure"* (sun, space, and green) to the city, i.e., to make the city into a huge "radiant" version of Howard's Garden Cities. His solution: open up the center of the city, erect a few towering skyscrapers, expand the parks and open spaces between them, and construct high-speed roadways and tramways on two levels radiating from the center. To achieve open space for those who live in apartments, build tall, thin apartment houses; equip these with elevators. Set buildings on pillars that expose the ground level (see Figure 2-4).

For convenience, place the superblock apartment complexes in a concentric band around the central urban core. Finally, Le Corbusier planned to construct, on the outskirts of some cities, low apartments, and factories, in a "linear city" pattern. See Figure 2-5.

In his book, *Can Our Cities Survive,*[13] Jose Luis Sert reflects the viewpoint of the C.I.A.M. which, as we have noted, has had great influence on the thinking of many architects and city planning authorities. Some of their premises for good planning, as given by Sert, are listed below.

1. *On the need for green open space.* "Progressive extension of the urban area has destroyed the green open spaces that once surrounded the dwelling districts of the city—denying the benefits of living near the open country."

2. *On creating open space.* "Widely spaced apartment blocks with elevators should be used to free necessary land surface for recreation, community services, parking, and providing dwellings with sun, air, and a view."

3. *On transportation needs.* "The absence of planned location of working places with respect to dwelling places has created excessive commuting distances. Traffic facilities are overtaxed during rush hours. Excessive space of a city is devoted to parking lots. Traffic is hazardous."

4. *On transportation improvement.* "Develop high-speed multilevel highways, space road intersections farther apart, widen streets."

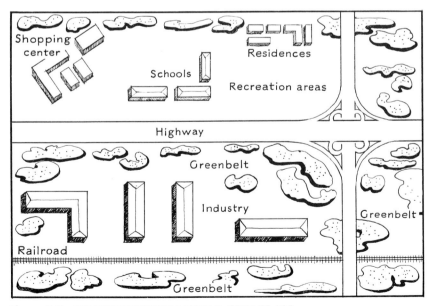

Figure 2-5 LE CORBUSIER'S LINEAR CITY PLAN

5. *On zoning.* "Without zoning the control of urban functions becomes impossible. There should be a master plan for industrial zoning. Plans should be developed to determine the needs of different districts according to their organic laws."

6. *On town planning.* "The point of departure for all town planning should be the cell represented by a single dwelling, conceived together with similar cells so as to form a neighborhood unit of efficacious size. With this as a starting point, dwelling, work, and recreation should be distributed throughout the urban area in their most favorable relationship."

We shall now see some of these proposed solutions challenged because they neglected certain social principles which (until recently) were not considered true or important.

2.4 Jane Jacobs and Diversified Use of Space

Jane Jacobs begins *The Death and Life of Great American Cities* with the statement: "This book is an attack on current city planning and rebuilding." Further on she remarks that in conventional city planning neighborhood open spaces are venerated in an amazingly uncritical fashion. "Ask a planner how his planned neighborhood improves on the old city and he will cite, as a self-evident virtue, More Open Space. Ask a zoner about the improvements in progressive codes and he will cite, again as a self-evident virtue, their incentives to More Open Space . . . More Open Space for what? For muggings? For bleak vacuums between buildings? Or for ordinary people to use and enjoy? But people do not use city open space just because it is there and because city planners or designers wish they would." She goes on to state that "American downtowns are not declining mysteriously because they are anachronisms, nor because their users have been drained away by automobiles. They are being witlessly murdered, in good part by deliberate policies of sorting out leisure uses from work uses, under the misapprehension that this is orderly city planning." Jacobs is concerned that our cities have secure streets—safe from muggings and other forms of crime. According to her observations, whenever streets are "lively" with people and activities, there are always people watching the activity of other people—always people around who feel responsible for what happens on their block and act as if they "own the street," and this interest helps to keep the peace.[14]

An example from St. Louis shows what can happen when this kind of diversity of people and activities is not made a part of an urban development scheme. There, a $36 million low-rent project was built in 1955 with plans that provided for tall apartment buildings separated with generous landscaping. In 1972 the project was demolished, for it had become three-quarters deserted, crime ridden, and wrecked by gangs.[15]

An important condition for a lively city life, according to Jacobs, "is the need . . . for a most intricate and close-grained diversity of uses [of streets, open spaces, and other public places] that give each other constant mutual support, both economically and socially."

Fundamental to Jane Jacobs's ideas is that children should be raised under the unstructured surveillance of, and in the presence of, meaningful adult activity on "lively streets."

> Garden City planners with their hatred of the street, thought the solution to keeping children off the street *and* under wholesome surveillance, was to build interior enclaves for them in the centers of super-blocks. This policy has been inherited by the designers of Radiant Garden City. Today many large renewal areas are being planned on the principle of enclosed park enclaves within blocks. The trouble with this scheme . . . is that no child of enterprise or spirit will be willing to stay in such a boring place after he reaches the age of six. Most want out earlier. These sheltered "togetherness" worlds are suitable, and in real life are used, for about three or four years of a small child's life.[16]

Another fundamental idea is that

> most city diversity is the creation of incredible numbers of different people and different private organizations with vastly differing ideas and purposes, planning and contributing outside the formal framework of public action. The main responsibility of city planning and design should be to develop—insofar as public policy and action can do so— cities that are congenial places for this great range of unofficial plans, ideas and opportunities to flourish, along with the flourishing of the public enterprises. City districts will be economically and socially congenial places for diversity to generate itself and reach its best potential if the districts possess good mixtures of primary uses, frequent streets, and close grained mingling of different ages in their buildings, and a high concentration of people.[17]

The latter become Jacobs's four conditions for reconstruction of our cities:

1. *The need for mixed primary uses.* "The district, and indeed as many of its internal parts as possible, must serve more than one primary function; preferably more than two. These must insure the presence of people who go outdoors on different schedules and are in the place for different purposes, but who are able to use many facilities in common."

2. *The need for small blocks.* "Most blocks must be short; that is, streets and opportunities to turn corners must be frequent."

3. *The need for aged buildings.* "The district must mingle buildings that vary in age and condition, including a good proportion of old ones."

4. *The need for concentration.* "The district must have a sufficiently dense concentration of people, for whatever purpose they may be there. This includes people there because of residence."[18]

The design for Compact City, which we will propose in Chapter 3, is in some respects based on Radiant City lines—it would have a central work core ringed by residences and there would be a general separation of functions. The Mid-Plaza belt of the city we propose would have a mix of several functions, however; e.g., local shopping, elementary schools, clinics, and recreation (a typical part of the Mid-Plaza belt is shown in Figure 3-7). Moreover, the flexible design of structures within the city would make rearrangements possible even in residential areas and could promote there the change to mixed primary use such as is recommended by Jane Jacobs.

Moreover, in Chapter 13, we present an alternative layout of the city which is designed to be even more conducive to developing lively neighborhoods. Such considerations are extremely important. According to Jacobs, "city diversity itself permits and stimulates more diversity." Cities are "the natural homes of supermarkets and standard movie houses *plus* delicatessens, Viennese bakeries, foreign groceries, art movies and so on, all of which can be found coexisting —the familiar with the strange, the large with the small. . . . This is because city populations are large enough to support wide ranges of variety and choice in these things. The diversity of whatever kind . . . rests on the fact that in cities so many people are so close together, and among them contain so many different tastes, skills, needs, supplies, and bees in bonnets."[19]

A new metropolitan area which is not sensitive to the ways that city design can foster diversity could well end up as just another unexciting, uninteresting place to live. In this country today, according to Jacobs, there are many vast urban areas that have long ago succumbed to the "Great Blight of Dullness."

2.5 Soleri's Arcology

One of the most persuasive and eloquent proponents of a more effective three-dimensional planning approach is the architect Paolo Soleri. Soleri, a native-born Italian, has lived in the United States since World War II. In Arizona, near Phoenix, Soleri hopes to build what he has spent his life dreaming of and working toward: a city in which the third dimension of verticality is as important as horizontal dimensions, a city he calls "Arcology."

In his book *Arcology, The City in the Image of Man*,[20] Soleri writes that man and society have evolved according to natural processes and patterns which, when discovered, can be extrapolated into the future and used to bring about the harmonious evolution of man and his society. He acknowledges man's ability to wreck the gradual patterns of evolution by his rapid progress in technology. To him, today's cities are evolving according to a pattern which is contradictory to the natural evolutionary patterns of man and society. These cities, he feels, must be replaced with new cities designed to be in harmony with natural processes and patterns.[21]

What is the natural pattern Soleri thinks the cities of the future must follow? It is the pattern of *miniaturization* (by which he means a compact rearrangement of space). It is Soleri's belief that miniaturization has been a key rule for all life. Soleri explains this belief by stating that as organisms evolved and developed greater complexity, time- and space-obstacles to performance were greatly increased. To maintain a level of performance adequate to sustain life, organisms have had to miniaturize to compact form in an effort to reduce these time- and space-obstacles. When they have not, like the dinosaurs, they have become extinct. Our reference here to dinosaurs is not merely metaphorical. Some scientists say the *Diplodocus* became extinct because the logistics of feeding its 35-ton 65-foot-long hulk became impossible when the swamps which were its habitat began to dry up. Others say that the major cause of its extinction was not its oversize, but its undersized, 6-cubic-inch brain.

According to Soleri, cities today are awkward, inefficient organisms and need to become compact through use of the third dimension to achieve efficiency. The complexity and size of cities make this the only solution. Man must turn to the fully three-dimensional city, the Arcology, for a better life.

Soleri writes that man may well be happiest in an environment in which he can satisfy his instinctive desire for the natural and his intellectual desire for the man-made, or neonatural. The Arcology, by allowing man to enjoy his city and still leave much of the natural countryside untouched, may be the solution needed to permit man to reach the fullness of life of which he is capable and deserving.

We are in general agreement with Soleri's characterization of the advantages of the Arcology as to beauty, harmony, efficiency, and spaciousness. But our approach differs greatly in the way the vertical dimension is to be developed. For example, based on the likely ratio of horizontal transportation speed to vertical lift speed, our calculations indicate that an optimally planned city should be less high and more spread out than those Soleri proposes. Nor does Soleri consider the possibility of making better use of the time dimension, which we do.

2.6 Two Principles

We will now say a few words about two concepts which we will call the principles of space and time. Properly exploited they can do much to alleviate the problems of oversized metropolises.

The Principle of Space

Thirty-five percent of the land surface of Los Angeles is used for transportation. Let us imagine a city, say Los Angeles, is laid out on a sheet; its various parts are cut apart and placed in layers—one on top of another—to form a three-dimensional structure. A striking feature

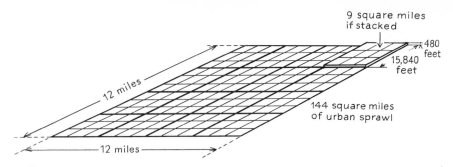

Figure 2-6 THE PRINCIPLE OF SPACE
Elimination of urban sprawl by stacking a city.

of this rearrangement is the frequency with which major highways will appear in each level of the layered sheets. It seems reasonable to eliminate some of the roads on each level and to move up or down to a neighboring level for horizontal transportation on the roads there, thus conserving space and considerably decreasing the total size of the city. In this connection, consider how much simpler the distribution of goods throughout the city might become. What once required a long time for transit between districts is now reduced to less than a minute by elevator to some desired vertical level.[22] See Figure 2-6.

The structures within the layered city could then be constructed of light interior materials because the outer surface of the city itself could be built to provide the desired protection against the elements. Architecture could be infinitely more varied because of the greater choice of materials and architectural forms. Interior open space around homes and apartments would become useful areas of activity the year round. Streets need not be monotonously straight because transportation time is no longer a major problem. Little use remains for the millions of cars with their consequent pollution, accidents, and the consumption of natural resources that is necessary for their manufacture, maintenance, and use. Public facilities, stadiums, and theaters become easily accessible to residents of all parts of the city, for people would be able to live on the various horizontal layers closer to facilities than they would if all lived on the same horizontal plane. Transportation back and forth to work would no longer waste human time. Even communication costs would be reduced because of the shorter distances involved.

Crowding or interference problems occur in two dimensions because the various types of flow paths tend to cross. On the other hand, flow paths can be easily positioned in three dimensions so as to have no blocking or interference of one part of a network with another or of different networks with each other.

Density is a factor used to estimate the availability of space. Two-dimensional density is measured in people per square mile, and three-dimensional density is measured per cubic mile. It is interesting to note that if all the people of the world were placed at arm's length, they would cover a plane of 625 square miles and if they were rearranged in layers eight feet apart, they would occupy less than one cubic mile.

The principle of space: In order to keep population densities low, conserve land use, and avoid the problems of urban sprawl, man must more effectively utilize the vertical dimension.

The Principle of Time

Of all the *curious* customs of man, perhaps the most curious is that everybody wants to do the same thing at the same time. Workers throughout an urban area arrange the time they awake, have their breakfasts, and kiss their spouses goodbye so all will arrive on the freeway at the same time. Of course, freeways are never quite wide enough to handle the load, so the peak becomes spread out somewhat. At noon, restaurants, which at other times are quite empty, line their customers up in queues. For some strange reason, everyone wants to quit work at the same time and to jam the freeways and other transportation facilities again. For all we know the custom of everybody doing things simultaneously may even include going to bed and making love.

We have called this phenomenon *"cicadian" rhythm.* Erich Fromm makes some observations about this in his *Sane Society.*[23] This term should not be confused with biological clocks that control *"circa*dian" rhythm. Cicadidae are a family of insects which include cicada (locusts) and grasshoppers; they make noise in rhythmic concert. See Figures 2-7 and 2-8. Circadian rhythm will be discussed later, in Section 14.3.

The consequences of man's cicadian customs have a drastic effect on the physical dimensions of a city. The size of rooms, the numbers

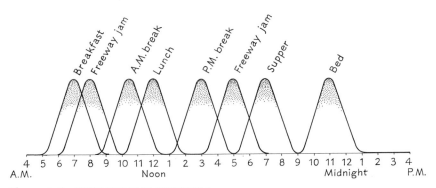

Figure 2-7 "CICADIAN" RHYTHM
The sound of insects rising and falling in concert; or, human activities conducted in unison.

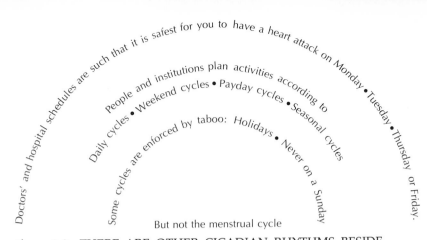

Figure 2-8 THERE ARE OTHER CICADIAN RHYTHMS BESIDE THE DAILY ONES

of desks and chairs, the size of facilities for distributing gas, water, and electricity are all designed to handle peak loads. The same is true for:

Highways
Factories
Sewers
Furnaces
Air conditioners
Offices
Schools
Check-out Stands
Toll Booths
Parking Lots
Power Stations

The size of a facility is several times the average hourly rate of use, but never enough to take care of the peak load.

Most congestion problems in large cities are related to man's time cycles. These cycles create the need for costly, large-capacity facilities. Roads are designed to handle the rush-hour traffic. See Figure 2-9.

As space has become a premium in large cities, there has been a growing trend toward activities that operate more evenly around the clock. For example, there are restaurants that are always open, and taxicabs that are in use day and night. Some stores are open on some week nights or Sundays. It is becoming evident that this trend is desirable for an unencumbered way of life.

In Japan, there are enterprises whose working-day habits do not follow the pattern of five days of work followed by a two-day holiday that is customary in the United States. The five working days are still there, but they are followed by a three-day holiday. A man may start a five-working-day cycle on Monday, take a three-day holiday and return to work on the next five-day cycle, starting on Tuesday. By varying the initial starting dates, there are always people working, and their work cycles are always shifting. The constant utilization of equipment can dramatically reduce the size of capital facilities. Their higher utilization rate means that they will be replaced sooner by new and more efficient equipment. All this adds up to reduced prices for products and a better quality of services.

Such work schemes alleviate the pressures on traffic, communication, and recreation facilities. People use them during their free days—and these times do not coincide for all the people. By using three shifts in a 24-hour period, further reduction in total costs is achieved because the peak demands are smaller and more evenly distributed. It is evident that the structure of a city could be further improved if the times that people go to work are distributed evenly throughout the day, night, weekdays, weekends, summer, and winter. Then there would be no peak periods for traffic, electricity, gas, shopping, clinics, restaurants, use of schoolrooms, use of factory equipment, etc. The result would be a great saving in the size and capacity of the capital stock, as well as in the time and cost of new construction. Take the case of a restaurant today used only for one hour at lunch: the savings in the size of that facility, used throughout the day, is 24 to 1. See Figure 2-10. Equipment could be amortized and updated more rapidly. Life becomes less complicated because the time principle allows one to do routine activities at times that are personally convenient.

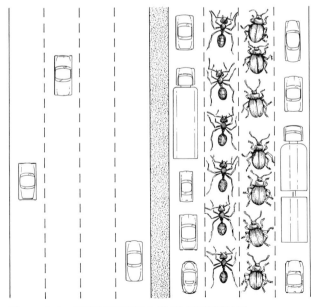

Figure 2-9 THE EIGHT-LANE FREEWAY
Built for handling peak loads. Some of the freeway space is underutilized at some times and in some directions.

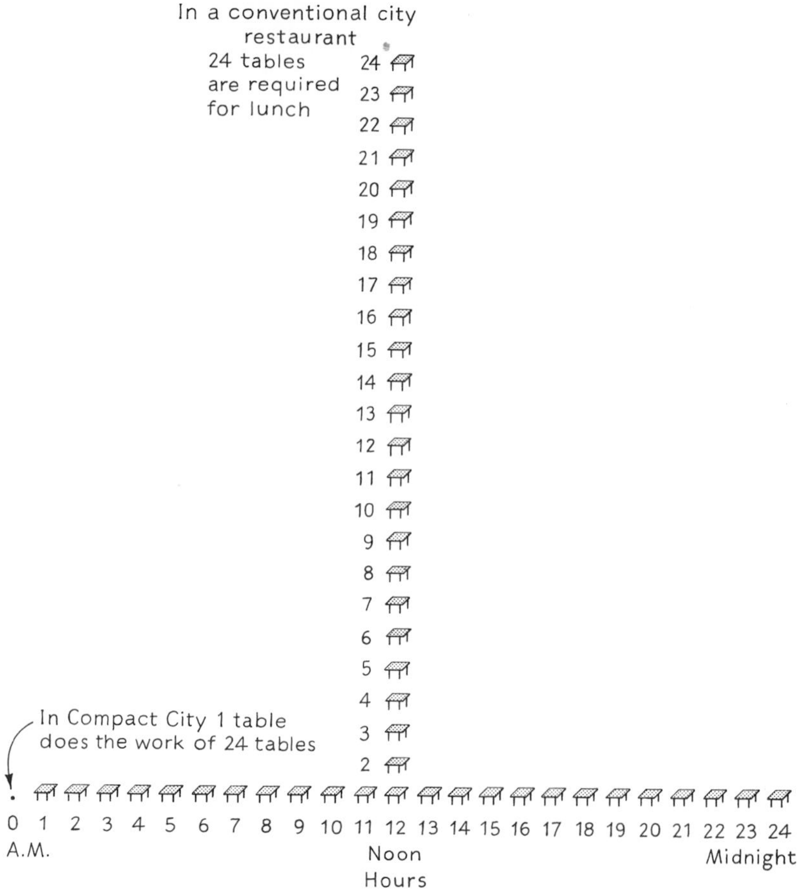

In a conventional city
restaurant
24 tables   24 🛏
are required   23 🛏
for lunch   22 🛏

21 🛏

20 🛏

19 🛏

18 🛏

17 🛏

16 🛏

15 🛏

14 🛏

13 🛏

12 🛏

11 🛏

10 🛏

9 🛏

8 🛏

7 🛏

6 🛏

5 🛏

4 🛏

In Compact City 1 table   3 🛏
does the work of 24 tables   2 🛏

🛏 🛏
0 1 2 3 4 5 6 7 8 9 10 11 12 13 14 15 16 17 18 19 20 21 22 23 24
A.M.   Noon   Midnight
                                    Hours

Figure 2-10 THE PRINCIPLE OF TIME
Around-the-clock use reduces the size of facilities needed to meet
peak loads.

*The principle of time: In order to conserve and maximize the effective
use of space and to lead a less encumbered life, man needs to free himself
from the syndrome of day-night cycles by utilizing the facilities of the city
more evenly throughout the twenty-four hour day.*

But there are problems. Man (unlike most animals) is a daylight
creature and it is not surprising that most people on the whole prefer
to work by day and to sleep by night. When clocks came into general
use, man standardized his daily cycle by synchronizing his activities
not to the sun, but to the movement of the clock.[24] In fact, so tied has
his cycle become to the clock that "daylight-saving" is used as a
device to "move the sun around" to give man more light in the evening hours. Each year man uses more and more artificial light in his
homes, offices, streets, highways, gardens, parking lots, stores, and

around his buildings. As a result, the daily patterns of people are beginning to be less rigid relative to one another.

Nevertheless, as long as the external environment remains more pleasant during sunlit hours, daylight will remain the preferred time for being awake. This still leaves a wide range of times to start the day. If these start-up times were spread more evenly, it would do much to dampen (or smooth out) peak loads. This is why, earlier, we poked fun at the custom of jamming the freeways, queueing for lunch, etc., and called it cicadian rhythm.

Cicadian rhythm has been "explained" in various ways. One explanation is that in some mysterious way man's internal biological "clock" is linked to the time the sun rises and sets and this in turn affects the time he goes to sleep and wakes up—i.e., it acts as the pace-maker for the cicadian rhythm. This seems hard to believe in view of Daylight Saving Time and the great variation in the amount of sunlight per day in extreme latitudes. Another justification is that it is necessary for all businesses to be open at the same time so that there is always someone around to receive orders. When business was a one-man enterprise and hence could not be open 24 hours a day, this was a good reason. Nowadays a considerable percent of transcontinental and intercontinental trade is transacted at odd hours by telephone. An important psychological reason, however, for cicadian rhythm, might be the desire to be at work during the same period of the day as the boss, so as to maximize one's chances of being considered for promotion; i.e., society enforces such rhythms.

If we can make the activities of the city efficient and inviting enough throughout the 24-hour day, then we can anticipate that most of the historical reasons for cicadian rhythm will disappear. On the other hand, the uniform use of time throughout a 24-hour day will not be without its problems. For example: can members of a family arrange their time for work and school so that they can be together at dinner time? What happens if a class is offered at a time when one is usually asleep? Suppose one wishes to go to a performance scheduled to be given once, at a time one is normally at work? All of these possibilities would occur and would represent a restriction on freedom of action just as now having to commute three hours each day in some present-day cities is an imposition on time, or having to take off from work to shop during store hours, or having to wait weeks for a doctor's appointment, or not taking a class because of a conflicting schedule, or having to wait until tomorrow morning to fix the TV because the TV repairmen don't work at night, etc. All are impositions on time and freedom of action, and they happen every day. We will say more about this later when we discuss the social implications of accessibility in Chapter 14. The interplay between man's cicadian and circadian cycles has been the subject of many recent studies.[25]

Having set the stage, let us turn, in the next chapter, to the Compact City proposal itself.

Notes and References

1. For a brief summary, see "New Architecture: Building for Man," *Newsweek,* April 19, 1971, pages 78–90.

2. Moshe Safdie, "Beyond Habitat," *Philadelphia Inquirer*, February 28, 1971, Sec. 7, page 1. See also, for the reactions of people who have been living in Habitat since it was built for Expo '67, *Time*, January 31, 1972, page 37.

3. Ebenezer Howard, *Garden Cities of Tomorrow,* reprinted by MIT Press (Cambridge, Mass., 1965).

4. Hans Blumenfeld, *The Modern Metropolis,* M.I.T. Press (Cambridge, Mass., 1967), page 5.

5. Frank Lloyd Wright, *The Living City*, Mentor-Horizon Press (New York, 1958), page 85.

6. Experimental City Project, *The Minnesota Experimental City*, Progress Report, University of Minnesota, May 1969. See also Ivan Menzies, "Europe's New Cities," *The Boston Globe*, June 8, 24, and July 2, 1969 (reprinted in 4 page booklet).

7. Victor Gruen, *The Heart of Our Cities*, Simon and Schuster (New York, 1967), pages 271–273.

8. Eliel Saarinen, *The City, Its Growth, Its Decay, Its Future*, Reinhold (New York, 1943), pages 290–291.

9. "The City: Starting from Scratch," *Time*, March 7, 1969, pages 25–26.

10. Hans Blumenfeld, *op. cit.*, page 5.

11. Le Corbusier, *The Radiant City*, Grossman-Orion Press (New York, 1967). English translation of *La Ville Radieuse*, 1933.

12. Norma Evenson, *Le Corbusier: The Machine and the Grand Design*, Braziller (New York, 1969). A penetrating short biography of Le Corbusier's work as an urban designer. The quote is from pages 108–109.

13. Jose Luis Sert, *Can Our Cities Survive?*, Harvard University Press (Cambridge, Mass., 1942, 259 pages.

14. Jane Jacobs, *The Death and Life of Great American Cities,* Vintage-Random House (New York, 1961) and Jonathan Cape Ltd. (London, 1961). Copyright © 1961 by Jane Jacobs. Quotations are from pages 90, 171, 14.

15. "The Tragedy of Pruitt-Igoe," *Time*, December 27, 1971, page 38.

16. Jane Jacobs, *op. cit.*, pages 79–80. For examples of what has been "inherited by the designers of Radiant Garden City" see Le Corbusier, *The Radiant City, op. cit.*

17. Jane Jacobs, *op. cit.*, pages 241–242.

18. *Ibid*, page 151.

19. *Ibid*, pages 146–147.

20. Paolo Soleri, *Arcology, The City in the Image of Man*, M.I.T. Press (Cambridge, Mass., 1969).

21. R. Kaiser, "Paolo Soleri, Urban Prophet in the Arizona Desert," *Saturday Review*, February 12, 1972, pages 37–43.

22. Irving Hoch, "The Three-dimensional City: Contained Urban Space," in *The Quality of the Urban Environment*, edited by H. S. Perloff, Johns Hopkins Press (Baltimore, 1969).

23. Erich Fromm, *The Sane Society*, Fawcett (Greenwich, Conn., 1955), page 102.

24. J. B. Priestley, *Man and Time*, Doubleday (Garden City, N.Y., 1964). 319 pages.

25. Gay G. Luce, *Body Time*, Pantheon Books (New York, 1971). 394 pages.

THE
GENERAL PLAN
FOR
COMPACT CITY

3.1 Its Shape and Layout

When we compare the skyline of our proposed Compact City with the skyline of any of today's cities we find the two are quite different. In the first place, in our Compact City there would be hardly any outward signs of a city at all, for Compact City's general silhouette would be low and flat—like an upside-down pie pan. One would see no tall buildings—only a landscaped plateau park raised 240 feet above the surrounding countryside. Into the tiered slopes forming the edges of this plateau would be built apartments, patios, and roads. These exterior roads would permit one to ascend (in a quarter turn about the perimeter) to the plateau atop the city. Inside, in the interior of the city, more apartments, also homes, offices, and work centers are built on several levels. See the lower part of Figure 3-1.

At completion of the first stage of its growth, Compact City would have a population of a quarter million. This choice of 250,000 people for the first stage is made only for the purposes of our discussion. The proposed city would, of course, be growing continuously. If the City were to grow beyond two million it would begin to lose some of its conveniences and so the latter figure could be used as an upper bound on size.

The "ideal" dimensions of a city depend on certain planning standards such as population size, the amount of space required per person, vertical versus horizontal travel speeds, and so on. Based on

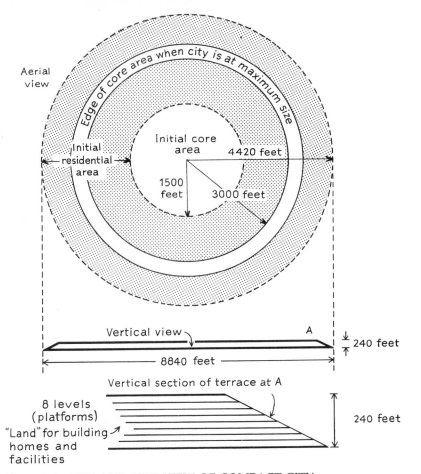

Figure 3-1 TOP AND SIDE VIEW OF COMPACT CITY
Population: 250,000. Base area: 2.2 square miles. As the city grows
to 2 million people, its height and diameter are expanded to
dimensions double those shown.

such criteria and others developed in Chapter 10 we can arrive at the
dimensions shown in Figure 3-1. The shape chosen is circular with a
radius eighteen times its height. (Later, in Chapter 13, we will discuss
variations of this shape.) When it reaches its eventual maximum
size, the city would have a base area of 8.8 square miles and a height
of 500 feet.

By constructing additional rings around the city and increasing
the number of levels, provision could be made for the city to grow
from its first-stage population to its eventual maximum. Its diameter
and height, however, would only need to double during this growth
process. (From geometry note that doubling the linear dimensions
increases the volume of the city, and hence the population it can
accommodate, eightfold.) When the city achieves full height, the

plateau roof becomes a landscaped recreational park that can be reached in less than one minute from any level within the city.

The plateau on top of the city gives a panorama of rural country-side. What would one see? Immediately beyond the city would be recreational areas, all within ten minutes by car or bus from any part of the city. (The Park-Roof and the surrounding environs of the city constitute 100 square miles of recreational areas immediately available to all inhabitants.) Truck farms supplying fresh produce are a little farther away than the recreational areas. Also visible from the city top is the airport. Underground all-weather roads connect the airport to the city. Railroad freight cars are marshalled beyond the airport and enter the city when they can be immediately unloaded or reloaded. Heavy industries, such as power plants and oil refineries, are located in an industrial park just beyond the airport, in the proximity of the railroad yards. But all other industry is inside the city. Figure 3-2 shows the city in its surroundings.

Exterior Dwellings

In Compact City people would have a wide variety of choices of dwellings. These could be apartments or homes, large or small; they could vary greatly in style, and could be located on the exterior with a view of the surrounding country, or in the interior close to work or shopping. No matter where they are located, the Park-Roof or surrounding countryside is only a few minutes away.

Under the plan proposed here, close to half of all housing units would be built around the periphery forming the outside surface of the city. The periphery can be terraced with apartments which have patios and an outward view. When the city grows to its maximum height of sixteen levels, additional apartment complexes can be built directly above the central core of the city, on, and looking out across, the Park-Roof. Homes on the top level directly below the Park-Roof would receive natural light through light wells. The apartment complex overlooking the Park-Roof above the city "Core" could consist of fifteen rings of six-story apartment buildings. These could be arranged in a variety of patterns with adequate green space and play areas. Such a complex would give an additional 80,000 apartment units directly above the Core. See Figures 3-2 and 3-3.

Peripheral apartments could vary in size. On the average, terraced apartments would have a 20-foot front facing the outside. To maximize the number of outside units, three apartments could be built between each level, each apartment being set back 20 feet from the one below it to provide surfaces for 20-by-20-foot patios. At completion of the first stage of construction there could be 32,400 such peripheral units and a somewhat greater number of interior households.

A computation: The total number of exterior terraced apartments can be computed by assuming an average exterior radius of 4,420 feet or circumference of 27,680 feet less 680 feet for roads. Multiply

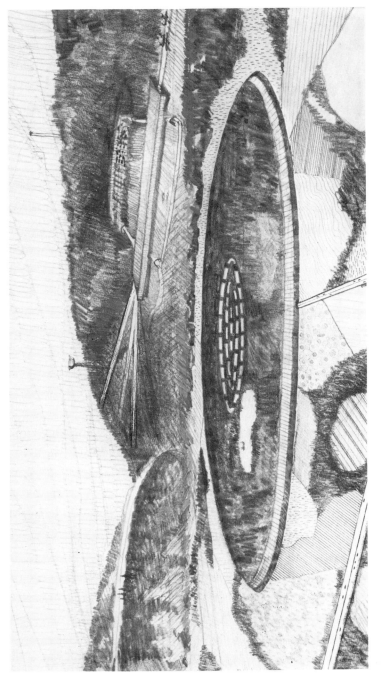

Figure 3-2 A VIEW OF COMPACT CITY
On the top is a park roof and a conventional ring of apartments above the core area. The city is surrounded by rural countryside. The airport is located close to the city, inasmuch as there are no suburbs.

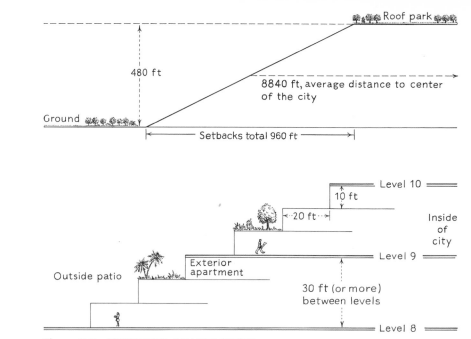

Figure 3-3 EXTERIOR APARTMENTS
As Compact City grows beyond the first stage, 130,000 apartments
could be terraced to face toward the outside, and an additional 80,000
could be located above the core area.

by 8 levels times the 3 units that are above each other per level and
divide by the 20-foot front per apartment. Thus there are 27,000
feet $\times$ 8 $\times$ 3/20, or 32,400 apartment units terraced around the sides
of the city. When the city reaches its maximum size an analogous
calculation yields 130,000 peripheral apartments.

The Interior

The city, in its first stage, has 8 *levels* which are spaced in excess of
three conventional stories apart. The total city height (240 feet) is
roughly the same as that of a conventional twenty-story apartment
building, but the proposed use of the interior space in Compact
City, as we shall see, is entirely different.

Physically, Compact City can be thought of as a three-dimensional
organic structure designed for convenient living for its inhabitants
during the various stages of its development. The essential idea is
that the city *builds* its own "land" instead of robbing nature. Various-
sized lots would be made available on different levels; on these lots
one could build offices, plants, stores, schools, apartments, and
houses very much like one would in a conventional city (except that
in Compact City a more flexible construction could be used since the
facilities are protected from the weather). On the lots one could build

homes in various styles and the remaining open space could be used
for patios and interior gardens. For our illustrations we have used,
as an average, a lot 60 feet wide and 100 feet deep. See Figure 3-4.

The choice of 30 (or more)- foot separations between levels is optional. The height shown in Figure 3-5 is largely based on the authors'
personal observations of lobbies, shopping malls, and protected
garden areas with high ceilings. When ceilings are higher than 25
feet and light in color, one enjoys a pleasant feeling of spaciousness —
the same feeling as being in open space. An example is the lobby of
the Union Carbide Building in New York — an elevated floor area
with two nicely landscaped interior gardens, island-like, beneath a
ceiling twenty-five feet above the floor. Dulles Airport in Washington, D.C., designed by Eero Saarinen, has a suspended acoustical
ceiling 30 feet above a base area of approximately 600-by-75 feet. In
spite of the length of the terminal building, one again has only a
feeling of spaciousness: there is no "tunnel effect." It is also note-
worthy that even during its busy time there are many hundreds of
people moving about talking and greeting each other, yet the noise
pollution is virtually zero.

The Core Area

Compact City's work area is called the *Core*. Similar to the central
commercial areas of present-day cities, the Core would contain offices, factories, warehouses, hospitals, high schools, and universities.
Only heavy industry, such as blast furnaces and refineries, would
be excluded from the Core area and located at some distance from the
city. The Core shopping area would resemble some of the attractive
covered shopping malls that are beginning to be built across the
country today.[1] The chief difference is that the proposed Core area
would also include major hotels, convention halls, theaters, movies,
sports facilities, as well as work, health, and education centers. The
three-dimensional layout, of course, makes the areas used for these
activities more readily accessible to one another — far more so than in
the central core area of a conventional city.

A large number of exhibit halls, museums, and auditoriums would
also be interspersed throughout the Core for exhibits, lectures, de-
bates, and for the conducting of public events and political processes.

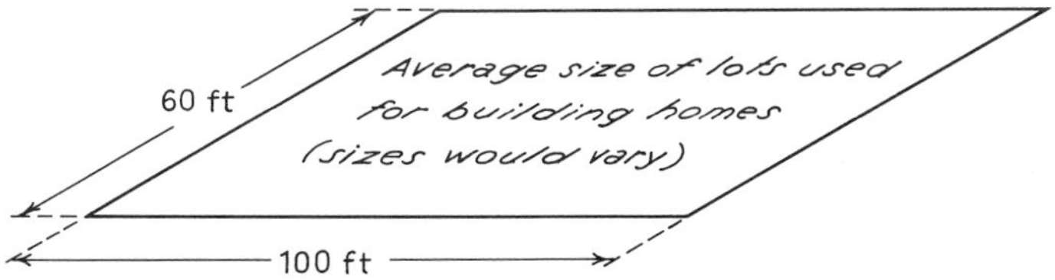

Figure 3-4 THE KEY IDEA OF COMPACT CITY IS THAT
IT PAYS TO "BUILD LAND" INSTEAD OF ROBBING
NATURE

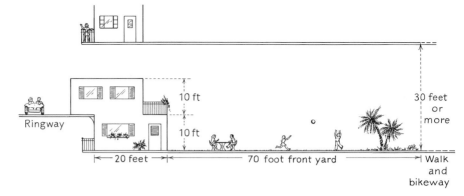

Figure 3-5 A TWO-STORY (2400-square-foot) HOME WITH A
SPACIOUS YARD
The "effective density" of the open space per person is less than in
present-day cities.

Also there would be many small parks and facilities for music and
visual arts. The Core area could be made very attractive: there could
be lights, mosaic decorations, and other uses of color; its sounds and
the hustle and bustle of its activities could make it an exciting place
to be. Figure 4-13 shows a view across the Core area.

One can anticipate that because of its central location the Core
would house the main fire, police, and municipal administrative
agencies. The latter would undoubtedly make use of computers (as
they already do in conventional cities) to maintain the vital functions
and flows throughout the city: electric power, air supply and air
conditioning, water supply, and the separation and recycling of
various types of sewage and waste. Computers could also be used
for short- and long-term planning and for determining the needs
for transportation, communication, and distribution of goods and
services.

Before passing on to a description of other parts of Compact City,
it is worth observing that we think the popularity of enclosed shopping malls in today's cities is an exciting and significant development because these may turn out to be the first step in the evolution
of Compact Cities. They could be used as a core; the next step might
be to combine an enclosed shopping mall with an enclosed hotel,
some businesses, a school, and some housing, all under one roof.

Other Areas

The broad band which surrounds the Core in Figure 3-6 is the residential area, which is located for ready access to the work area and
to rural environs surrounding Compact City. As already noted some
houses and apartments would have terraces overlooking the countryside. In the uppermost layers of Compact City the houses could be

built with indoor gardens and sunlight wells; some apartments would also be built directly above the Core area overlooking the Park-Roof. The residential ring shown in Figure 3-6 is actually two concentric rings separated midway by the city's Mid-Plaza, and is representative of the residential area on each level of the city. The residential area is separated from the Core area by the Core Edge when the city eventually reaches its maximum size. At that time the city map of each fully completed level would show five distinct rings (see Figure 3-6):

Core
Core Edge
Inner Residential Area
Mid-Plaza
Outer Residential Area

The main function of the Core Edge would be to provide facilities for parking cars just outside the Core Area. The Core Edge would also contain ramps with mechanical devices for pulling electric autos to

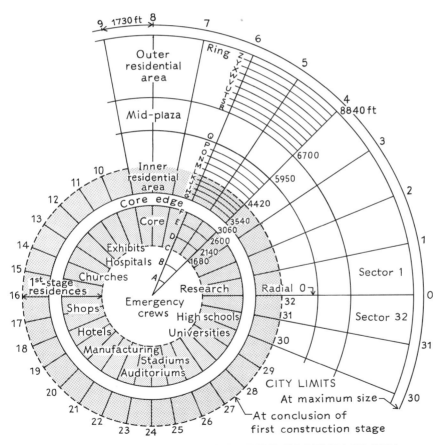

Figure 3-6 A TYPICAL PLAN FOR ONE LEVEL IN COMPACT CITY

higher levels and regular ramps for cars descending to lower levels (how these would work is outlined in Section 4.6). The Core Edge has a promenade (or mall) with small parks and recreational areas. Shop windows and exhibits line the core side of this ring.

The Mid-Plaza is conveniently located between the Inner and Outer Residential Areas and provides local facilities such as elementary schools for children, clinics, neighborhood shops, parks, and play areas. It too has ramps similar to those in the Core Edge. See Figure 3-7.

The main system of roads within the city consists of 32 radial two-way roads which radiate from the Core Edge like spokes of a wheel. These spokes divide the city on any level into 32 sectors. For example, Sector One is the wedge-shaped area between Radial 1 and Radial 0. The cross streets are alternating one-way roads. These total 26 rings, starting with the innermost A Ring and ending with the outermost Z Ring, as shown in Figure 3-6. Automobiles would be electric-battery-powered; they could be privately owned but more likely they would be rented because of low family usage. In Figure 3-7 and also in Figure 3-9 they are shown parked in the residential sections along the radials.

Radials, rings, and levels provide a good frame of reference for locations within the city. An address like 1621 K6 could be used to refer to residence number 21, located between radials 16 and 17, Ring K, Level 6.

Initially, during the first stage of the city development, only rings A, B, . . . , L would be built. Part of the residential area, at first, would be inside the eventual Core area and then would be moved outward as the city core grows in size. Flexible construction would facilitate this outward movement. During the first stage, the Core Edge would serve as an interim mid-plaza for the residential areas, but later it would become the edge of the Core and a new Mid-Plaza would be created between rings Q and R.

3.2 Interior Houses and Apartments

Most houses in Compact City would have two floors in order to conserve base area. Design of both the interior and exterior of these houses would vary according to the preferences of the residents. The ringway would provide access to the *rear* of the upper floor of a house. To facilitate home deliveries by electric-battery-powered trucks from the ringway, it would probably be convenient to have the upper floor of a house built to open directly onto the ringway. The lower floor, however, could be offset 10 feet from the ringway 30 feet below, creating an appearance of openness and spaciousness there. See Figure 3-8.

As noted earlier and illustrated in Figure 3-4, lots would vary in size: some would be large, others small. Views of the rear of homes

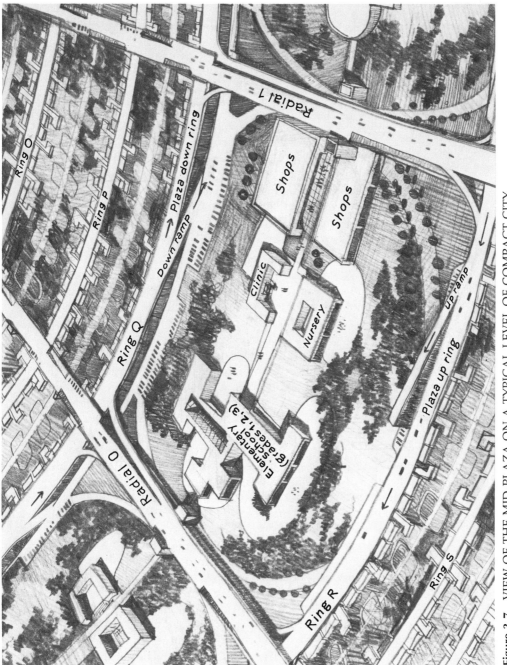

Figure 3-7 VIEW OF THE MID-PLAZA ON A TYPICAL LEVEL OF COMPACT CITY

Residences are along the ringways on both sides of the Mid-Plaza (center), where the local neighborhood shopping, elementary schools, nursery, clinic, and other local recreational facilities are all located. The roof and any upper levels have been cut away for this view.

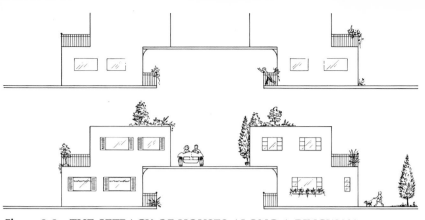

Figure 3-8 THE SETBACK OF HOUSES ALONG A RINGWAY
The general plan of Compact City would open the interior views to give
a feeling of spaciousness. This would be done with lighting, and with
the setbacks, high ceilings, interior terraces, and decorative effects.

along a ringway are shown in Figures 3-8 and 3-10 and the front
along the walkway in Figures 3-5 and 3-11. Houses also would vary
in size: some of these would be large, others small. An average house
could occupy the entire 60-foot width of the lot along the ring. The
lower floor could be 20 feet deep and stand 9 feet high. The top floor
(as noted above) would usually be offset 10 feet and would have, on
the average, the same dimensions as the floor below it. The total
house area, therefore, on the average, is 2,400 square feet (Figure
3-5). With this arrangement the open space on the lot would be a
front yard, 60 by 70 feet. The front of the lot would border a walkway
and one would normally enter his home along a path from the walkway. Access to the front yard from the ringway in the rear would also
be possible with stairs located along the side of the house, but the
route would usually be blocked to keep children out of the ringway
and away from cars. See Figure 3-9.

Interspersed among the houses could be, for example, L-shaped
apartment buildings, each consisting of two flats, one above the
other. Flats would vary in size; we allot an area of 1,400 square feet,
on the average, for planning purposes. See Figure 3-9.

The treatment of open space around homes and apartments in
Compact City will probably be more utilitarian than in today's cities.
In present-day suburbia the exteriors are largely decorative, making
the neighborhood look nice with the least amount of upkeep. On the
other hand, in Compact City the children will be able to play in
front yards and walkways without the danger of being run over because there are no streets or driveways there. Landscaping needs will
also be different since (1) the entire city is immediately accessible to
the rural environs and (2) it takes only a minute to reach the Park-
Roof from any level. The vegetation around households in the

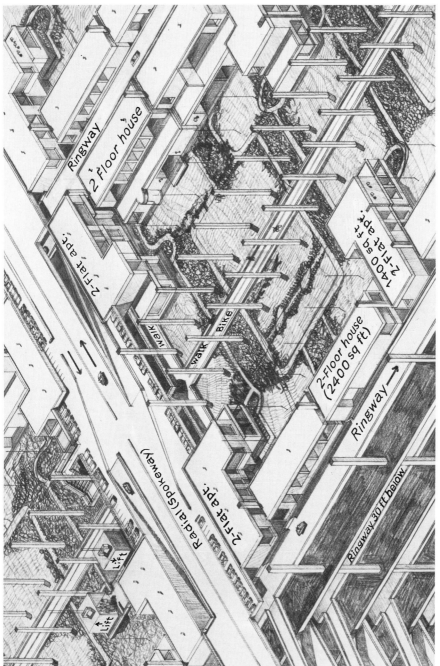

Ringway

2 floor house

2-flat apt.

2-flat apt.

Radial (spokeway)

2-flat apt.

walk

Bike

walk

Lift

Lift

1400 sq ft
2-flat apt.

2-Floor house
(2400 sq ft)

Ringway →

Ringway 30 ft below

Figure 3-9 DETAIL OF A RESIDENTIAL SECTION

Individual two-story houses and flats could vary greatly in style and design. Lots could vary in size also, though the average size would be 6,000 square feet. The city has eight levels, each separated from the next by at least 30 feet (an increase to 16 levels as the city grows to maximum size). For this view the roof and upper levels have been cut away.

Figure 3-10 THE BACKS OF HOMES FACE THE RINGWAY
Cars and trucks could make deliveries to the backs of homes, which open directly to the ringways. At the top of the figure is the underside of a ringway. Note that from the lower floors of houses one can look over the next lower ringway.

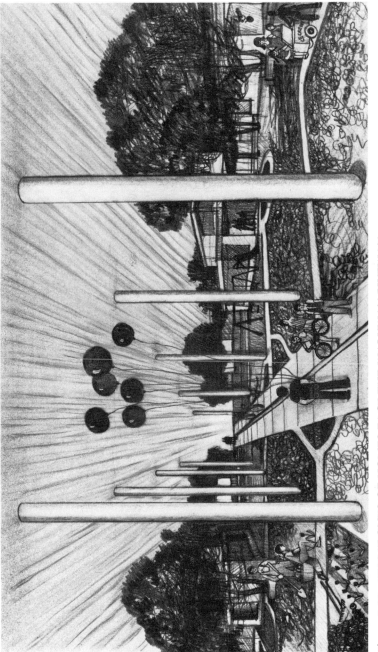

Figure 3-11 THE FRONTS OF HOMES FACE THE WALKWAY-BIKEWAY
Because the front yards and walks are not in contact with roadways, they are safe places to play.

interior of the city would, for practical reasons, be limited to foliage that can be maintained for long periods under indirect or artificial light, and new ways would have to be found to make the interior open space around homes decorative (such as small waterfalls, rock gardens, colorful garden furniture). Because front yards will not be subjected to seasonal variations in climate, the outsides of houses will undoubtedly become a more integral part of the living space. We shall speak more about this point later.

We have so far only briefly mentioned Compact City's facilities for movement about the city (e.g., its ringways and walkways). Since accessibility of any part to any other part of the city is one of the chief advantages of Compact City, we will describe in the next chapter how one can get about in Compact City.

Reference

1. "Shopping Centers Grow in Shopping Cities," *Business Week*, September 4, 1971, pages 34–38. A picture of A. Alfred Taubman, a leading developer of shopping malls, is displayed on the cover of the magazine. An example of one of his developments is Eastridge Mall (with 150 shops) in San Jose, California; it was designed by the architect Avner Naggar.

THE PLAN
FOR TRANSPORTATION

4.1 Walkways, Bikeways, and Roads

We analyzed a number of different plans for circulation in Compact City before arriving at the one which we will present here. This analysis will be found in Part Two, Section 13.4. We found to our surprise that the three-dimensional arrangement of Compact City gives rise to a very simple solution.

From the general plan for the city, shown in Figure 3-6, note that the average distance to the Core center from the residential areas, at the first stage of development, is only a half mile and that most parts of the city would still remain within easy walking distance of each other even if the city's linear dimensions were eventually doubled to maximum size. In the detail of a residential section shown in Figure 3-9 also note that the walkway that runs between the front yards is at the same elevation as the lower floor of homes. The ring and radial roads, however, are at different elevations relative to each other and to the walkway within a level as shown in Figure 4-1. The bikeways and the walkways as planned run alongside each other, separated by lane dividers.

Children and housewives would find the short walk to schools and local shopping in the Mid-Plaza safe because the walkways are placed at different elevations away from all roadways. A child walking to school would start out along the walkway in front of his home. When he reaches the spoke (or radial) he would proceed on the walkway going in the radial direction. To bicycle to high school, he would

Radialway

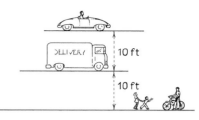

Ringway (at rear of house)

Walk-bikeway (at front of house)

Figure 4-1 ELEVATIONS WITHIN A LEVEL
The elevations where people walk and bicycle are separated from the roadways. The radials are separated from the rings so that no road intersects another.

follow the same route but in a separate bike lane. For safety, the lanes for bicycles in the radial direction are one-way and arranged so that someone using a walkway to go to school or downtown from his home would not have to cross a radial bikeway (where the bicycle flow is apt to be faster and denser). Thus no major bikeway need intersect with the main pedestrian flow from homes to shopping and work areas. See Figures 4-2 and 4-3.

4.2 Why Not Walk?

What life have you if you have not life together?
There is no life that is not in community . . .

And now you live dispersed on ribbon roads
And no man knows or cares who is his neighbor
Unless his neighbor makes too much disturbance.
But all dash to and fro in motor cars,
Familiar with the roads and settled nowhere.
Nor does the family even move about together.
But every son would have his motorcycle,
And daughters ride away on casual pillions.
When the Stranger says: "What is the meaning of this City?
Do you huddle close together because you love each other?"
What will you answer? "We all dwell together
To make money from each other?" or "This is a community?"

Selected lines from "The Rock,"
T. S. Eliot (1934)[1]

Even though T. S. Eliot's poem is now many years old, the lines above are remarkably up to date. In today's cities, because of over-extended urban areas, we have become captive to the very cars which, at one time, held out the promise of giving us the freedom to go where and when we please. In Compact City, although electric-battery-powered cars would be available, distances would be so short that people would probably find it far more convenient to walk, bicycle, or ride the mass-transit system we describe in Section 4.5. Walking should foster community life, because it is a natural way for people in a neighborhood to meet. People with similar interests could get to know each other in Compact City while walking in the neighborhood or walking to a shopping center, or to a meeting, a sporting event, a theater, or a musical event. In this way common concerns of individuals could become known and, we hope, translated into relevant community action. Such contacts are virtually impossible in today's cities because of the dependence on the auto-mobile as a primary mode of transportation. Moreover, walking could contribute in a major way to public safety. Not only are pedestrians freer from accidents but, as pointed out by Jane Jacobs and discussed in our Section 2.4, active use of sidewalks provides some unstructured supervision of children and promotes the general security of the neighborhood against crime.

In Compact City we might want to limit use of cars for a number of reasons: First, because there would be very little real need for cars for transportation; second, the increased walking should contribute to the general health and well-being of people (as a relaxing form of exercise) and to community life through the neighborhood contacts

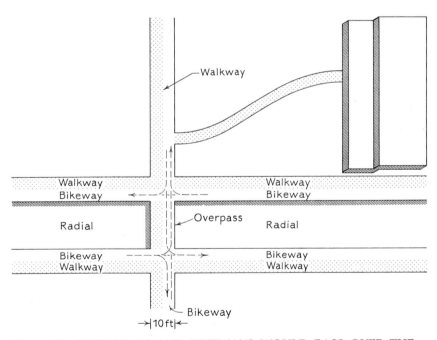

Figure 4-2 WALKWAYS AND BIKEWAYS WOULD PASS OVER THE ROADWAYS
For increased safety, no major bikeway need cross a walkway.

Figure 4-3 THE VIEW IN A RADIAL DIRECTION
Because the crosswalks pass over the roadways and have protective screens, they are safe for the pedestrian.

Figure 4-4 CHILDREN GOING TO SCHOOL
The walkway in the foreground leads to a 2-flat apartment complex. Cars travel along streets completely separated from places where people walk. The safety of the walkways means that mothers would no longer need to spend time chauffeuring their children.

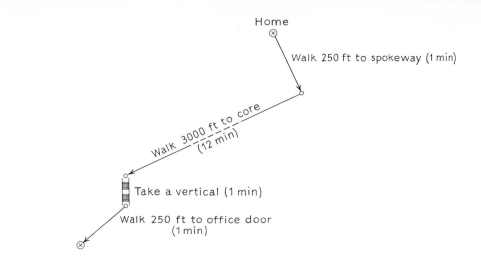

Home

Walk 250 ft to spokeway (1 min)

Walk 3000 ft to core
(12 min)

Take a vertical (1 min)

Walk 250 ft to office door
(1 min)

Figure 4-5   TOTAL WALK-TIME FROM HOME TO OFFICE:
15 MINUTES
The diagram represents distances and times in a city at first-stage
size.

made while walking; and third, because it would conserve natural
resources and reduce noise levels and other forms of pollution.

It takes a person walking at a moderate pace a little under one
minute to walk 250 feet. The average distance of a residence from the
Core in the city at completion of the first stage of development would
be roughly 3,000 feet, a 12-minute walk. The reader can visualize such
a walk by referring to Figure 4-5 and comparing it with the plan
shown in Figure 3-6.

Even if the city were to grow to eight times its first stage size, the
average walk time would only increase to 27 minutes—just enough to
qualify as a healthy walk (or, if one likes to jog, about 12 minutes).
A typical walk for a housewife (or child) from a home in the Outer
Residential Area to the Mid-Plaza for shopping (or elementary
school) is illustrated in Figure 4-6. The total walking time would be
10 minutes. Thus, even at maximum size, the city would still be a
convenient place for walking.

4.3 Up and Down

Ramps, escalators, stairs, and elevators would, of course, be used to
move vertically between levels or within levels. The main mode of
transportation from one level to another would be the elevator. Suppose we were to locate elevators every 1,000 feet along the spoke
roads. Let us see how far people would have to walk to reach an
elevator from their homes. The average distance between spokes
along a ring direction would be less than 1,200 feet when the city is

at maximum size (and half that if it were at the first stage of development.) From the simplified street layout of Figure 4-7, it is evident that a typical walk to the nearest elevator would be 275 feet plus 250 feet (about two minutes) and the maximum walk would be 550 feet plus 250 feet (about three minutes) at a moderate speed of walking.

Surprisingly few elevators would be needed—no more than eight per radial, or $8 \times 32 = 256$ main elevators for the whole city when it reaches its maximum size. Additional elevators, of course, would be required along the Mid-Plaza, Core Edge, and Core. There would also be a need for special elevators, escalators, and ramps to knit together those functional units that occupy several levels or floors within one level.

One drawback of conventional elevators is the time spent waiting for the elevator cage to arrive.[2] One scheme for reducing this waiting time is to have several cages in the same elevator shaft, one above the other. This system of multiple-cage elevators has been in use in Europe for a long time; the cages circulate continuously without stopping. See Figure 4-8. Their popular name is "Pater Noster" (Latin for "Our Father . . .") because one is advised to say his prayers before jumping into an open cage as it goes by. To increase the safety of Compact City citizens, however, it would be necessary to design a multiple-cage elevator system that would stop to pick up or drop off passengers and to close doors before moving. The 30-foot space between levels (and hence between cages) should make such a system practical to develop. The 256 main banks of elevators (each consisting of 16 cages continuously going up and 16 going down would have a capacity to deliver over 30,000 passengers per minute to the middle level of the city where the mass transit system is located. This obviously should be more than adequate to meet demand because even if (for a maximum-sized city) some 2,000,000 people wanted to make seven trips downtown per day, the demand per minute would be far less than 10,000 passengers.

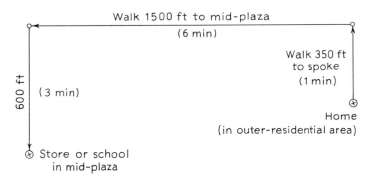

Figure 4-6 TOTAL WALK-TIME FROM HOME TO STORE
(OR SCHOOL): 10 MINUTES
The diagram represent distances and times in a city at
maximum size.

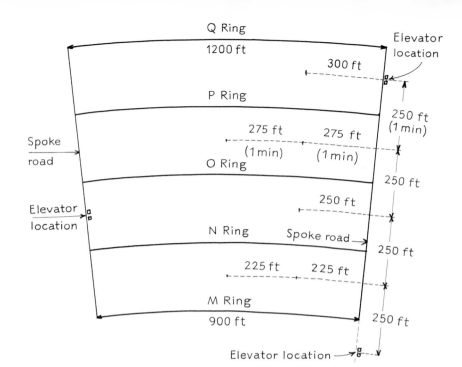

Figure 4-7 TWO MINUTES WALK-TIME TO ELEVATOR LOCATIONS
Average time from home to an elevator location is two minutes. Add one
minute to reach the mass transit level, one more minute to wait for
the mass transit vehicle, and three minutes more to arrive in the Core
area; the average time from home to Core is seven minutes in a city
at maximum size.

A high speed elevator can reach the top of the Washington Monument (500 feet) in about one minute. Its speed is six miles per hour
without stops. With a multiple-cage system, all cages within a shaft
would move and stop simultaneously; all doors would open and close
on the various levels simultaneously.

It is possible to make the elevator alternately act as a fast express, a
slow express, and as a local, by having it go through a cyclic pattern
of passing some levels between stops. For example, all cages could
rise one level, then stop, then rise two levels, then stop, then rise
three levels, then stop, and then repeat the cycle by rising one level
again, stopping, etc. In order to assist the passenger in knowing
which cage to take (in order to arrive at the level of his destination), a
panel of signal lights would be provided both inside and outside the
elevator door. Assuming 10 seconds, on the average, between cage
stops, the average speed (including stop time) would be four miles
per hour; a passenger arriving at a random time would wait, on the
average, 12 seconds for an elevator cage that would take him to the
level that is his destination; the average time to go eight levels
(including stops and wait time) would be less than one minute.

From these considerations it is evident we could design the city so that the typical time (including walk time and wait time) to reach the Park-Roof or the mass transit on the middle level of the city from one's home or any part of the city would be about three minutes.

4.4 Bicycling

Bicycling could very well become the most popular mode of personal transportation in Compact City because the bicycling paths would be relatively flat. Bikeways would be safe because they do not come in contact with car traffic. All distances would be short and the weather always ideal. As in conventional cities, bikes would probably be privately owned. Typical users would be children going to school and people on routine household errands. Cycling also would provide a good way for going to work in a hurry. Normally a person

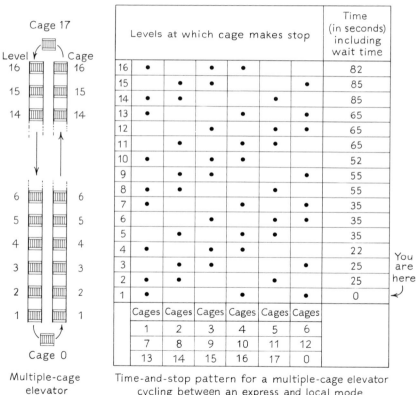

Levels at which cage makes stop						Time (in seconds) including wait time
16	•		•	•		82
15		•	•			•	85
14	•	•			•	85
13	•			•		•	65
12		•		•	•	65
11		•		•	•	65
10	•		•	•		52
9		•	•			•	55
8	•	•			•	55
7	•			•		•	35
6		•		•	•	35
5		•		•	•	35
4	•		•	•		22
3		•	•			•	25
2	•	•			•	25
1	•			•		•	0
Cages	Cages	Cages	Cages	Cages	Cages	
1	2	3	4	5	6	
7	8	9	10	11	12	
13	14	15	16	17	0	

Cage 17

Level — Cage

You are here

Multiple-cage elevator

Time-and-stop pattern for a multiple-cage elevator cycling between an express and local mode

Cage 0

Figure 4-8 MULTIPLE CAGE ELEVATORS
To reduce time spent in waiting for elevators, a multiple cage system is used. Average time (including wait-time) spent in traveling between any two randomly chosen levels is 1/2 minute. Only 256 such elevator systems are needed in a city of maximum size.

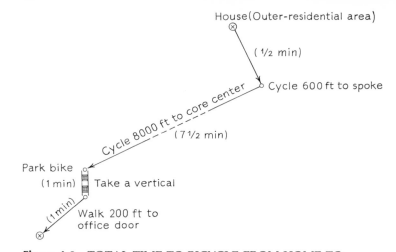

Figure 4-9 TOTAL TIME TO BICYCLE FROM HOME TO
OFFICE: 10 MINUTES
The diagram represents distances and times in a city at
maximum size.

would keep his bicycle on the same level he lives on. Starting at his
home, he could ride first along a pathway bordering his garden, then
turn into a bikeway bordering a spoke. When he reaches a downtown
vertical, he could park the bicycle, take the vertical to the level he
wants, and then walk the rest of the way to his destination.

Even if the city were to reach maximum size, by bicycling at 12
miles per hour one could cover a route from a point in the extreme
Outer-Residential Area to a point near the center of the Core in under
10 minutes. See Figure 4-9.

4.5 Mass Horizontal Transit

For those who wish to travel downtown but do not walk, bicycle, or
use autos (which will be discussed later), a mass transit system is
proposed. One simple arrangement would be to have the mass transit
located on a middle level with routes along each radial and along the
Mid-Plaza Ring.

One criticism of the design of transportation vehicles (cars, buses,
trolleys) used in today's cities is that they are *not* designed for very
small children, the handicapped, or very old people who, as a result,
become very dependent on other people in order to move about. It is
therefore a challenge to see what can be done under the ideal road
conditions provided by Compact City.

One possibility for a mass transit vehicle that would overcome
these drawbacks would be a conveyer (which we will refer to as a
tram) consisting of a simple open platform which seats a total of 28

people. People would walk onto the tram at floor level through inward opening gates (as depicted in Figure 4-10) without having to step up or step down. Note that space for standing or for bringing in a wheelchair is provided behind the driver's seat. Including standing room, this tram would have a capacity of 32 people. Because the tram floor would be at street level, it would be easy for children and for people in wheelchairs to board. Each tram would be suspended from above. Powered by individual motors, its rubber-tired wheels would ride on overhead rails and would transport the vehicle. These rubber wheels would also keep the noise level low. If direct-current electricity is used to run the trams, then energy could be conserved

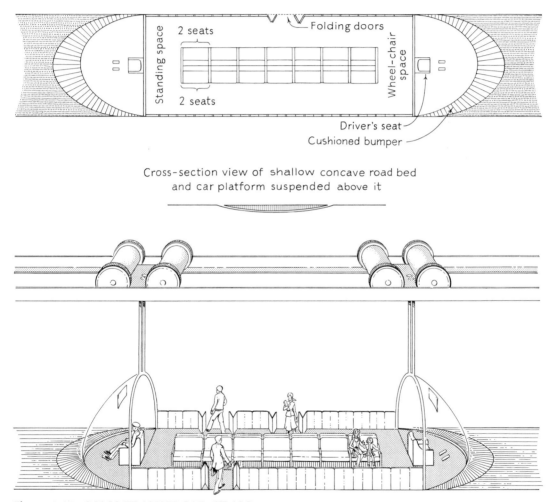

Figure 4-10 MASS TRANSIT CAR (TRAM)
The vehicle has (1) car platform at floor level, (2) easy entrance for children and wheelchairs, (3) no fare collection, (4) overhead suspension, (5) cushioned "cow-catcher" bumper, (6) capacity: 32 people, (7) safe shallow roadbed.

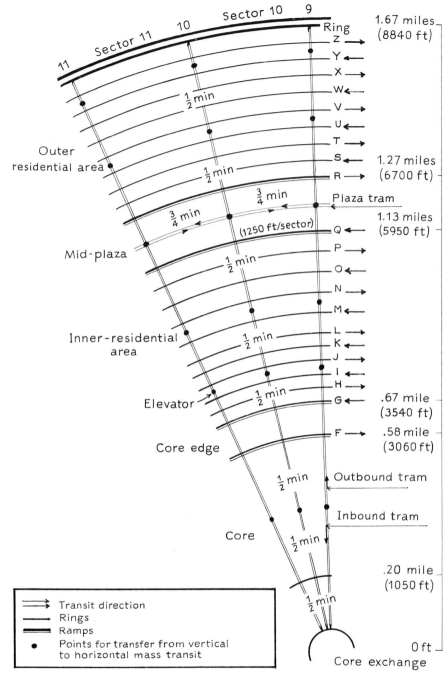

Figure 4-11 MASS TRANSIT SYSTEM ROUTES
For a city of maximum size, the average time spent in traveling to the
Core area is 3 minutes and the maximum time is 5 minutes. The stops are
at elevator locations 1,000 feet apart.

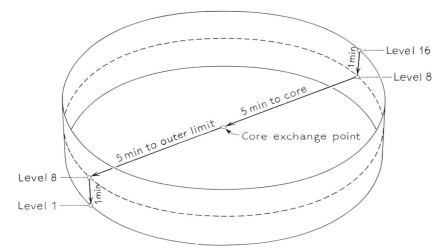

Figure 4-12 MASS TRANSIT TIME
From top to bottom and across the city in twelve minutes.

by using direct-current motors, which (by reversing the input contacts) can be turned into electric generators that brake the vehicle to a stop.

Turning to the route plan for the mass transit (Figure 4-11), we propose to have all the routes located on the middle level along the thirty-two spoke roads and around the course of the Mid-Plaza. Trams could probably average 20 miles per hour or 1,760 feet per minute including passenger pickup. If so, it would take less than five minutes to go from the outer limits of the city to the center of the Core of the city at maximum size, and half that time for the city at first-stage size.

People wishing to take a tram would walk from their residence to an elevator located every 1,000 feet along a radial. There they could ascend (or descend) to the mass transit level to a tram stop adjacent to the elevator and board a tram for downtown. The routes a person could take to do this are also shown in Figure 4-11.

How long would it take to cross the city? Suppose the city has grown to maximum size and we are on the top level in the outer limits (Ring Z) and we wish to travel to a point diametrically opposite on the bottom level. The time to travel, as seen from Figure 4-12, would be 12 minutes plus the time spent in waiting for the tram. Note that the "Core Exchange" area of the middle level serves as the main transfer point from one spoke route to another. We will assume that the mass transit cars are spaced two minutes apart so that the average waiting time would be one minute for any transfer. Figure 4-13 shows the Core Exchange.

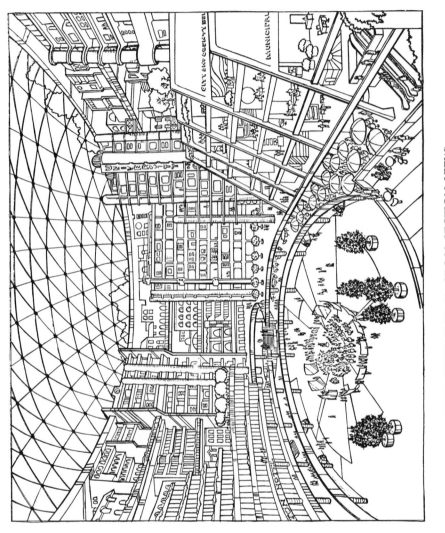

Figure 4-13 THE CORE EXCHANGE (A CROSS-SECTION VIEW)

The Core Exchange is a large open lobby area in the center of the Core building at mid-level (Level 8). Mass transit trams converge from 32 radial directions to discharge their passengers at the edge of the open area and to start new runs (the front ends of four trams are visible near columns on the floor of the Core Exchange). The diameter of the Core Exchange is 250 feet. Tiered around it are theaters, hotels, restaurants, and shops. The supporting rim of a dome is at Level 14. Levels 14 to 16 would rise around the outside of the dome.

Typical times between home in the Outer Residential Area and an office (using the plan we've outlined) would be somewhat like these:

Leave home	8:00 a.m.	⎫	
Walk 600 feet to elevator	8:03	⎪	
Descend to Level 8	8:04	⎬	Mass transit:
Wait for tram along a spoke	8:05	⎪	12 minutes from
Arrive at Core location	8:10	⎪	home to
Ascend to office level	8:11	⎪	office door.
Walk to office door	8:12	⎭	

Thus the city would still be a convenient place in which to travel even if it were of maximum size.

Let us now see just how many transit cars would be needed, based on the assumptions we have made about speed and spacing. We shall again assume the city is at maximum size since it is only when the city goes beyond the first stage of development that there would be much need for a mass transit system. Our calculations are shown in Table 4-1.

4.6 Autos and Trucks

Considering how easy transportation throughout Compact City would be by walking, bicycling, or by using the relatively simple mid-level mass transit system, it seems likely that people would decide to relegate the auto to a minor role. Cars for use outside the city could be of conventional design and would be used for rides into the country or for trips between cities. Such cars would be parked at the periphery of the city. Because their use would be only occasional, they would probably be rented rather than owned.

Compact City's *internal* auto or taxi needs, as we will see in a moment, are very minimal. Indeed, fewer than 10,000 battery-powered autos would be needed even if people were to use them instead of walking, bicycling, or mass transit. These could be parked along the radials, as was depicted earlier, in Figure 3-9. If parked there, the average time for a walk from home to a parked auto would be only two minutes (even if the city were to grow to maximum size).

Ramps would have to be provided so that autos could move between levels, but it would probably be more convenient for the driver not to shift levels. One way he can do this is to drive to the Core Edge or Mid-Plaza, staying on one level, and then park at the point closest to one's destination, finally taking an elevator and walking the rest of the way.

Autos need not be powerful or geared for climbing steep grades since all streets could be made level and the ramps on which they would move could be made one-way downhill in the residential areas. To complement the downhill ramps, uphill ramps in the

Table 4-1
*Details of a mass transit system operating at maximum capacity within
Compact City (to serve ultimate city population of two million).*

Spoke cars (for travel along radials)	
Route distance (one way)	8,600 feet
Average speed including pickups (20 miles per hour)	1,760 feet per minute
Time for one way trip	5 minutes
Time between car arrivals	2 minutes
Number of cars per radial (both directions)	5 cars
Total cars (5 × 32)	160 trams
Trips per day	23,040 trips
(1,440 minutes × 32 radials/2 minutes apart)	
Mid-Plaza cars (for travel around the Mid-Plaza ring)	
Route distance (2π × 6,300-ft radius)	40,000 feet
Average speed including pickups (20 miles per hour)	1,760 feet per minute
Time of complete circular trip	24 minutes
Time between car arrivals	2 minutes
Number of cars (12 each direction)	24 trams
Totals	
Capacity per car	32 people
Total mass transit cars (160 spoke cars + 24 plaza cars + 8 percent reserve)	200 trams
Maximum passenger delivery to Core area per day (23,040 trips × 32 passengers)	737,280 people

Mid-Plaza and Core Edge would be mechanized; i.e., cars would be
equipped with a device for grabbing (or hooking onto) a cable which
would pull them up a ramp. In this way vehicles would be able to
negotiate inclines without the use of battery power and special gear-
ing systems. A ramp system of this kind would make battery power
practical, would be smog free, and would be quiet. The shortness of
trips, the even use of cars throughout the 24-hour day, their relatively
low speeds, their quiet motors, and the availability of other means of
transportation, mean that electric cars would produce little noise
pollution. Because of their infrequent use, these battery powered cars
for use within the city also would probably be rented rather than
owned. The practicality of the battery-powered cars will be discussed
further in Section 13.4. Regarding the practicality of sharing the use
of rented cars, we note that in Montpellier, France, a system of
sharing has been introduced in which a subscriber acquires a key
and buys chips which "wear out" with distance travelled. A car may
be picked up and left at a large number of points.

   Even if every family were to dispense with walking, bicycling, or
riding mass transit, and were to use an auto as much as one hour a
day on the average, the total requirement for autos would still be
quite low. Thus for a maximum-sized city, car-hours used per day
would equal 600,000 families × 1 hour, or 600,000 car hours used
per day. Assuming that residents of Compact City would require the

use of cars fairly uniformly throughout the 24-hour day, then the number of autos needed would be 600,000/24, or 25,000 autos. But note that one hour of use per day represents about 20 separate trips since a typical trip would be from .5 to 1.5 miles and would take only two to four minutes per trip. Now 20 separate trips per family seems obviously excessive, so it follows that the requirement of 25,000 autos is also excessive. It is for these reasons that we say that *10,000 or fewer battery-powered autos would more than adequately service the transportation needs of Compact City (at its maximum size).*

By way of contrast, today more than 1,000,000 cars can be found within an urban area of California in which 2,000,000 people live, and these cars are used primarily for travel within that area.

4.7 Automatic Delivery System

In Compact City deliveries to homes would probably be made in much the same way as in a present-day city. Very large objects, of course, would be delivered by truck. Distances are short, so smaller objects could be carried by hand or in grocery carts. But it is possible Compact City residents would avail themselves of the use of an automatic conveyor system for delivery of small objects directly to the home. Such a system appears to be practical in a compact environment, though it is definitely not in a conventional city. Its availability in Compact City could change our ways of doing routine shopping and it could simplify the collection of solid waste.

We considered a number of possible automatic delivery systems. Figure 4-14 shows what we found to be the simplest. It is one in which each dwelling unit would have a vertical duct equipped with a vertical moving belt for lifting boxes containing the objects to be delivered—a kind of modern automated dumbwaiter. Objects to be delivered to a home (say) would be placed in a container equipped with a bank of dials which could be used to set up a delivery address that could be read mechanically as the container passes various transfer points. A container originating in the Core area, for example, would first be taken to the Mid-Level. There it would be placed on a horizontal conveyor belt system located along the radials at the Mid-Level which would take objects from the Core and transport them first along one of the spoke directions (probably every fourth radial would be sufficient). Next, transfers are made to other horizontal conveyor belts moving around the concentric rings; finally transfers are made to belts in the vertical duct leading to a home. These vertical belts lift (or lower) the conveyor boxes to the appropriate level. At each home there could be a device which automatically opens a small door to the duct and shoves the container box off the vertical belt onto a small receiving "dock" in the home. Such a dock is shown in Figure 6-8 in Chapter 6. Like all delivery systems, it is possible that misrouting could occur. But the dial spelling out the address for the

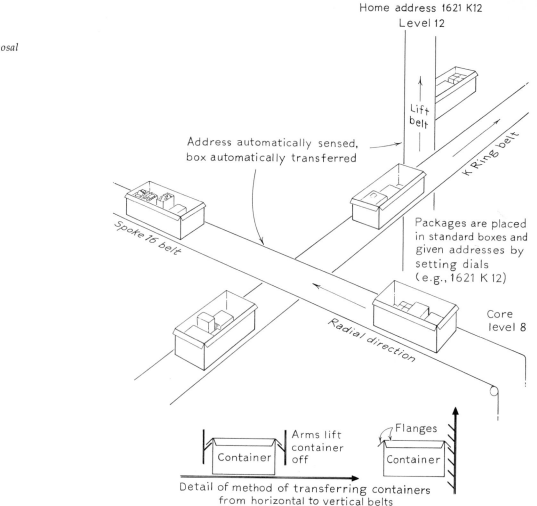

Home address 1621 K12

Level 12

Lift belt

K Ring belt

Address automatically sensed,
box automatically transferred

Spoke 16 belt

Packages are placed
in standard boxes and
given addresses by
setting dials
(e.g., 1621 K 12)

Radial direction

Core
level 8

Arms lift
container
off

Container

Flanges

Container

Detail of method of transferring containers
from horizontal to vertical belts

Figure 4-14 THE AUTOMATIC CONVEYOR BELT SYSTEM
Packages are placed in standardized boxes and dispatched from any
point in the city to any other point. The system plays a role analogous
in many ways to the arteries and veins of the human circulatory system.

automatic sensory apparatus could easily be compared with the address written on a package in the delivery container, an adjustment could be made, and the box correctly rerouted.

A parallel conveyor system would operate in the reverse direction. This could be used to return empty containers or to dispose of solid waste, and the woman in Figure 6-8 is doing just this. To prevent possible contamination of the system by trash, it might be advisable to place the trash first inside a special closed container or plastic bag that can be sealed before placing wastes into the conveyor box for transmission.

If the city grew to maximum size, it would need, for the 600,000 dwelling units, 600,000 divided by 32 or 18,750 two-way vertical conveyor lifts. Note that we divide by 32 instead of by 16 because two adjacent houses on a level and all those above and below them on all the different levels could share a common vertical duct. Similarly the two apartment units one above the other on a level and all those on all levels above and below them could share a common duct. The conveyor system appears extensive but the proportion of the system that would need to be paid for by each family turns out to be trivial: about 2 feet of horizontal conveyor belt in each direction and 15 feet of vertical lift belt in each direction. To see how this is calculated, note that the amount of belt in the 8 spoke directions is about 8,000 feet × 8 spokes = 64,000 feet, and the amount needed in the ring directions is 2 π × 6,000 feet × 17 residential rings × 2 (there are residences on both sides of a ring street). This yields about 1,300,000 feet; dividing by 600,000 families yields a little over 2 feet each direction per family of horizontal belt.

Similar analyses could be made of the Core area. Because of the compact arrangement of the business facilities, it is likely that the shared costs of the conveyor belt system in the Core area would be low also.

4.8 Airport Logistics

The automatic delivery system would make it possible to eliminate all baggage handling by a traveller to or from the airport. A suitcase packed at home could go directly to the hotel room at the traveller's destination without the traveller ever having to check it or carry it.

Because of the even 24-hour use of the airport by residents of Compact City, airplanes would need to be processed through the airport in a steady, efficient way. Because there would be no suburbs, there would be no need to locate the airport beyond the suburbs, and it could be located close to the city, say six miles away. With no suburbs, nearly everyone landing at the airport would have the city as their eventual destination. It seems reasonable that the airport could be designed so that passengers leaving an airplane could transfer directly into waiting buses (instead of, as in today's airports, having to make a long walk through terminal lobbies). Because of the short distance between airport and city it would be economically feasible to have the airport connected to the city by a roadway protected from the weather (e.g., a tunnel). Buses moving at an average speed of 60 miles per hour could reach the Core in six minutes. See Figure 4-15, which shows how a passenger could land at 12 o'clock, board a bus, and arrive at a conference located in a lecture room in the Core area by 12:08 or at his home in the Residential Area by 12:15. This includes time for transfers. At the same time the passenger is reaching his destination, his bags could be automatically delivered to his hotel room or home.

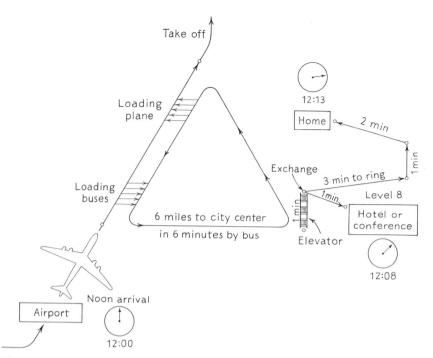

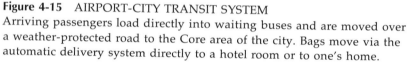

Figure 4-15 AIRPORT-CITY TRANSIT SYSTEM
Arriving passengers load directly into waiting buses and are moved over
a weather-protected road to the Core area of the city. Bags move via the
automatic delivery system directly to a hotel room or to one's home.

Summary

This concludes our proposal for transportation within Compact
City. In this chapter we discussed, for the most part, alternative ways
for people to circulate internally about the city. We anticipate that
transportation to the countryside, to heavy industry plants outside
the city, or between cities would not change much from the forms
these take today. Because most distances are short within the city,
walking and bicycling could become the principal means of transportation in the city. With the use of the elevators and the mass transit,
one could reach any point in the city from any other point in less than
12 minutes, even when the city reaches maximum size. Battery-
powered cars present another option for getting about in the city,
but we expect they would play a minor role. Because of the effective
use of the vertical dimension in the city, it would be feasible to install
an automatic conveyor belt system for deliveries of small packages to
and from houses and apartments. This conveyor system would be
a convenient way of collecting solid wastes and recycling them
economically.

1. From "Choruses from 'The Rock'," in Collected Poems 1909–1962, by T. S. Eliot. Copyright 1936 by Harcourt Brace Jovanovich, Inc. Copyright 1963, 1964 by T. S. Eliot.

2. G. R. Strakosch, *Vertical Transportation: Elevators and Escalators*, John Wiley and Sons (New York, 1967). See also G. Bouladon and P. Zuppiger, *Continuous Vertical Transport for Skyscrapers*, Institute Battelle, Centre de Recherche, (7 Route de Dreze, Geneva, 1966), 29 pages.

5

IT'S A BARGAIN

5.1 Housing and Facility Costs

The cost of building tall structures in a conventional city increases rapidly with height. To haul materials to great heights consumes energy, time, labor, and therefore, money. As examples, we cite the John Hancock Building in Chicago, which has a height of 1,200 feet and a floor area of 2.9 million square feet at a total cost of $96 million,[1] and the World Trade Center in New York, two towers rising to 1,350 feet (110 floors) and four surrounding structures with a total floor area of 10 million square feet at a total cost of $600 million. The difference in cost per square foot jumps from 30 dollars in Chicago to 60 dollars in New York (at 1969 costs). Differences in height, time of construction, and land costs are partial reasons given for this doubling of price per square foot of space.

Another important observation is that the taller a building is, the more of the total horizontal space is used to house shafts for vertical transport (between 13 and 25 percent, depending on whether a trip from the ground floor to the top floor is to be made in one elevator or will require several). The taller the building, the longer the time spent in vertical transport; hence, at a given time more people are moving up and down from some horizontal level. Most of the time for vertical transport is spent in waiting and in stopping. To compensate for this, structures are often designed with increased horizontal area and with several parallel elevator shafts, some housing express elevators. Although these reduce the time spent in waiting for elevator travel, they also reduce the amount of useful floor area in a tall building.

The costs of tall structures are more than two to three times higher per square foot than what one pays to build a suburban house. But in suburban residential construction there are no costs for elevator space, for moving men and material up and down, and for expensive land acquisition. Moreover, skyscraper costs include excavation (sometimes rock-blasting) and the building of extensive foundations below the ground.

Compact City's height of 240 feet at the first stage of development (and 480 feet at maximum size) is low compared to the height of the John Hancock Building and the World Trade Center. (There are over 75 buildings in New York City with heights above 500 feet.) Compact City's maximum height would be about that of a conventional 36-story building. Note, however, that Compact City would exert less pressure at the base because it would have only 16 levels inside instead of 36. Hence, as far as height or weight is concerned, the construction of the city should not cause any unusual building problems. The 256 or so main elevators (spaced about 1,000 feet apart along radials in the city) use up a negligible area. The system of ramps within the city make it easy for trucks to bring materials *to any level* during construction. What this means is that it should be no more costly to construct the higher levels of Compact City (per square foot) than to construct a low one- or two-story building. Accordingly, in the analysis that follows, we have used, as standard cost factors for building Compact City, the same costs per unit area as those for building low structures in present day cities.

In estimating costs we have used 1969 dollars throughout. These are useful in calculating *comparative* costs; the conclusions would not be different after adjustment for the inflation that has taken place since that date.

Cost of Homes and Apartments

In determining what it would cost to build Compact City, we note that the major expense (just as it is in today's cities) would be in residential housing. Recall that since trucks could use ramps to bring materials to any level of Compact City, construction would be easier. Building techniques would also be simpler because (1) houses would not be subjected to severe weather conditions, (2) mass production techniques could be used (later, we will discuss the possibility of greater variety in construction through prefabrication and modular construction), (3) there would be no need for furnaces, hot water heaters, or air conditioning equipment (since centralized equipment would be used instead), nor need for garages or slanted roofs. All these contribute to keep costs low. And it is possible that owners of Compact City lots could participate in construction of their houses, thus further reducing costs. We can, accordingly, assume that housing units in Compact City can be built for $10 a square foot (in 1969 dollars). Admittedly, this may be on the low side. Whatever the cost of future housing, that cost will be incurred whether a conventional house is built in sprawling suburbia or in Compact City. The cost of $10 a square foot for a house or apartment unit assumes the use of modular construction referred to above. It excludes the cost of the cement-slab floor-base of the lower floor of a house or apartment complex since this will later be included in the cost of building the lot.

For figuring costs, we will make use of certain construction standards that we will develop later. In particular, we assume (1) that Compact City's typical house is 2,400 square feet and hence would cost $24,000, and (2) a typical apartment would have 1,400 square feet and hence would cost $14,000. We also assume that there are an equal number of house and apartment units so that the average cost per unit is $19,000 — exclusive of the cost of the lot.

Commercial Space

The cost of developing commercial space will depend on how many floors are built between each level of the city, and on what it costs to build a square foot of floor space. We will use for the latter an average factor of $30 per square foot. Based on certain standards, which, as we have said, will be developed in Part Two, about two-thirds of the commercial space would be devoted to exhibition halls, stores, and factories. These typically have high ceilings and hence could be priced at $30 for each square foot of 30-foot-high space. The remaining third of the commercial space would be office facilities, consisting (on the average) of two floors of offices to each level. These would hence be priced at $60 for each square foot of 30-foot-high space. We can now calculate the combined cost of developing 30-foot-high space for commercial purposes: two-thirds at $30 per square foot plus one-third at $60 per square foot results in an average cost of $40 per square foot.

5.2 The Cost of Building "Land"

A crucial figure in determining Compact City costs would be the cost of building "land"; primarily this is the cost of laying the cement-slab bases for the various levels on which apartments, houses, and their yards or gardens would be placed. The cost of pouring a 4-inch reinforced concrete slab for a patio in present-day suburbia costs a homeowner around 60 to 70 cents per square foot (1969 retail prices). Naturally the unit cost of large production jobs is less. The costs also vary depending on the thickness of the slab, the concrete mix, and the amount of reinforcing steel used. If a slab for the yard and the base of a house in Compact City could be laid at a cost that is close to 60 to 70 cents (including the costs for supports for the slabs) the cost of the residential part of the city would run about 30 percent less than that shown later in Table 5-2, and the total cost of the city would run about 22 percent less. The authors have received all kinds of estimates for costs. These costs were five dollars and higher per square foot, but included the costs for expensive distribution systems (water, electricity, etc.), which are excluded from the costs we are estimating.

A catenary-supported parking area and roof for a large supermarket area recently built in San Francisco ran six dollars per square foot, and this was considered inexpensive. Multiple level parking facilities are usually costed at five dollars per square foot (1969 prices) in the United States. The cost to build a mile of highway (6 lanes with dividers and shoulders—a concrete strip about 100 feet wide) runs about a million dollars per mile or about $1.90 per sq. ft. This figure is of interest because mass production techniques are used for paving highways. Presumably similar equipment could be developed for laying slabs rapidly and inexpensively in Compact City.

We have used the cost factor for building "land" in Compact City of *three dollars per square foot*, or $83.63 million per square mile. This cost assumes the slabs are six inches thick and it includes the cost of structural supports. We think that such slabs could be assembled or poured (or that both methods will be combined) on a production-line basis. One possibility is to pour sections of slab on a previously constructed level using specially designed high-speed pouring equipment; when the slab sections have hardened, they are raised into position to form the level above.

At the rate urban areas are expanding in the 1970s, it would be necessary (in order to curtail urban sprawl) to develop a high rate of building. For example, suppose 100 new families a day wished to settle in Compact City. To accommodate them, close to half a million square feet of "land" would have to be poured per day. This is roughly 1/10 the daily rate used for highway construction in the United States.[2]

If it turns out that our cost per unit area of slab is out of line with what could, in fact, be achieved, it will be necessary to lower the costs per household by decreasing the generous size of the lots.

The cost of *public* land—roads and interior parks—is also calculated at three dollars per square foot (or $83.63 million per square mile), the same cost factor used for residential lots.

The amount of space in Compact City that we assume will be devoted to apartments, houses, yards, walkways, work areas, and interior parks is derived from certain standards set forth by Hans Blumenfeld in his book, *The Modern Metropolis*.[3] We will discuss these standards, which are quite generous, later in Part Two. It is convenient, for costing, first to summarize the amount of area needed for each function in a maximum-sized Compact City (with a population of 2,000,000 people) and then to reduce these proportionally to determine what would be required for a first-stage city of 250,000. See Table 5-1.

Table 5-1

*Amount of "land" (reinforced concrete) needed at $3
per square foot, or $83.63 million per square mile*

Space needs	Square miles of slab required
Residential Areas	
(600,000 housing units)	100
Mid-Plaza	
(includes 4 square miles of facilities)	17
Core	
(includes 8 square miles of facilities)	17
Core Edge	
(includes 1 square mile of roads)	6
Total area on all levels	
(when the city is at maximum size)	140 sq miles

Additional Costs for Initial Construction

Land, of course, is not the only thing that costs money in a city. Both
present-day cities and Compact City have capital costs also for the
installation of various systems, which would have to be compara-
tively evaluated before a cost analysis is complete. We have, however,
omitted from the cost analysis that will follow (in Table 5-2) the costs
for certain systems which we have listed below. (1) These are usually
paid for indirectly through the tax structure or with monthly bills for
service and (2) the sum of the costs for all the systems, when totalled,
appears to be about the same (or possibly less) for Compact City.

Systems not
included in
cost estimates
in Table 5-2 { Electrical
Water recycling
Air conditioning
Communications
Mass Transit
Automatic delivery

Both present-day cities and Compact City require elaborate distribution networks, central facilities, and substations for electricity,
communications, and water recycling. The installation costs are
estimated to be lower in Compact City than in conventional cities
because of the shorter distance from the central input source of these
utilities to the points of use; moreover, pumping and transformer
capacities would be lower in Compact City because of the more even
distribution of demand through a 24-hour period.

The air conditioning system would be centralized in Compact City
whereas in conventional cities individual homeowners must all

purchase their own cooling equipment, furnaces, and air circulators. In a present-day city, before a factory that causes air pollution can cleanse its own air, it must install elaborate equipment on the premises. In Compact City, the air used by factories could be easily isolated from the general atmosphere and could be gathered with that of other factories for special reconditioning. This would drastically reduce the amount of filtering equipment needed. In conventional cities there are also appreciable extra costs for antipollution devices on cars and for special gasolines which would not be used in Compact City. Based on these considerations it appears that the comparative cost of installing air conditioning equipment would be considerably lower in Compact City.

Similarly, the water used by a factory could be conveniently isolated from the water discharged through general city use. Industrial water could be consolidated with that of several commercial plants and then upgraded through use of specialized recycling equipment—again, with resultant savings in cost.

Mass transit installation costs are not included in the cost of the basic Compact City structure shown in Table 5-2. These are estimated to run about one-fourth that currently being spent for a modern mass transit system in a present-day city. The costs would run lower in Compact City because of the shorter distances involved, the slower speeds of travel required, and because vehicles of simpler design could be used.

The automatic delivery system installation costs are also not included in Table 5-2. As noted in Chapter 4, these would require a shared cost for only 4 feet of horizontal belt and 30 feet of vertical belt per family. It does not appear to be a costly system. Such a system would not be feasible in a conventional city.

Considering the *total costs* for installation of all these central facilities and distribution networks (where feasible), they appear to be about the same if installed in a present-day city or in a Compact City of comparable population. As noted, all of these costs have been omitted from the "land" development costs since they would be paid for indirectly just as they are in present-day cities via the tax structure or with monthly utility service charges.

We are now in a position to summarize the cost of building "land" and facilities. These are presented in Table 5-2. In the next section we shall make a comparison between costs for housing plus transportation in a present-day city and the costs for housing and transportation needed in a comparable Compact City.

5.3 Comparative Costs

Now let us compare directly the cost of housing and transportation in a present-day city with that of Compact City, using as our reference point moderate living standards[4] which we hope will be representa-

Table 5-2

The cost of building "land" and facilities. Table includes the
cost for building "land," houses, apartments, commercial facilities,
and roads. Omitted are costs of (1) initial planning, (2) developing
equipment for high speed pouring of slabs, (3) services usually paid
for via taxation: namely, water, electric power, and sewer systems.
Roads and parks, however, are included in the costs.

Areas and their facilities	Cost in billions of dollars for city at maximum size*
Residential	
Dwelling Units: 600,000 × $19,000	11.4
Lots, Roads: 100 sq miles × $83.63 million per sq mile	8.4
Mid-Plaza	
Facilities: 4 sq miles × $5,280^2$ sq ft × $40/sq ft	4.5
Interior Park: 17 sq miles × $83.63 million per sq mile	1.4
Core	
Facilities: 8 sq miles × $5,280^2$ sq ft × $40 per sq ft	8.9
Interior Park: 17 sq miles × $83.63 million per sq mile	1.4
Core Edge	
Roads: 1 sq mile × $83.63 million per sq mile	.1
Interior Park: 5 sq miles × $83.63 million per sq mile	.4

Totals		
	Maximum-sized city:	36.5
	First-stage city:	4.56
	First level of the first-stage city:	.57 (570 million dollars)**

*The city would of course be built in increments—probably one level at
a time and neighborhood by neighborhood within a level.
**Includes the cost of 10,000 dwelling units and .2 square miles of commercial facilities. Such investments are presently going into urban sprawl.
Thus the costs involved can be viewed as simply a rechannelling of current
investments with some savings.

tive of future living. In Table 5-3, "Comparative Costs," presented
at the end of this chapter, all costs are in 1969 dollars and will need
to be corrected for the inflation which has taken place since 1969. The
annual costs shown in the table are computed by multiplying the
total cost of land (or of the house) by eight percent. The eight percent
represents a "normal" interest of five percent plus average payments
of three percent on the original principal. Unfortunately, inflation
has the effect of increasing interest rates above five percent. A higher

interest rate, if used, would not change the results of our analysis. Another cost factor used in the table is one dollar a square foot for the average cost of land purchased in a present-day city.[5]

There are indirect costs associated with time spent in travelling. The time the principal wage earner requires to go from his home to work and to return increases with city size and income level. A half hour each way, or one hour a day, is typical. In the New York area, however, it is not unusual for moderate-income wage earners to commute for one and a half hours each way, or three hours a day. Because of the possibility of traffic tie-ups, most commuters allow extra travel time, say, 15 minutes. Thus, total travel time for the principal wage earner varies between 1.25 and 3 or more hours per day.[6]

What is the time spent in travel worth? Assuming the lower figure of 1.25 hours travel per day, 250 work days per year, and $3.50 salary per hour for time wasted in travel, one could arrive at a total economic loss of about $1,000 per year for moderate-income families. Under what circumstances would a wage earner, given a choice, be willing to pay an additional $3.50 per day just to avoid travel time? He might if it also meant his car would be free for use by other members of his household. He might if it meant that he could use the extra time to work longer hours, and thus increase his total take-home income. He might, if he could use the free time to do more upkeep himself around the home and thus save money currently payed to others to perform such services. Thus whether or not he would be willing to pay $3.50 (or more) per hour to save time now spent in travel depends on what opportunities he has to use the time.

There are other indirect costs due to an auto-based transportation system. For example, free parking lots around a shopping center are really not free but are paid for by the merchants within the center, who pass on that cost through increased prices for items shoppers purchase. Life insurance and health insurance rates include a cost to cover the possibility of highway accidents. There are indirect economic losses due to smog: this affects agriculture, natural foliage, and human health. Then too, the wage earner is not the only person whose travel time constitutes an expense; travel time by other members of the household is growing, and most families can probably place a value on this time if it were freed for other uses. Finally, if the people presently earning their living in some aspect of automobile transport were eventually freed to perform other services in the economy, this could significantly increase the general standard of living (perhaps as high as ten percent). The indirect costs of auto-based transportation require a more elaborate evaluation than we have been able to sketch here. We believe, however, for moderate income families that the figure of $1,000 per year which we computed earlier is a conservative economic estimate and we have used it in the table of comparative costs (Table 5-3).

In Table 5-3, we compare the direct and indirect costs of transportation and housing in Compact City with that in a present day city

Table 5-3

Comparative costs per family (1969 prices)

Item	Present-day city		Compact City	
2,400 sq ft HOUSE	$2,880/year	$15/sq ft	$1,920/year	$10/sq ft
			The lower per sq ft cost of a Compact City house is due to a simpler roof, no weatherproofing, no garage, no driveway. Cost includes prefabrication and mass assembled construction, and assumes that heating, cooling, and hot water will be supplied from a central source.	
6,000 sq ft LOT	$ 480/year	$ 1/sq ft	$1,440/year	$ 3/sq ft
SUBTOTAL: HOUSE AND LOT	$3,360/year		$3,360/year	
TRANSPORTATION	$1,000/year		(nominal)	
1 to 3 hours lost per day and other indirect costs.	$1,000/year		(nominal)	
GAS AND ELECTRICITY	$ 500/year		$ 500/year	
Citywide lighting, hot water, air conditioning, heat removal	(nominal)		$ 350/year	
TOTAL OF COSTS LISTED ABOVE	$5,860/year		$4,210/year	

Plus whatever it is worth to you to get rid of these:
Traffic deaths
Traffic injuries
Smog, pollution
Traffic jams
Noise
Unsafe walk and play areas
Inaccessible natural and
   recreational areas
Inconvenient, expensive shopping
Inconvenient entertainment
   and cultural centers
Depletion of natural resources
Bad weather
Future slums

Moreover, a better quality of life results

WE PRESENT THE DOLLARS BUT FEEL THE IMPORTANT DIFFERENCE
IS THE IMPROVED QUALITY OF LIFE

for a moderate-income family living in a 2,400 square foot home on
a 6,000 square foot lot. If our estimates are correct, the comparative
annual costs would be $4,210 in Compact City versus $5,860 in a
present-day city (based on 1969 prices) — a saving of over 25 percent.
A similar calculation based on the alternative design presented in
Section 13.1 yields a savings of 35 percent.

Notes and References

1. Ruth Wagner, and Wolf von Eckardt, "Chicago's Hancock Building,"
   The Washington Post, July 6, 1969, pages H1 and H4; two commentaries:
   their theme is "Park and work where you live." See also Skidmore,
   Owings, and Merrill, "John Hancock Center, Chicago, Illinois," News
   Release (155 E. Superior St., Chicago, August 1968).

2. *American Almanac 1972,* "Statistical Abstract of U.S.," Grosset and
   Dunlap (New York, 1972). Table 838, page 572.

3. Hans Blumenfeld, *The Modern Metropolis,* M.I.T. Press (Cambridge,
   Mass., 1967).

4. *American Almanac 1972,* "Statistical Abstract of U.S.," Grosset and
   Dunlap (New York, 1972). Table 536, page 341.

5. See James Q. Wilson (editor), *Urban Renewal,* M.I.T. Press (Cambridge,
   Mass., 1966) — in particular, the paper in it by William L. Slayton. On
   page 224 Slayton states that disposition prices for cleared land have
   averaged out at about $1 per square foot. This is the price for urban
   renewal project land made available to developers and is comparable to
   similar land used elsewhere in the community.

6. Stanford Research Institute, *Future Urban Transportation Systems, Final
   Report,* Stanford Research Institute (Menlo Park, Calif., March 1968).
   See also Wilfred Owen, *The Metropolitan Transportation Problem,* Double-
   day-Anchor (Garden City, N.Y., 1966). A Brookings Institution study.

ADVANTAGES

Let us now group together the advantages of Compact City, some of which we have already discussed, and introduce some others about which we will say more in the sections that follow.

6.1 What Are the Advantages?

Compact City

1. Eliminates many of the inconveniences related to urban over-size.

2. Makes it possible to build a modern, convenient metropolis in a natural setting at a low cost, indeed, at costs which can be largely financed out of the savings now spent on transportation in present-day cities—on vehicles, accidents, roads, parking facilities, and gasoline.

3. Saves money. The preliminary analysis (outlined in the preceding chapter) indicates that the cost for housing plus transportation for people with a moderate standard of living would be 25 percent *less* in Compact City than in present-day cities and would result in superior housing and superior transportation. The cost for good housing and transportation proposed for Compact City would run about 30 percent more than what people with a low standard of living are presently having to

pay for poor housing plus poor transportation. For people presently enjoying a high standard of living, Compact City would cost 50 percent less for comparable housing and superior transportation.

Moreover the expenditures for building Compact City represent a rechanneling of investments rather than a new burden. The cost of its construction should be weighed against the costs of further construction and renewal in today's cities, work that is outmoded before it is started.

4. Conserves the use of time. From one to three hours of time spent by wage earners in travel could be saved each day. Assuming 250 working days and $3.50 per hour wages, this amounts to a saving of from half a billion to one-and-a-half billion dollars of lost time each year in a city of 600,000 wage earners — a potential portal-to-portal income bonus of between 12 to 36 percent. Mothers no longer would need to spend their time chauffeuring children. Distances are short and free from danger of accidents.

5. Saves lives. About 500 lives would be saved from death on highways and 6,000 accidents would be avoided each year in Compact City as compared to a present-day city, assuming both have 2,000,000 inhabitants. It would no longer be necessary to fence in yards or to engage in chauffeuring in order to protect children from being run over by cars.

6. Conserves the use of land. The city at maximum size could be built on less than nine square miles of land, whereas a comparable conventional city would require 178 square miles. The 170 square miles or so thus freed for use as farms or recreational areas would be within ten minutes distance of all the inhabitants of Compact City. Calculated at $1 per square foot, about $5 billion worth of land would be permanently preserved. In the next section we shall make a comparison with the use of land in present-day cities.

7. Makes it possible to locate the additional 70–100 million people who are expected to populate the United States in the period between 1970 and 2000, but without the destructive effect urban sprawl brings to the countryside, the environment, or the ecosystem.

8. Conserves use of energy. The redesign of the city would mean a different pattern of use of energy. In Compact City use of petroleum in autos and trucks would, of course, be dramatically reduced. So would direct use of petroleum for heating. On the other hand, there would be new needs: yards and interior open areas would need to be lighted artificially, air conditioning would be required to remove heat generated by people, lights, and appliances. Overall, there appears to be a reduction of energy use of at least 15 percent.[1]

9. Conserves material resources. Automobile and gasoline costs per capita today in California run in the neighborhood of $500 per year. For an urban area with a population of two million, there are over one million cars. Transportation costs run over one billion dollars a year. As noted earlier, more than a million cars could be replaced in Compact City with less than 10,000. The round-the-clock use of facilities would drastically reduce the amount of equipment needed to handle peak loads. Installed equipment would be used more evenly and intensively. It would be renewed and modernized more often.

10. Makes possible flexible construction so that the city could adjust to changing needs. Present building methods are so rigid that it is not economical to relocate parts of the city or to modify existing parts. In contrast, the interior of Compact City would be protected from the weather so that less permanent construction could be used. The need for flexible construction is extremely important in today's fast-moving world. More will be said about this need in Section 6.3.

11. Could provide opportunities for the economically disadvantaged. Basically, because it is new and not bound by past customs, the city could provide a new start. In addition, educational and health facilities would become readily accessible to all because of the short distances involved.

12. Makes a city-wide automatic delivery system possible. Such a system might well have benefits for a city that are analogous to the function of arteries and veins in the human body. How the automatic delivery system could affect life in Compact City is discussed later in Section 6.4.

13. Permits consolidation and centralization of certain urban services. Urban sprawl causes the duplication of hospitals, schools, and many other institutions. Later, we shall see that many specialized services could be made available in Compact City which are presently not economically possible in cities because of the time and distance.

14. Makes it possible to have an ideal living environment almost anywhere. For example, if Compact City were located in a place with an extreme climate, large populations could live there—and thrive—in its comfortable interior climate while taking advantage of opportunities—economic or other—that might exist in the natural surroundings. The potentialities of an ideal, controlled, climate will be discussed in Section 6.5.

15. Eliminates air pollution. Because the atmosphere of Compact City would be controllable, air of the highest quality could, through better waste management, recycling, and air filtering techniques, be in constant supply for all the inhabitants. See Section 6.5.

16. Makes possible economical water- and solid waste-recycling systems. How the automatic delivery system can contribute to solid-waste disposal will be developed later in Section 6.6.

17. Reduces noise pollution and congestion because of round-the-clock use of facilities, the less frequent use of cars, and the use of cars with battery power. See Section 6.7.

6.2 Elimination of Urban Sprawl

With its initial population of 250,000, Compact City would occupy about 2.2 square miles of land. If one lived on the outer periphery and wished to walk to the city center, the total distance covered would be 4,420 feet. As we described earlier, the city at this stage would consist of eight levels, one above the other, 30 feet or more apart. A level in Compact City is thus the equivalent of a conventional piece of land, and like any land, a level can be used for open space around homes, recreational areas, or for building structures with a height limitation of three conventional floors (30 feet). The city grows by increasing the size of its base and the number of its levels. If it were to grow to a maximum size of 2,000,000 people, it would have a base of nine square miles and 16 levels. The same city, if laid out flat on the earth's surface, would cover an area of 140 square miles. But in that case a network of highways and extensive parking facilities would be needed; a present-day city built to the same standards would occupy an area of 178 square miles.

At its maximum size Compact City would still be a convenient place to live. It would house more people than the Borough of Manhattan in New York City, but at only one-fifth the effective density of Manhattan and in only one-third the land area. Manhattan is a classic example of dense use of land. Figure 6-1 shows Compact City superimposed on Manhattan Island. It need not be circular as shown. With some loss of efficiency its shape could be made to conform to the natural shape of the island.

San Diego, California and its suburbs, by contrast, constitute a sprawling metropolitan area with 1,318,000 people spread over 4,262 square miles. Compact City could provide this many residents— and more—with ample-sized lots and homes; its climate would be ideal; recreational facilities within and near Compact City would be readily accessible to all. Yet Compact City would occupy only 1/500 of the land area of San Diego County. Indeed, if it were located in central San Diego, as depicted in Figure 6-2, it would occupy only a fraction of the area within the boundaries of the city proper.

Parts of the greater metropolitan areas of Cleveland and Washington, D.C. each have a population of roughly 2,000,000 and both spread out over hundreds of square miles. See Figure 6-3, for a comparison of sizes if Compact City were to be located in the Cleveland area, along the shores of Lake Erie. Originally the land set

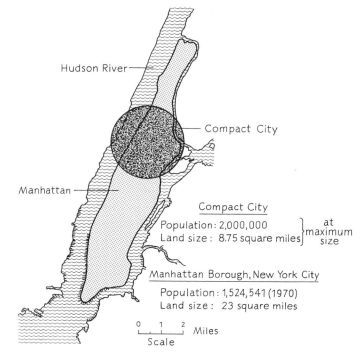

Hudson River

Compact City

Manhattan

Compact City

Population: 2,000,000
Land size : 8.75 square miles } at maximum size

Manhattan Borough, New York City

Population : 1,524,541 (1970)
Land size : 23 square miles

0   1   2   Miles
Scale

Figure 6-1 COMPACT CITY IS ONE-THIRD THE SIZE
OF MANHATTAN
New York's Manhattan Island is an example of a
high-density city. By contrast, Compact City at its
maximum size would contain more people, be more
convenient, have better access to business and recreational
areas, and have an effective density that would make it
one of the least dense cities in the world.

San Diego County

Population: 1,318,000 (1970)
Land size: 4262 square miles

San Diego

San
Diego
County

Compact City

0 5 10   20   Miles
Scale

Figure 6-2 IF COMPACT CITY WERE
LOCATED IN SAN DIEGO
Nine square miles could replace a sprawl of
4,262 square miles.

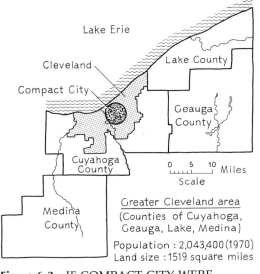

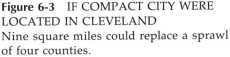

Figure 6-3 IF COMPACT CITY WERE
LOCATED IN CLEVELAND
Nine square miles could replace a sprawl
of four counties.

aside in Virginia and Maryland for the capital of the United States
covered 100 square miles, in the shape of a square 10-by-10 miles.
Because it was not at first used, the part of the square west of the
Potomac River was returned to Virginia. Now the greater metropolitan area of the District of Columbia spills out over a vast area
of Maryland and Virginia and it, in turn, is part of the huge mega-
lopolitan belt illustrated in Chapter 1, which sweeps many hundreds
of miles up the Atlantic Coast, all the way to Boston. In Figure 6-4
the small circle represents the area that would be occupied by Compact City if it were located in the center of Washington, D.C.

6.3 Flexible Construction

In his book *Future Shock,* Alvin Toffler testifies about the effect
of the "accelerative thrust" of change in the socio-economic life of
man. In *The Death and Life of Great American Cities,* Jane Jacobs discusses how lively streets, those that have many diverse uses, can
contribute in an important way to the safety and well-being of a
neighborhood, particularly when there are some people in the
neighborhood who form a core of stability in an otherwise constantly changing scene. And an interesting, active street is the kind
people wish to remain living near. The challenge is to design a city
in such a way that it can economically adapt to changing functional
needs. The following paragraphs tell how Compact City could be
made flexible in its construction to meet this challenge.

Greater Washington D.C. area
(Counties of Montgomery, Prince Georges,
Fairfax, and city of Arlington)

Population : 2,547,200 (1970)
Land size : 1485 square miles

Figure 6-4 IF COMPACT CITY WERE LOCATED IN
WASHINGTON, D.C.
One tenth the size of the District of Columbia, it
could absorb 1,400 square miles of urban growth
that now sprawls over the three surrounding
counties.

As we pointed out earlier, part of the failure of the "Radiant City"
approach to urban design is that it can, through its zoning off of
various functions, isolate one area from its neighbor by permitting
separating barriers of traffic and by using green space not for people but to make buildings look more attractive. It often creates
lonely places where people have no defense against criminal attacks.

Some might criticize us by pointing out that we also propose to
separate various functions in Compact City. For example, in the
plan presented in Chapter 3, residential areas are separated from
work and commercial areas. There are, however, four important
differences. First, there is the obvious one of ready accessibility of
any part of the city to any other part. Second, the internal structures
can be made less permanent. They could be made to be rearrangeable
to suit changing needs. Third, there would be greater stability of
populations within a neighborhood because a change of jobs within
the city would not require that a family move to another neighborhood; a family break-up would not mean a change in one's shopping
patterns or schools. Fourth, there is in the plan as we have presented
it considerable diversified use of interior open space. (In Section

13.1 we present an alternative arrangement of Compact City which is even more conducive to diversified use of space.)

Today's exterior construction materials—concrete, stone, bricks, or cement blocks—are bulky, rough, heavy, and clumsy to handle. Once the many individual building units of a conventional urban development are finished, they are rigid and expensive to alter or replace. Thus, whether we like it or not, what we build in a conventional city is what we are stuck with for several subsequent generations. By way of contrast, the only rigid part of Compact City would be its outer three-dimensional shell and the concrete slabs that form the "land" base for each level. The housing and work areas could be constructed upon these slabs and the terraces and parks could be planned in such a way as to permit easy modification and rearrangement. For example, lightweight less sturdy materials could be used to build the interior units. These could be designed to be mounted rapidly with ease and also to be dismounted and altered with effort that is small when compared with what is required to tear down or put up individual new building units in our current cities.

In brief, in Compact City houses could be made to be assembled rather than constructed, disassembled rather than wrecked. Parts of houses could be designed so that they could literally plug into each other. The same is true for office space, school rooms, and other arrangements within a neighborhood. The keynote of Compact City construction is its flexibility.

One of the saddest aspects of conventional building is its irreversible character. Irreversibility starts at the design stage. Changes in the blueprint involve work, and expense, so planners and clients tend to accept rather than modify them. Once bids are accepted on various systems of a house—plumbing, tiling, lighting, appliances, painting, masonry, or flooring—it is costly to alter plans and changes create delays. When it actually begins, construction can be so rapid that an error can be committed before it is caught. The wrong kind of plumbing fixtures are uncrated and tiled in, or the wrong sized windows are framed and sealed. After the house is completed modification is costly. Replacement by a more suitable design requires a bulldozer and a wrecking ball.

Thus we see that "custom" housing is more of an illusion than a fact. Whether one buys a tract home, a used home, or a "custom" home, one is (for all practical purposes) buying a home "off the shelf." After living in a house for a while, the needs of the family can change but the family finds it easier to make the old home do, for exchanges are not easily arranged. If, finally, one must sell his home and relocate, this involves high agent fees, delays, and location of temporary housing. The net result is that structures of a neighborhood remain as they were built; slowly they deteriorate into rotting, unattractive slums. The same is true for superblock projects—cities are stuck for a generation or two with what is constructed: society pays a high price for inflexible, rigid construction that is initially cheap.

The organization of the housing industry in Compact City, by way of contrast, could be built around the concept of change that could make it possible to redesign and rearrange homes, neighborhoods, work areas, and various other functions easily into new patterns to suit individual taste and changing community needs.

A house-planning center could be set up in Compact City to help people *learn* about the design possibilities. A variety of model homes could be continuously on display. These could include different configurations of living rooms, kitchen displays, bathrooms, closets, lighting, stairs, lifts, built-ins, cabinets, hardwood fixtures (knobs and pulls), lighting fixtures, wall panels, flooring, window framing, and landscaping possibilities. Pictures of homes designed by various architects and designers could also be on display. The center could have guides, conduct classes, and have a training program to assist people in assembling their own homes from prefabricated parts. There could be special kits available for putting together a model of a preplanned home or a preplanned modification of an old one.

We will now illustrate one way to achieve flexible construction in Compact City. Let us suppose first that the upper story of a house in the residential area would have its own horizontal base slab which is *not* supported by the walls of the 1st floor but is independently supported. (A proposed design for such a slab-support structure will be presented in Section 11.2.) This would permit walls to be used throughout both floors of the house which would not need to bear weight, and hence, these could be made of lightweight fire-resistant panels. To build a house, a light frame for a lower story might be put up first. These frames, as illustrated in Figure 6-5, could be slotted so that wall panels could be easily inserted into a slot at the top of the frame and then allowed to drop into a slot in the bottom of the frame.

The roofs and exterior surfaces of houses could, if it is desired, be made of the same materials as the interior surfaces since there is no need for them to furnish protection against rain or cold. Present-day technology is constantly developing new building materials. Light, sturdy, colorful heat- and sound-insulating materials of plaster board, plastic, or fiber glass would be particularly suitable for this purpose, if made fire-resistant. Such materials could be modeled in various sizes and shapes so as to fit together perfectly and sturdily, and they could be made more attractive than most materials in common use today. Indeed, panel surfaces—exterior and interior—could be made in a great variety of styles just as wallpaper comes in various styles.

Among the many advantages of such materials is the ease with which they could be moved, assembled, disassembled, or put to-

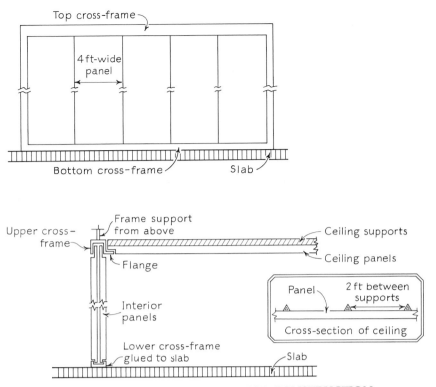

Figure 6-5 PREFABRICATED ASSEMBLY FOR CONSTRUCTION
OF HOMES

- Walls would be made from double panels—an exterior panel and an interior panel, which would come in various sizes. One side of a panel could be finished in various styles and the other side would be sound-insulated. Electric wiring and outlets could be installed in the panel, at the factory, with plug-in connections.
- A panel would be inserted into the slot of the upper frame until the bottom clears the lower frame. It would then be dropped into the slot of the lower frame.
- Ceiling panels are attached to prestressed light-weight concrete cross supports.
- Wall panels carry no loads.

gether in various ways to enclose space. Also, exciting designs, colors, and unusual shapes could be used to provide an aesthetically pleasing effect. Special surfaces could be used to deaden noise. Beside the need for easily rearrangeable walls and ceilings, there would also be the need for easy installation and replacement of floor coverings, kitchens, bathrooms, nooks, and decorations. Indeed, all aspects of home construction would have to be designed to be completely flexible.

An automatic delivery system, if combined with the water-recycling system to be discussed later, could be viewed as the analogue of the circulatory system for the human body. In time it could play an equally fundamental role. It gives promise of a simpler way of life. Physically, as we have described it earlier, the system would consist of a series of horizontal beltways on the middle level of the city; these would move objects to be delivered from distribution points to vertical belts which then raise or lower them to the house level where they would be finally deposited. A parallel system would work in the opposite direction. As described in Figure 4-14, objects to be delivered would be placed in special containers with a coded address. This address would be read by a photo-eye and the container would be transferred by lifting it off the belt and placing it on another beltway, or placing it so that it is picked up by the vertical belt.

To be truly effective the system would have to be tied into a "communication ordering system." For example, routine household items could carry special "reorder labels." The housewife would then place her order by feeding the reorder labels into a special "reorder reader" in her kitchen. The reorder reader would trigger a mechanism controlling a container in, say, a grocery store, and the container would move down a belt past loading points for the various items, stopping wherever the automatic control of a computer dictated. Once collected, the order would be placed on the return automatic delivery system and dispatched to the automatic delivery "dock" in the home, which is shown later in Figure 6-8.

Many special services could be rendered in this way which are not now economically feasible. For example, food prepared in specialty kitchens could be sent directly to individual residences. Laundry could be sent out automatically and returned within, say, three hours—washed and dried.

The automatic delivery system might also make convenient the rental of many things only occasionally used around the home. Example of objects that are cluttering shelfs and occupying space around the house are tool kits and home decorating equipment, sewing and cooking equipment, extra bedding, and camping equipment. It might be feasible to rent such items as well as magazines, toys, sports and catering equipment, and liquor and bar supplies.

In case of illness, prescriptions, thermometers, vaporizers, bandages, alcohol for rubs, basins, and other small paramedical items could be obtained around the clock, seven days a week, without having to leave the patient unattended. A service like this, combined with the possibility of a direct videophone conference between doctor and patient (such as we describe later in Chapter 15) might turn out to be almost as satisfactory as a doctor's visit. In fact, it might turn out to be *more* satisfactory in some cases, because diagnosis and treatment would take place sooner.

Because in Compact City all arcades, passageways, shopping centers, streets, and many of the homes and gardens would be beneath the protective cover of the city roof, problems associated with rain, heat, and cold would not exist. There would be a significant decrease in the amount of energy needed to cool or heat a single three-dimensional urban environment insulated from the outside, compared with that required for present-day cities.

Many parts of the world are inhospitable to human life because of severe weather conditions—that is, they have climates with temperatures below zero,[2] with excessive heat and humidity, or with desert heat and dust. Compact City would provide an attractive and economic protection in such environments. Even the weather on the Park-Roof could be controlled so that it would be comfortable throughout the year, for, if Compact City were to be constructed in a cold climate, excess warm air from the city's interior could be vented into the roof park area to keep it from freezing. In hot desert or moist tropical climates it would be possible to have areas of the roof protected from heat and rain by small covered domes.[3] Compact Cities located in such climates would undoubtedly tend to have more indoor recreational facilities, and the population there could be oriented more towards the internal opportunities of the city.

Obvious problems of air quality will need to be considered in planning Compact City. In a present-day city the air we breathe is the same as the air into which we dump our automobile exhausts, industrial fumes, and various kitchen odors. In the winter we use energy to heat the air; in the summer we use energy to cool it. The amounts of pollution we emit into the atmosphere is truly staggering. About five pounds of pollutants is dumped daily into the air per person in the San Francisco Bay Area (population about four million)—the total pollutants are shown in Table 6-1, broken down by source and type.

It should be noted (from the table) that most of the smog problem would disappear if the automobile could be phased out. Instead of

Table 6-1
Air pollution in the San Francisco Bay Area (measured in tons of pollutants added per day, 1967).

Type of pollutant	Source of pollutant					Total
	Automobile	Automobile related	Residential incineration	Organic solvents	Other	
Carbon monoxide	5,220	444			1,239	6,903
Organic materials	1,027	192	272	327	341	2,159
Nitrogen oxides	279	47			188	514
Sulfur oxides	20	128			281	429
Particulates	38		26		146	210
Total	6,584	811	298	327	2,195	10,215

doing this, however, all our efforts are going to salvaging the auto by refining gasolines and redesigning engines in an attempt to reduce their harmful effects. The effect of smog on the health of people has not been precisely determined. It does cause respiratory and eye irritation. During peaks of concentrations of carbon monoxide, the rate of fatal heart attacks has been shown to increase.[4] Smog is definitely unpleasant!

And it does more than merely obscure distant views. It has a deleterious effect on agriculture and plant life. The acids in smog have a corrosive effect on paint and stone surfaces. There is always the possibility that smog levels could become highly dangerous if inverse temperature layers or other weather conditions conducive to smog were to persist for long periods of time. This has happened in the past. Heavy London "killer" fogs, particularly the famous one that lasted from December 5 to 9, 1952, which caused four thousand deaths due, in this case, to presence of coal smoke in the air, led to controls on the burning of soft coal in fireplaces to heat British homes. Animals that live in open-air environments, like those in municipal zoos and animals grazing near cities or smelting plants have died of lead poisoning. Some researchers believe the cumulative effect of the lead compounds in the air everyone breathes has already adversely affected the mental health of many people.

Some progress in the control of air pollution has already begun to take place, and some cities now issue "smog alerts" when rates of particular emission surpass a predetermined danger point. Devices that reduce the amounts of pollutants are required on automobiles in some states and there will undoubtedly be new laws further restricting the amount of lead used in gasoline. The increased use of automobiles and the growth of human populations have overloaded the atmosphere, however, and smog has become a familiar phenomenon the world over. Population gains appear to be more than offsetting what improvements do result from corrective half measures, and the prospect is that air pollution will undoubtedly get worse.

In addition to the problems of controlling particulate pollution faced by cities, an important environmental problem is also heat pollution. All use of energy produces heat, and as the world becomes increasingly industrialized, so it also becomes increasingly heated. The largest concentrations of heat-producing activities are in and near cities. We anticipate that in Compact City, in addition to industrial processes, humans will also give off heat into the city air (for even biological organisms release heat through their use of food energy—for example, each person converts food into energy for use as heat or for work, and even the energy expended in work eventually results in heat that is diffused into the surrounding air). The same is true of the electrical energy used within cities for lights, appliances, vehicles, etc. According to our studies the heat that would be given off by human bodies would be small relative to the total generated by all other sources. Since Compact City would be effectively insu-

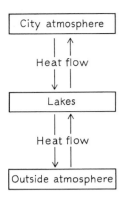

Figure 6-6 HEAT FLOW EXCHANGE
Because the area of exposed surface of the city
is small relative to its volume, it will be necessary
to cool the city. Its overall use of energy for
lighting, transportation, cooling, and heating
could be at least 15 percent less than present-day
cities.

lated from the outside atmosphere, it would, in time, become un-
bearably hot unless its internal heat were "pumped" out, and hence,
it would be necessary for Compact City to have an air conditioning
(cooling) system.

Lakes near Compact City could serve as a reservoir for coolant
water. The city would pass on its excess heat to the lakes and the
lakes, in turn, would discharge heat into the atmosphere as depicted
in Figure 6-6.

It is of course not necessary that all parts of the city be controlled
to the same temperature or to a temperature unvarying through time.
People may prefer a *variable* controlled climate. If so, then energy for
cooling and heating could be conserved by mixing warm air from
one part of the city with cool air from another part. The air conditioning process takes place in several steps which are outlined in Figure
6-7.

The input of outside air would provide oxygen to the system.
Human oxygen needs are small—less than one cubic foot per person
per hour. The air man breathes is not all oxygen. Seventy-nine percent of it is nitrogen, so the one cubic foot of oxygen is in fact diluted
by four of nitrogen. Thus humans have need of 5 cubic feet of fresh
air per person per hour. It is also essential that the concentration of
carbon dioxide in the air we breathe be kept very low, in fact, less
than one half of one percent. Removing carbon dioxide requires a
flow of 400 cubic feet of fresh air per hour per person. In Compact
City, balancing the input of fresh air would require that an equal
volume of air from inside the city be expelled. The various passages
leading out of the city and to the Park-Roof would function as air
vents. Air would naturally flow outward because pressure would be
maintained at a slightly higher level within the city. This outward
flow could keep various gardens, terraces, and the Park-Roof warm in
the winter so that year-round growth of plants—even tropical
plants—might be possible.

Air inside a home would need to be circulated several times an
hour not only to prevent the buildup of carbon dioxide but also to

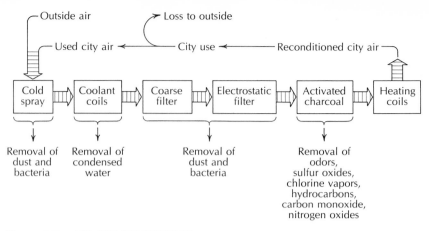

Figure 6-7 AIR CONDITIONING
In Compact City air contaminated by various processes never comes in contact with the general atmosphere of the city. Only air of the highest purity, at the temperature and moisture best for individual comfort, is circulated to the homes.

remove body odors that can give air a stale smell. It would be easy to arrange the flow of air to move from the insides of homes to their outsides. This would be desirable for it would keep airborne dust, pollens, and odors from accumulating. Only air of the highest purity, at the temperature and moisture best for individual comfort, would be used in homes.

It would be possible to keep the concentration of oxygen in the air of Compact City at the same level as that found in natural surroundings. This level is somewhat higher than that found in some closed crowded places of present-day cities, where the oxygen level can be depressed by a percent or so due to oxygen consumption by people, cars, and industrial processes.

The air recycling system of Compact City could be arranged in such a way that air contaminated by various industrial processes would be kept separate from the general interior atmosphere of the city. Such contaminated air, including that generated in household kitchens and bathrooms, could be carried efficiently by a separate system of ducts to appropriate independent air cleaning systems. The air to be reconditioned, in certain cases, could be first "cascaded." By this, it is meant that the air, although contaminated, is still of sufficiently high quality that it can serve one or more uses. Each use contaminates it a little more until finally it must be cleaned up and recycled. These subsystems could be designed so as never to come in contact with the general atmosphere of the city.

In a similar way the reconditioning of liquids and solid wastes could also be efficiently tailored to each application because of the multilevel arrangement of Compact City.

The system of disposing of household trash in Compact City would be easier than current practice. Trash would never need to accumulate about the house or yard or be deposited in the street for collection on a designated trash-collection day. Instead, at any time trash could be disposed of by placing it in a special container and dispatching it immediately by way of the automatic delivery system for recycling as depicted in Figure 6-8. The automatic delivery system could supply any number of containers so that one would never need to mix the different types of trash but could keep them separate from each other at all times—a step considered essential in making recycling economically feasible. For example, it would be an easy matter to process soiled paper, clean newsprint, journals (printed on glossy paper), plastics, metal alloys, aluminum, reusable bottles, broken bottles, and glass, and other materials at recycling factories if these are not mixed together in the first place.

We mentioned earlier that the automatic delivery system could function as an important artery for bringing items to the consumer. It would function also as a vein through which waste would be removed to other organs of the city body for reprocessing.

Figure 6-8   SOLID WASTE RECYCLING STARTS IN THE HOME
The automatic delivery system could supply trash containers immediately as required; therefore one would never need to mix the different types of trash but could keep them separate at all times—a step considered essential in making recycling economically feasible.

The more effective use of the third dimension and the time dimension in Compact City would reduce dramatically the number of people passing any particular point within the city at any particular time. All the parts of the city on any level would become easily accessible from any other level and any other part by foot, bicycle, car, or by the efficient mass transit system. Because of the continuity of activities around the clock, it is hard to imagine an occasion when one would ever encounter a fraction of the traffic congestion that characterizes present-day metropolises.

According to George Wilson, an acoustical consultant, the general ambient noise of present-day cities is caused by the highway system. He states that a long train could be designed to go 80 miles per hour with less noise than one high-speed automobile. In Compact City, congestion, noise, inconvenience, and costs due to highway repair would be inconsequential because (1) roads are protected from weather, (2) auto traffic is sharply reduced in quantity and speed, (3) trucks could be designed to make less noise and would not need to travel long distances at high speeds. Thus rapid deterioration of roads could be prevented.

Because of the balanced demand day or night for travel to or from other cities there would be no time wasted in traffic jams in travelling to airports or to railway stations and this could materially decrease the total transit time between major cities. Compact City's airport for its size would be far more efficient. Note that although the airport would be located close to the city (inasmuch as there would be no suburbia) the interior of the city is fully protected from the noise of airplanes.

Having stated the arguments for Compact City, we address, in the next chapter, the far more difficult question of how to implement such a proposal.

Notes and References

1. A preliminary analysis indicates that the household electric bill in Compact City would be about the same as the electric plus heating bill in conventional cities. Because of the increased energy needs for lighting the open space in the interior of the city and for heat removal, the total energy needs for heating, air conditioning, appliances, and lighting are likely to run 70 percent higher than for present-day cities. However, this increase is more than offset by a reduction in the energy needed for transportation. Overall there appears to be a reduction of total energy use (all forms) for all purposes (including industrial) of 15 percent or more.

    Moreover, savings greater than 15 percent in total energy use can be anticipated if nuclear energy becomes the mainstay for electric power. This is because nuclear power is more efficient than petroleum power when there is an even distribution of demand during a 24-hour period.

2. "A Climate Controlled City for Alaska," *New York Times*, September 21, 1969, page R4.

3. R. Buckminster Fuller has designed and built a number of lightweight domes which are called *Fuller Domes*. For an interesting description of their potentialities, see his book *Utopia or Oblivion*, Bantam-Matrix Books (New York, 1969). See also his article in "The City of the 21st Century," *Stanford Daily Magazine*, February 23, 1968, 11 pages.

4. Alfred C. Hexter, "Carbon Monoxide: Association of Community Air Pollution with Mortality," State of California Department Public Health. (Unpublished draft, February 1971). Hexter states: "Regression analysis of daily mortality in Los Angeles County shows community carbon monoxide levels to be significantly associated with mortality."

WHERE DO WE GO FROM HERE?

7.1 Rechanneling Funds and Effort

Up to now we have been concerned with how to redesign urban development to avoid many of the problems of urban overgrowth. We selected one possible Compact City arrangement and examined it in some depth to show that it is both technically and economically feasible. We now come to the far more difficult challenge: how can Compact City be made a reality? Inasmuch as each realization of Compact City would have its own special problems, the answer to the question, except in general terms, goes beyond the scope of this short book. Nevertheless, we will now sketch some of the tasks that would be necessary for its implementation.

We have shown that Compact City would be economically feasible because of the savings from transportation costs alone. In Chapter 6 we listed seventeen important advantages that could be realized by making the city compact. We authors believe that the more one studies the various facets of the Compact City design and its advantages, the more the proposal we have outlined for Compact City will appear to meet most of the criteria, standards, and goals that one could reasonably hope for in a city of optimum design.

The proposed city we have presented is, however, just a sketch. There are many possible variations in its details that need to be examined. Implementation would require a detailed master plan, many special studies, and the development of specialized construction equipment. Furthermore, implementation would require drawing on a technology that synthesizes the know-how of architects, builders, and operators of the municipal services of our present-day cities.

tion equipment. Furthermore, implementation would require drawing on a technology that synthesizes the know-how of architects, builders, and operators of the municipal services of our present-day cities.

Since urban construction—and reconstruction—will take place in one form or another—in order to meet population increases, rising aspirations of city residents, and the renewal needs of inner cities—equivalent labor, material, or funds could instead be made available for construction of Compact City. What we need to do is to rechannel funds and energies away from currently inadequate solutions to the fundamental problem of urban sprawl and to redirect energies towards something better.[1]

Earlier we reviewed some of the progress that has already been made in integrated town planning in the United States at such locations as Reston, Virginia and Columbia, Maryland; progress is also being made in England, France, Sweden, and other countries too. Such planned communities have many objectives in common with Compact City. If restructured, a planned town could serve as an ideal way to pioneer the development of a "mini"-Compact City. This could be followed next by a first stage city of 250,000 people with the idea that such a city would serve as a real trial of the concept. If successful, the trial city should be allowed to grow quickly to maximum size. For, vast as the undertaking to build one Compact City would be, more than one city like it are, in fact, urgently needed.

How Many Compact Cities?

Earlier, in Section 1.1, we listed the socioeconomic pressures leading to urban sprawl. Population increase is one of them, but there are other factors—for example, the idea that improved economic status is reflected in residence in the suburbs. Let us cite some statistics: the population of the United States increased during the period from 1960 to 1970 by 24,000,000.[2] The United States Bureau of the Census has made four estimates of the expected increase in population based on four assumptions about the average number of children per 1,000 women at the end of child bearing; these are shown in Table 7-1. Assumption B is that 3,100 children are born per 1,000 women; Assumption C, that 2,775 are born; Assumption D, 2,450; Assumption E, 2,100. Assumption B, the highest birth rate, is lower than the rate actually observed in the 1962–1966 period and may be considered the most pessimistic assumption of what rate of population increase could materialize in the 1970–1980 decade. On the other hand, the annual rate of increase in total population appears to have dropped from 1.7 percent in 1958 to 1.0 percent in 1968. If this encouraging trend persists, Assumption C could become a reasonable forecast. Curtailing the increase in urban sprawl that will occur due to population increases in the period 1980–1995 alone will require the building of somewhere between 15 and 25 Compact Cities (of two million people each).

Table 7-1

Projected increase in the population of U.S.
(in millions of people), according to four different
assumptions explained in the text.

5-year period	Assumptions and projected increases			
	B	C	D	E
1980–1985	20	17	13	11
1985–1990	21	17	14	11
1990–1995	20	17	10	9
15-year total	61	51	37	31

Source: U.S. Bureau of Census, "Statistical Abstract of the U.S.," Table 5 in *American Almanac 1972,* Grosset and Dunlap (New York, 1972), page 7.

The great magnitude of the task of building so many cities is obvious. Let us keep in mind, however, that in one form or another this magnitude of building *will* take place. Population plus other pressures will probably double the amount of area covered by urbanization by the year 2000.

Where Should Future Cities be Built?

Certain parts of the United States have dense populations while other parts have vast areas that are largely vacant. Apparently dense populations have been necessary in the past for certain socioeconomic activities to evolve. Undoubtedly the development of the airplane, television, good communication, and fast long-distance rail and truck transportation have reduced this historical need. Nevertheless, travel between major cities remains expensive, is tiring, and takes time. At the present time, socioeconomic factors still pressure people to keep close to their friends and members of their family, for businesses to stay near related business and labor markets, for scientists to be near their scientific centers, and for entertainers to be near their entertainment outlets. This is probably why New York City remains the center for finance; Pittsburgh serves as the center for metals; Detroit is the center for automobiles; Los Angeles and New York are centers for entertainment, and so on.

We feel that no meaningful solution to the urban crisis can be achieved by building another suburbia or new town followed by still another, and then still another, farther out, but rather to build, once our proposal has been thoroughly tested, many *population absorbing centers* in the form of Compact Cities, which would be allowed to grow to an eventual maximum population of about two million people each. These concentration points would probably have to be located in the more populous areas of the country in order to induce people and industry (or perhaps it is better to say it the other way around, to induce industry and hence people) to move into them. At the same time, smaller Compact Cities that offer protection from extremes of weather could be developed in the less populous areas of the United States and Canada with the hope that they will develop industry, become popular, and attract people to move into them.

7.2 Growth by Modules

Let us suppose that a new city, Compact City, is to be built in the outskirts of an existing metropolitan area. Do we begin by building the business core and have people commute to work from the old city to the new core area? Should Compact City be built sector by sector with people moving into each sector as it is completed? Or should the whole city be built first and then people and industry be invited to move in all at once? Obviously, Compact City even at the first stage of 250,000 would be too vast an undertaking for the latter approach. But granted that it would have to grow a sector at a time, should it be built in vertical slices or in horizontal slices? Would residents have to wait 15 years or so before enjoying the Park-Roof on top?

Let us first examine the rate of growth. Suppose we set as our goal the completion of a compact city for a population of two million in 16 years; the building schedule would then average one level per year. At this rate 37,500 families per year could move into the city —about 100 families per day.

One possibility is to settle the incoming families on the ground level of each sector as it is completed—first on the ground level of the first sector, then on the ground level of the second sector, etc. There are 16 times 32, or 512 sector-levels (modules) in all. For a city built to accommodate a maximum population of two million, each module would need to accommodate about 1,200 families. Several such modules could be under construction at the same time— each taking several months to complete. The necessary completion rate would average one module every 12 days. See Figure 7-1.

A different growth pattern probably would be used if the residential part of the city were designed so that the interior open space would have as much diversified use as possible. This alternative is described in Section 13.1. It consists of building a series of neighborhoods of about 5,000 people, each neighborhood occupying eight levels and sharing a common elevator, local market, school, and mass transit facilities. By this plan the city would be built in vertical slices a neighborhood at a time, each neighborhood being a kind of superblock as depicted in Figure 7-2.

Is one module every 12 days too rapid a construction rate? Remember that from 15 to 25 times this rate of building will be taking place *somewhere* in the country, in some form or other, during the

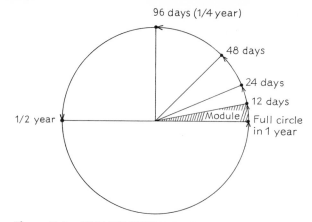

Figure 7-1 ONE POSSIBLE GROWTH PATTERN
FOR A COMPACT CITY
One possible way to curtail the increasing urban
sprawl is to build a maximum-sized Compact City
during a period of 16 years. The city could grow
by modules consisting of sectors shaped like pieces
of pie. There are 32 sectors on a level and 512
sectors on all 16 levels. A module contains part
of the Core and Residential areas for 1,200 families.

period from 1980 to 1995. So it might as well be organized on a mass
production basis, be done efficiently, and with worthwhile results.

A precedent in rapid construction of giant buildings was set in
1930 when excavation for the Empire State Building was begun.
The building was opened one year and 45 days later. It was erected
on one of Manhattan's busiest intersections without interference
with the traffic flow. If such a monumental feat of construction engineering could be done in 1930, it is reasonable to expect that in the
1980s several such projects could be going on simultaneously, each
one busily constructing modules for a Compact City.

The various levels of Compact City consist of concrete slabs covering wide areas. These must be laid out rapidly and be "dirt cheap."
The concrete requirement (for houses and open space) for 100 families per day is about 400,000 square feet (6 inches thick). This is
less than one percent of the daily concrete production for the country as a whole, production which in 1969 amounted to 150 million
cubic yards.[3]

7.3 Developing Detailed Plans

A more substantial guideline for development of detailed plans is
obviously the next step. In this section we will try to present the
beginnings of such a guideline. Establishing detailed plans will be

a major project—a project involving architecture, systems engineering, sociology, and economics. First, an assessment must be made of the trade-offs of various alternative ways to build a compact city. What are the benefits and debits of these alternatives? Thus, the ideas need to be built first on paper. Problems of architecture and engineering—stresses and strains, the foundation, modular construction, special plumbing, and so on—all must be resolved. Prototypes for internal transportation by tram must be designed and studied. The problems of recycling must be reckoned with too. The computer's uses and functions within the city need to be developed. Educators must decide on the facilities for the education system. Lawyers and criminologists must decide on legal codes appropriate for a Compact City. New administrative methods to supervise the actual construction of the city as well as the subsequent internal management of the city must be explored in depth. Part of nearly every technology and discipline that have arisen in civilization to date will in one way or another need to be harnessed into the effort. We hope a completely new "Compact City Technology" will emerge, leading to an urban design which reflects the best that science and imagination have to offer.

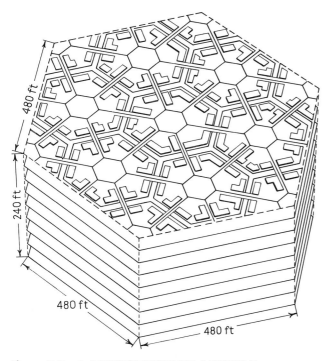

Figure 7-2 A NEIGHBORHOOD MODULE:
AN ALTERNATIVE PLAN FOR A COMPACT CITY
Another possible growth pattern is to build the residential part of
the city superblock-by-superblock. The one displayed in the figure
is based on an alternative street plan described in Section 13.1.

Every developer in present-day cities undertakes preliminary planning before beginning construction. Much of what is known will be applicable to Compact City. The scope of Compact City is of course far more extensive than anything planners have yet encountered or contemplated. The design of Compact City, though anchored within current capabilities, demands a certain break with tradition. This is necessary because of the exponential growth of urban sprawl and the fundamentally incorrect premises on which the development of present-day metropolises are based. What has been learned from the efforts with new towns may or may not be readily applicable to Compact City. The proponents and developers of the Compact City idea may have to review their planning and start afresh.

To start developing a detailed overall city plan requires forming organizations of highly competent people and gathering financial support for their efforts. To support a staff of the top men in each field for the length of time that the effort will demand will in itself require large sums of money. Funds undoubtedly exist for developing such detailed plans, but to obtain them the idea of Compact City would have to be more completely presented than is this sketch—a sketch developed largely to explore the feasibility of planning cities that make more effective use of third and fourth dimensions.

The federal government has become more concerned about city planning and planned towns than it was in the past. This reflects, of course, the increasing concern of citizens at regional and local governmental levels for the environment both inside and outside our cities. Congress has said that the urban plight is "the most critical domestic problem facing the United States." As long as sentiments like this are voiced, the better are the chances that an idea like Compact City will come to be accepted.

In the Congressional Act of 1966 titled "Demonstration Cities and Metropolitan Development," Congress appropriated funds to provide "additional financial and technical assistance to enable cities of all sizes to plan, develop, and carry out locally prepared and scheduled comprehensive city demonstration programs containing new and imaginative proposals to rebuild or revitalize large slum and blighted areas." Certainly Compact City modules should be considered to fall within the scope of such language. If the Department of Housing and Urban Development were interested in exploring further the idea of a Compact City, it could provide money for a study in the form of a grant under Title I of the Demonstration Cities Act, and could provide up to "80 percent of the cost for formulating such plans." The National Science Foundation and other agencies have sponsored studies of new city developments. Besides governmental agencies, there are wealthy private sources to turn to, such as the Ford or Carnegie Foundations and ambitious land-developing corporations.

The universities offer a natural place for preliminary investigations, but the systematic development of the plan would probably be best carried out by industrial groups. Whatever organizations conduct the research, they should in any case consist of eminent men not only knowledgeable in their narrow speciality but broad enough in their thinking to participate in a total-system approach to city design.

7.4 Organizing the Construction

Our cost estimate for building a Compact City for a population of two million is $36.5 billion (1969 prices). For an initial city of 250,000 the cost would be about $4.6 billion. For the individual family the proposed average cost per household unit is about $2,700 per year. Families living in large houses would, of course, pay more than this average. Those living in smaller houses or flats would pay considerably less. We have seen that directly or indirectly society is currently paying a high cost for transportation and for the inconvenience of congestion and pollution. We have already concluded that the proposed new design would pay for itself out of transportation savings and produce a higher quality of life. The problem then is how to get it started financially.

Since there will be high initial planning and development costs associated with building the first compact city there is bound to be an agonizing decision process that will have to take place before undertaking what will eventually become a major multi-billion-dollar program.

Experiences with planned towns indicate that private enterprise and individual owners would join to provide money. The government could build the superstructure for a module and the "land" (lots within the city) could be turned over to individual developers on a *lease* arrangement. We recommend that these lots, slab-space, be leased because the *sale* of slab-space to private individuals could destroy the city's very important advantage: flexible arrangement of its functions. We recommend also that sites in the city be initially very inexpensively leased in order to attract industry and people to the city. After the first few years, the lease price could be raised above the break-even level.

In a later chapter we will present a detailed cash flow analysis of funds needed for development of a city for two million people. The assumption is the city would be built on a module-by-module basis over a period of sixteen years. The cost for the government and for private groups to finance the initial year of construction would be roughly 1/16 the total cost, or $2.2 billion which, in the light of current budgeting and investment, is affordable. Finance costs each year would be about 300 million less than the previous year, and the amount of debt outstanding would become progressively less as those home owners and businesses that have moved in begin to pay off their mortgages.

The large scale of construction will, of course, have its impact on the construction industry. Presently that industry is made up of many individual contractors whose work is not highly automated. While it is essential that many parts of the city be mass-produced, we don't recommend a full commitment to automated construction. In order for there to be a wide variety of designs for houses and work centers, it is important to maintain individualistic efforts. This is best achieved in our opinion by having small contractors offering a variety of special services, arts, and crafts.

After the city has been designed and an estimate has been made of the cost of constructing it, a detailed construction schedule would be prepared. At present, there is probably a shortage of the type of equipment best suited to build Compact City and probably also a shortage of qualified contractors. There would undoubtedly be increased demands on local suppliers to supply such materials as portland cement, structural steel, sand, and gravel. Assuming that this necessary expansion of the construction industry and the training of skilled workers occur, then it appears possible to build a maximum-sized Compact City in 16 years. Such a development would undoubtedly have to be part of a pervasive nation-wide federally sponsored plan to alleviate the urban crisis. Even so the development of Compact City could probably be left largely to private enterprise and to semiprivate groups. Competitive bidding for the various subsystems within the city could take place as usual. Local, state, and federal governments would undoubtedly need to assume the responsibility of subsidizing low-cost housing projects, public facilities, utilities, schools, hospitals, and other institutions in cities.

References

1. W. Baumol, "Macroeconomics of Unbalanced Growth, The Anatomy of the Urban Crisis," *American Economic Review, 57* (1967), pages 415–426.
2. *American Almanac 1972,* "The Statistical Abstract of the U.S.," Grosset and Dunlap (New York, 1972), Table 5, page 7.
3. Portland Cement Association, *Cement and Concrete Reference Book,* Portland Cement Association (Chicago, 1951), 111 pages.

**Part
Two**

OPERATIONS RESEARCH
AND THE
TOTAL-SYSTEM
APPROACH

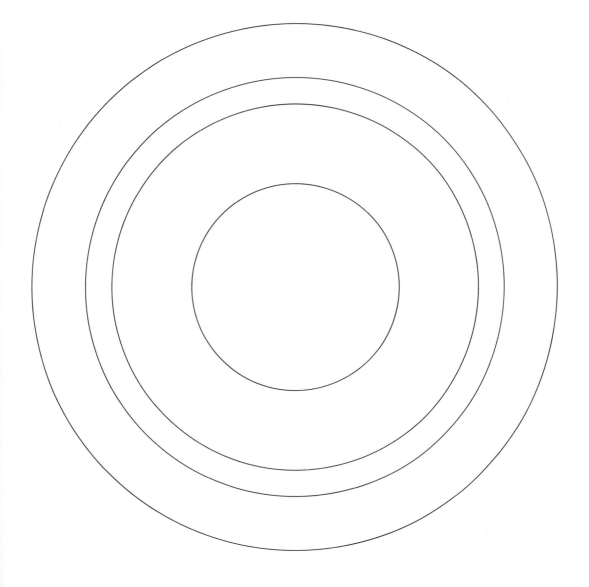

In Part One, we outlined the need for redesigning urban areas, listed what some of the goals of such a redesign should be, and described some of the solutions that have been proposed. We then developed two basic principles — the space principle and the time principle. In order to see what the potentialities of more effective use of the vertical and time dimensions might be, we proposed a plan for a possible city that could be built with present-day technology and pointed out its low costs and other advantages. We then discussed some of the tasks involved in the implementation of the proposal.

This proposal, however, is based on certain standards and goals and an analysis of the total urban system, which we will now present in Part Two. Since there is an infinite variety of possible ways to develop the urban system, some means of reducing the number of choices to be examined are obviously necessary. In Chapter 8, Urban Models, we outline the ways computers, mathematical models, and certain optimization techniques — operations research — could be used to help narrow the selection and for other analyses. Chapter 9 sketches some of the broad conservation and ecological considerations that enter into — or should enter into — a good urban development plan. We then turn, in Chapter 10, to the specific problem of setting up the space standards for Compact City and use these to determine its shape and height.

In Part One we described briefly the systems for transportation and for air and solid waste recycling. In Chapter 11 we return to these systems to give further details about structure and system design, in particular the water recycling system and the electrical system. This is followed in Chapter 12 by a financial analysis of the capital outlays that would be required year by year in order to finance construction of Compact City and of the expected cash flow receipts that could be expected as mortgages are paid off. It turns out the latter could generate enough reinvestment capital to build additional new Compact Cities. Moreover, the proposed expenditures do not constitute a new burden for taxpayers; instead they could be made by rechanneling funds that already exist. Since there are other ways to develop the urban environment to make effective use of vertical and time dimensions, we describe in Chapter 13 some of the advantages of these alternatives.

Later, in Part Three, we shall speculate briefly about what some of the social and economic effects of the Compact City proposal might be.

8

URBAN
MODELS

8.1 What Is Total-System Planning?

Planning, as we visualize it, is an adaptive, self-corrective process, one which avoids the assumption that the objectives we set forth for the future will remain forever inviolate. A good plan should contain procedures for changing proposed solutions quickly as new conditions and policies arise. A flexible approach is necessary if we are to meet the exigencies of rapid change.

The plan is, or should be, the result of the evaluation of many alternative possibilities. We live in an era in which it is possible to make plans based on an overall analysis of the entire system—this kind of planning is called the total-system approach. Expert planners are no longer satisfied with ideas that appear to solve problems for only part of a system but leave problems in other parts unresolved.

Patchwork solutions are not enough. Too often society, over-burdened with problems, shifts attention from one crisis to the next and accepts some piecemeal remedy for each ill. Concern with traffic congestion today replaces the monetary crisis of the 1930s, housing subsidies take precedence over agricultural price supports, narcotic control replaces liquor prohibition, water supply becomes more crucial than reclamation of the Dust Bowl. In short, "planning" has, for the most part, been short-run reaction to crisis.

Most proposals for improving living conditions do not consider the effect of a proposal on the system as a whole. For example, as depicted in Figure 8-1, a solution like a new freeway encourages new

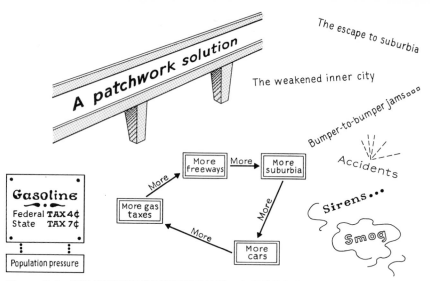

Figure 8-1 WE INVEST IN FREEWAYS — A SELF-PERPETUATING MISTAKE

Unfortunately, the tax money derived from gasoline taxes is earmarked for maintaining and expanding the road system; thereby it becomes a mechanism for perpetuating urban sprawl and all its consequences.

suburban development which in turn increases the traffic on the road systems (hence more smog and accidents), adds to the peak-hour traffic congestion within the city, and weakens the ability of the city to finance solutions to slum problems (or to implement other city improvements). Such patchwork planning is not in the spirit of the times. Society should reject this kind of *sub*optimization because it now has methods that can take all the various subproblems simultaneously into consideration.

The simplest approach to total-system planning is to use computers to construct many alternative plans which can then be compared — the best plan being selected according to some criterion of excellence such as low "cost" where cost may be measured in terms of money, pollution, delay time, etc. The well-known city planner, Constantinos Apostolos Doxiadis, has stated his own comparisons of city designs with the help of a computer this way:

> Why should we prepare a plan without studying the alternatives? For example, there are 49 million alternatives for one American city by the year 2000. We reduced these to 500,000; then our second approach led to 11,000; then to 312; then to 40; to 10; to 7; to 3; to 1 . . . if no computer or systems approach had been used, it would have taken 800 to 900 years![1]

The procedure Doxiadis used is called *system simulation*. Narrowing down the selection and ruling out alternatives is done by means of a "heuristic procedure"—a procedure whereby the computer is provided with "common sense" rules on which it bases its selection. Sometimes the alternatives are classified into several groups called branches. For example, *A, B, C* in Figure 8-2 might refer to alternative designs for a city with respect to vertical height, which might be divided into three categories: flat, medium-height, and tall. Each alternative is classified into subbranches (*A1, A2; B1, B2; C1, C2*), which might refer to the shape of the base of the city, say round or square. Each subbranch in turn is classified into subbranches that might refer to the alternative location of facilities within the city or alternative modes of transportation, etc. It is easy to see how the total number of alternative possibilities can grow astronomically and it is clearly not practical to explore all alternatives in detail to make a selection. However, by examining certain common aspects of, for example, branches *A1* and *A2*, without going into the detailed differences of their various subbranches, it is often possible to come up with some upper-bound estimate of the "cost" of *any* plan for the *A* class. The *A* branch is then temporarily set aside and the other branches (and possibly their subbranches etc.) are then explored. The procedure is stopped if it becomes evident that a lower-bound estimate of their costs is greater than the previously determined upper bound of the *A* branch. If this should happen then all branches (except *A*) are eliminated and comparisons between subbranches of *A1* and *A2* are made in a manner similar to that made earlier for *A, B, C*. The results gained with this procedure often work surprisingly well when implemented. It is referred to as *branch and bound*.

Often computers are used in conjunction with mathematical techniques to find the optimum plan. A minor example of this approach is the determination of the optimum ratio of height to radius of the city, discussed in Section 10.2. There are, in theory, an infinity of

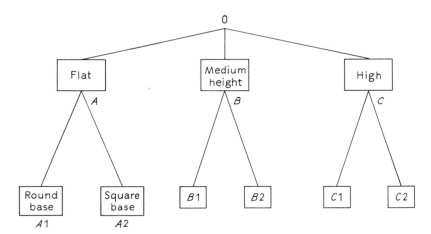

Figure 8-2 BRANCH AND BOUND
One technique that can be used in conjunction with computers to select a good plan for urban development.

possible ratios to choose from. With the aid of calculus, however, it is possible to find the best ratio without examining each ratio individually. Linear Programming, Dynamic Programming, Integer Programming, Inventory Theory, Reliability Theory, System Theory, Queueing Theory, and Network Flow Theory are the names of some of the Operations Research methods used. Whatever procedure or system of procedures is used, the solution arrived at is the "best" that can be practically obtained. Moreover, these procedures can explore which changes in plan should take place when future contingencies become the realities of the present.

When we speak about a plan as "optimum," we have in mind a plan that reflects an individual's need for happiness, satisfaction, leisure, knowledge, freedom, and an exciting creative life that challenges his capabilities. The objectives of the citizens of a city are important. For example, we might decide to develop a city in which the emphasis is placed on the acquisition of material things. Or we could try to develop a new city more in tune with a post-industrial and post-technological era, a city that would maximize opportunities for man to develop his mental powers and his potentials for emotional and artistic expression. Here man becomes more than just a physical input-output system consuming an endless stream of new gadgets and spewing out a mountain of waste and pollution. Just what mix of materialistic, intellectual, or "goof-off" pursuits should exist for citizens of a city is something which must therefore be decided upon. The decision could affect the choice of the optimal design for a city.

Reconciliation of Multiple Goals

The goals we might wish to achieve in a well-designed city might include:

1. An aesthetic environment
2. As many labor-saving conveniences as possible
3. Rapid access to any part of the city
4. A suitable climate
5. Low-cost living
6. Conservation of agricultural land
7. Easy access to natural surroundings
8. Elimination of delays
9. Reduced pollution
10. The elimination of auto accidents
11. The prevention of sabotage
12. The minimization of the possibility of being trapped in the city in case of a disaster.

The final plan must somehow reconcile these multiple goals. If they conflict with one another, the plan must make clear how much of one goal would have to be sacrificed to attain more of another. Presented in this form it is possible for the citizens or their designated representatives to make intelligent decisions as to whether or not to accept a plan or to request modification of it.

Finding the Global Optimum

Earlier we spoke about the fact that no amount of patchwork is going to help find good solutions to problems of urban crisis. If we settle for patchwork planning we become locked into what mathematicians call a local optimum whereas what we want is a global optimum. Improving an optimum is a little like climbing a hill. The view from the top of a small hill may be better than a view from its slopes, but it is still not as good as the view from a distant, higher hill. But to get to the top of the higher hill one must first descend to a valley where there may be no view at all. A local optimum is like the small hill. The global optimum is like the highest hill. If we consider the "view" to be analogous to quality of life, then achieving a global optimum may involve making some temporary sacrifices to get there. See Figure 8-3. We do not claim that our version of a compact city is necessarily the global optimum. But it appears to us clearly to be better than any local optimum which might be achieved through patchwork planning. As depicted in Figure 8-4, there is some evidence that present-day cities are attempting to make more effective use of the third dimension inefficiently, and at high cost.

We the authors advocate the total-system approach — the systematic collection of data in a tractable form, the setting down of goals, the modeling of the full system, the using of computers and analytical techniques to select the best solution, and finally the comparing of solutions obtained by using different assumptions. A word of caution: the art of optimization is not so advanced that all of these steps can be done without introducing some aggregation and simplification of detail. But we will say more about this later. For the moment let us see how urban developmental planning takes place in large cities.

8.2 How Cities Currently Do Their Planning

A recent University of Pennsylvania study, "Prospects of the American City,"[2] studied three ways that municipalities approach urban development:

Planning by Extrapolation: The Inactive Approach

In many cities a "plan" (if you wish to call it that) is based on a simple extrapolation or extension of the present-day city. The new city budget consists of small changes in the current city budget. As a result of such "planning" one can expect, in general, that in such

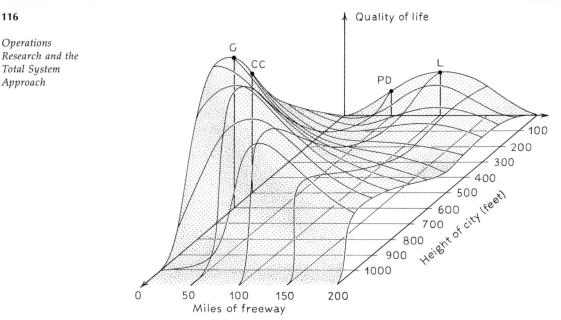

Figure 8-3 LOCAL VERSUS GLOBAL OPTIMA

The hilly surface displayed in the figure is purely illustrative. Suppose
we are at *PD*, a present-day flat city, and we look around to see if there
is some way to improve things. Building a few more miles of freeway
seems to help and so we build more freeways and move towards *L*. But
from *L* there is no gradual patchwork action that we can implement to
improve things; we're stuck; we are at a locally best solution. Our city
is still flat. Way off in the distance, we can dimly make out *CC*, a
multilayer compact city. The quality of life (in many ways) is much
higher there than at *L* or *PD*, but we have no patchwork way of moving
to *CC* from where we are without making a little sacrifice at first. Nor
do we claim that our particular version of Compact City is necessarily
the best. The fact that it is better than *L* only shows that *L* is some sort
of *local* optimum. What we are really looking for is *G*, the *global* optimum.

cities populations will continue to grow and become more dense.
There will be (as there is now) unemployment among the disadvantaged. Housing and education will be available to all, but it will be
of a lower quality than at present. Industries will continue to shift to
the suburbs. Because of this, the poor will continue to migrate away
from the slums surrounding the city core. The present difference
between personal income per capita in metropolitan and suburban
areas will decrease (suburban income was 60 percent greater than
metropolitan income in 1960 and by 1985 it will be only 24 percent
greater). Revenues for state and local governments will increase but
less rapidly than in the past. The trend in the mechanization of
physical work will continue.

According to the study, sexual taboos will continue to crumble and
more permissive social attitudes towards sex and households with

Figure 8-4 CONVENTIONAL CITIES ARE BECOMING THREE-DIMENSIONAL INEFFICIENTLY, AND AT HIGH COST.

unmarried partners will develop. There will be a further decline in church attendance. Crime will continue to increase among the young in urban areas and the suburbs will become less safe. Pollution and other health hazards will continue to increase. Health program subsidies will grow but at a slower rate than the need. In short, the problems of today will multiply and magnify in cities whose future planning consists of minor changes of current budgets.

Planning by Reacting to Crisis

Some municipalities plan their futures, according to the Pennsylvania study, by initiating programs that resolve current crises just enough to maintain stability, i.e., by alleviating problems in some areas but letting others persist, perhaps to deteriorate. Functional agencies are created at metropolitan and regional levels to study and meet crises. Various citizen groups form at different levels to pressure corrective action when it suits their own particular needs. As each new pressure arises, just enough effort is concentrated (in the form of budgeted money) to serve as a psychological palliative.

In cities where planning takes this form it is anticipated that income will rise for the majority of citizens, though it will rise slowly for the disadvantaged, thus increasing the economic gap. More welfare will be made available but not enough to improve standards of living significantly. Civil demonstrations will be tolerated, but if they become violent the violence will be resisted by the police and the army.

The study predicts that prosecution of civil rights violations will intensify, and that service industries will grow to absorb a greater number of untrained workers. Support for low-cost housing will increase but not by enough to meet the housing shortages. Universities will increase aid to capable underprivileged students, and hospitals will develop more community services, but the number of people depending on welfare for income will also increase. No significant change in the crime rate or in the treatment of criminals seems likely. More people will be armed and will use protective devices (locks and burglar alarms) against crime in their homes. Young people will exercise a greater influence on government policies. In sum, under meet-the-crisis planning, more in the way of major projects will be attempted, but few of them will be brought to full fruition because of shifting priorities.

Planning by Principles: The Total-System Interactive Approach

The third approach to city planning discussed in the University of Pennsylvania study (which is more along the lines we envision for Compact City) is one that boldly conceives of actions that would benefit society—actions which, it is hoped, will yield life, liberty, the pursuit of happiness, equality of opportunity, and an effective participatory democracy for *all*. A city whose approach to planning is based on such principles would maintain an ongoing experimental attitude toward the solution of its problems.

In such a city, according to the study, citizens would take action to reduce income inequality between different groups that could result in disparity in the education of children or in the satisfaction of fundamental needs. The study asserts that the long-run cost of maintaining inequality in society exceeds the cost of removing it. The city with a principled approach to planning would seek equality of opportunities for health, recreation, and other public facilities, and for employment and suitable housing. The city guided by principles would be sensitive to the needs brought forth by a democratic participatory process. The people within the community could undertake much of the detailed local planning consistent with technology supplied by experts. Such planning would be a continuous, intense process beginning with formulation of plans, and moving on through implementation, evaluation, and successive modification of plans. This process could be the basis of a new style of politics in which continuous dialogue and bargaining serves to accommodate the self-interest of various elements in society. It could prove to be an effective method for evaluating and reconciling programs developed by individuals, groups, and city agencies. The hoped for result would be the emergence of a society in which failure to use relevant knowledge constructively for the benefit of the total system would be regarded as a cardinal sin.

8.3 Modeling a City

The idea of a model is to express relationships, some of which we can control or change, and some of which are as immutable as a law of physics. The model is the framework which allows us to consider the alternatives and select the "best" plan. Thus the term "model" as used here means a "model generator," i.e., a way to generate many particular "model realizations" for comparison and selection.

Modeling a total system is a serious art, the systematic assembly of an enormous amount of information in a form that is tractable for prediction and intelligent action. There is no such thing as *the* model for the economic life of a region, or for a city within that region; nor is there a single total framework to serve for modeling the world. The best that can be achieved are simplified (but not oversimplified) aggregate models which are constantly being revised, improved, and made more detailed.

Ecologists, conservationists, urbanists, and the young work under a handicap because they have no formal analytical model to help them understand the total system and its interacting parts. All they can be sure of is that something is wrong. The rest is hindsight. Many public agencies view their jobs as consisting in the preparation of a special report instead of as requiring a continuing effort — an integrated responsibility for action. For example, suppose evidence shows that an insecticide has a bad side effect. Immediately some planning body should engage in a reevaluation of policies affected by such evidence and this should be followed rapidly by a coordinated series of corrective actions based on a total-system model. We hope our book (to cite a second example) will spark some agency to evaluate our findings and to initiate studies of a detailed urban development plan emphasizing fuller and more effective use of three dimensions in order to eliminate the sprawl resulting from growth that is predominantly two-dimensional. Such studies will lead to new thinking about what form future urban development should take.

An urban development plan is primarily guided by local considerations. Nevertheless it forms part of—and is affected by—regional, national, and even world trends. The latter consist essentially of estimates of the status and growth of the world population, of the availability of world-wide land and sea resources, and of projections of world-wide manufacturing capacity and needs. National plans and studies are concerned with these same factors except at a national and regional level. They are also concerned with the effects of human activities on the ecosystem, with the allocation of water and energy for farm and city use, and with the recycling of water and waste. Studies might include the merits of avoiding the generation of waste in the city by completely processing and packaging food where it is grown. Or they might consider the desirability of reprocessing plastics versus the use of waste plastics as a fuel supplement. Ideally, it is within these broad world, national, and regional considerations that the details of an urban development plan should be developed.

Suppose, for example, it is decided at a national level to curtail urban sprawl. To do this, Compact City (and many cities like it) would have to be started and allowed to grow rapidly (perhaps at the rate of 100 families a day). This growth means in turn that the rate of building Compact City must take place faster than conventional construction. Such a construction rate would imply, undoubtedly, more extensive use of specialized equipment and prefabricated materials.

The planning of Compact City could begin with such overall considerations. Like a master plan for a conventional city, detailed plans would need to be made for the layout of streets, the location of residences, shopping centers, offices, light and heavy industries, schools, civic centers, utilities, and transportation. Since Compact City contains many small facilities within a big facility, the plan for Compact City must very closely integrate the building of all subunits —houses, schools, etc.—with the building of the structure itself.

While we have tried to consider as many aspects of a total urban system as we could, we do not want to give the impression that we put together a complete planning model which allowed one to consider all possible alternatives and that Compact City was its particular result. Rather, Compact City is the outgrowth of a first attempt to visualize a new city that makes more effective use of space and time dimensions.

We will now outline how one might go about constructing a total-system model for a city:

Step I: Set down certain goals or standards. Some of these goals might be:

Traffic fatalities ≤ 5 per year per million population
(Our current rate is 50 times greater)

Transportation time to work ≤ 25 minutes walking time

Transportation time to work ≤ 5 minutes vehicular time
(Our current time is over 8 times greater)

Housing + transportation costs ≤ $4,000 per year for a 2,400 square-foot home on a large "lot"

Accessibility to nature ≤ 5 minutes walking time

Accessibility of facilities to each other ≤ 5 minutes

Ideal climate (defined in quantitative terms)

Low pollution (defined in quantitative terms)

Low-energy needs (defined in quantitative terms)

Flexible construction (defined in quantitative terms)

And so on . . .

The list in fact would be quite long. Parts of it are also likely to be contradictory. For example there may be no way physically to arrange all housing on large lots if, at the same time, another goal is to have them within walking distance of work centers, or to have as one goal flexible construction while another is to have low-cost housing. It would be the purpose of the model to determine whether or not a feasible solution exists for any given set of goals. The goals are treated as "parameters" which are varied until feasible solutions (designs) can be arrived at. The simplest way to get a feasible design is to relax the goals (standards) so that they are nearly the same as those currently prevailing in present-day cities. After one achieves a "feasible" solution using relaxed goals, one then tries to tighten up the goals. Eventually one might produce a feasible design which would to some degree meet every desired goal with only a few exceptions.

One goal many people say they put a high premium on is having sunlight pour through every window. (Actually people are seldom at home to enjoy this amount of sunlight and when they are home they may even close the drapes—but let's pretend nevertheless there is such a goal in a city for the future.) The question now becomes one of deciding what, for all inhabitants, is the "price" of getting more sunshine through their windows. If it turns out (as is likely) that the price is an elaborate transportation system (in order to convey residents to regions where houses can be located in spacious rural surroundings), a 50-fold increase in traffic fatalities, two hours a day commuting, and a host of other inconveniences, one may be led to conclude that it would be preferable after all to live in Compact

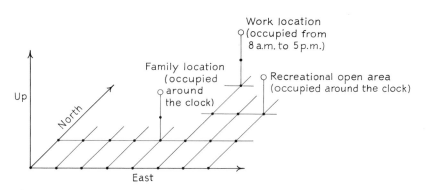

Figure 8-5 THE SPACE-TIME GRID
The space-time grid could be used to help determine the optimal
location of facilities and residences in a new city. In this figure the
time coordinate is not shown.

City and to walk to work by taking a one-minute detour through the
park on the roof in order to breath fresh air and to enjoy the sunshine.

Step II: List certain functions (or activities) that would be performed within the city by its inhabitants. Obviously, such a list
can be very complicated and would have to be represented in its
simplest terms to be useful for overall city planning.

The key idea begins with the concept of a space-time grid and the
assignment of the various activities to grid points. For example, a
family unit might be assigned to a set of grid points with fixed space
coordinates 4 East, 1 North, 2 Up, with time coordinates 1, 2, . . . , 24
representing the 24 hours in a day. The interpretation to be made
from this is that the family unit would be assigned to some corresponding location in the city when it is built and would presumably
occupy this location around the clock. The purpose of the planning
technique is to determine the optimal assignment of households and
other functions to grid points. If we omit the time coordinate for
purposes of illustration, then the assignments can be depicted as
shown in Figure 8-5. We *will* need the time coordinate, however,
because a work function like that shown at point (5, 3, 2) may require
the location for times 8 a.m. to 5 p.m. only. This leaves open the possibility that other functions could be assigned to the same space
grid point provided they would not overlap in the time coordinates.

If the space-time requirement of a family unit might be depicted as
a single grid point (somewhere in the city) continuously over time,
the requirement for a restaurant could be depicted as a cluster of adjacent grid points in the space grid, each point of which must remain
there for 24 hours a day. Alternatively, the restaurant could be depicted so that the points (representing the "units" or rooms available
for dining) could also be used at certain times of the day for other
functions—perhaps for meetings; another restaurant could be de-

picted as a cluster of points that move from one location in the space grid to another during the course of a day (a mobile lunch wagon).

The list of major functions and their admissible variations is very large. It is complicated by the fact that various functions are quite adaptable. There could be trade-offs between size and convenience. For example, a restaurant could be designed to occupy a very small space near a work center. If so, it would occupy a convenient location but would have a limited capacity for service.

Step III. Once the major functions are tentatively assigned to points on the space-time grid almost everything else (at least in theory) falls into place: for example, the best layout of the network of basic utilities and roads could be determined. One could also compute the transportation time and other indexes that measure the efficiency (or the inconvenience) of the total system so that they can be compared with the desired goals. If one is not careful it is entirely possible for the tentative assignment to be infeasible. For example, it could result in insufficient room for roads or insufficient space for certain facilities associated with maintenance of roads. Clearly the major functions must be assigned positions in the space-time grid so that when the grid is translated into a physical plan there will be room left for supporting services. Space-time allocations cannot be made willy-nilly.

It is here that one can make effective use of linear-programming models, for these allow one to consider easily many alternative assignments of functions to grid points. (Almost all the other simulation techniques for large-scale systems can bog down because of the magnitude of the computational work or because they find a local optimum such as we described earlier but can find no way to move from there to a global optimum.) Nevertheless, severe limitations restrict the applicability of the linear programming models. It will also be necessary, for this reason, to consider many "scenarios." For example, what is the "best" one can do if planning is limited to what is feasible in a flat city (one in which the vertical dimension is not exploited); *or* what is feasible in a vertical city where most activities follow an eight-hour work-cycle; *or* what is feasible in a fully three-dimensional city where time is exploited evenly around the clock?

C.A. Doxiadis uses the term "Ekistics" to describe the "science of human settlements."[3] In 1968 he published a comprehensive, easily read treatise on this subject. In his book he sets forth his premise "that human settlements are susceptible of systematic design." He lays down several principles which can help us to understand why man constructs his cities in certain ways:

1. Man tries to shape his settlement so as to maximize his personal human freedom, i.e., so as to give him easy access to "elements of nature (such as water and trees), . . . other people, and . . . works of man (such as buildings and roads)."

2. Man tries to evolve a technology so as to minimize the effort required to attain a high level of personal human freedom.

3. Man tries to optimize his "protective space, which means the selection of such a distance from other persons, animals or objects so that he can keep his contacts with them without any sensory or psychological discomfort."

4. Man tries to optimize "the quality of his relationship with his environment. . . . This is the principle that leads to order, physiological and esthetic." It also "influences architecture and, in many respects, art."

5. Man tries to strike a balance between the first four principles.

In the authors' view, the accelerative thrust of modern society will force yet another principle into the foreground of our consciousness, one that will operate to protect man over the long term, namely:

6. Man tries to optimize his future on this planet as well as that of other species.

This completes our outline of how mathematics, operations research, and computers could be used by an interdisciplinary team of architects, economists, social scientists, engineers, and city planners to explore the many possible ways of assigning functions to the space-time grid and to select those plans for urban development that most nearly meet the goals set down.[4]

The goals of city design, which we outlined earlier, can now be seen to be merely a detailed expression of Doxiadis's five principles. Let us next turn our attention to the "sixth principle," which is the central theme of the next chapter.

Notes and References

1. C. A. Doxiadis, *SCD Magazine*, System Development Corporation (Santa Monica, Calif., December 1969), page 9. See also C. A. Doxiadis, *Ekistics*, Oxford University Press (New York, 1968), 527 pages. On page 388 Doxiadis applies computer simulation to the analysis of the Urban Detroit Area. A short summary can be found in Doxiadis's paper entitled "Ekistics, the Science of Human Settlements," *Science*, Vol. 170, Number 3956 (October 23, 1970), pages 393-404.

2. Russel Ackoff and others, "Prospects of the American City," Management Science Center (University of Pennsylvania, 1969), 114 pages.

3. C. A. Doxiadis, *Science, op. cit.*

4. For an elementary introduction to the art of formulating linear-programming models, see Chapter 3 *in* George B. Dantzig, *Linear Programming and Extensions*, Princeton University Press (Princeton, N.J., 1963).

CONSERVATION

9.1 Repaying Our Debt to Nature

> The great question of the seventies is: Shall we surrender to our surroundings or shall we make our peace with nature and begin to make reparations for the damage we have done to our air, to our land, and to our water?
>
> Richard M. Nixon, State of the Union Message, 1970

Man is beginning to assume his responsibility: in a very real sense man has become more than the master of nature; he has become its custodian.[1]

Of course, man is always in balance with nature. After all, he is part of it. The balance is bad if at any time, anywhere, now or in the future, people live at starvation level. The balance is bad if man destroys the vegetation, or the wild life, or pollutes the sky. The balance is bad if man strips the earth of basic resources and has no plan for restoration.

Through his greed, man may have already set natural forces in motion that endanger his future on earth. To establish a good balance with nature requires a way of life that is less demanding on resources; one that returns wastes gracefully to the earth. Almost every intelligent individual now believes that man must begin controlling population growth. But what else can be done? Resolving environmental problems requires a better way to develop urban areas, a change in certain human customs, and a modification of some of man's industrial practices. In the end, of course, all will be of no avail unless world population is stabilized soon.

Man treats his environment selfishly, stripping away what he wants and dumping what he doesn't. This he does in the name of "economics." Indeed, in planning, the future is discounted so heavily that only the immediate present (for example, the next five years) has any value. About the only thing we hesitate to do is to remove our ancestors from their graves to make room for highways and housing.

But now we are faced with investing larger amounts of our efforts into restoring and preserving those processes of nature which may in the future determine whether or not man survives. Often the process of trying to make amends for man's environmental destruction becomes a vicious cycle. Eliminate air pollution and you create water pollution. Build a treatment plant for the fouled water and you've got solid waste to dispose of. The environment is complex. There appear to be no easy solutions to problems of environmental abuse; their resolution requires gathering the knowledge from many fields and using good planning techniques to make the most effective use of this knowledge. This is why we have placed so much emphasis on modelling the total system and making use of operations research and computers.

Examples of Environmental Abuse

Let us look at some well-known examples of man's abuse of the biosphere—that part of the earth which supports life—and let us examine some of the possible consequences of this abuse. Later, we will examine how the design of cities can help attack some of the problems of preserving the environment.

Everyone is now aware of why the use of insecticides such as DDT, which once seemed nearly miraculous in their effectiveness against destructive insects, had to be controlled or banned. In large part this awareness began with publication of Rachel Carson's book, *Silent Spring*. Indiscriminate use of pesticides upsets the very delicate ecological balance, creating all kinds of unforeseen repercussions. Now it is realized that chemical controls on plant and insect life often means man ends up poisoning himself.

Use of chemical fertilizers on agricultural land has deprived the soil of its natural ability to fix nitrogen. These chemicals have also penetrated deeply into the underground waters, making them hazardous to drink. Use of industrial chemicals also contributes to water pollution. Pollution of the waterways (as well as the air) is prevalent around Tokyo, the Rhine, and the Great Lakes. Waste products from the manufacture of pesticides, paints, and paper often contain relatively harmless mercury compounds that eventually reach the waterways where they have unforseeably been converted by biological processes into mercury compounds not harmful to certain types of sea life but harmful to man, who eats that sea life. Now oceans, rivers, and lakes have all become so contaminated with mercury that man cannot eat the fish he catches in some locations.

Example:

The U.S. Environmental Protection Agency on March 12, 1972 banned all pesticides containing alkyl mercury and the use of all types of mercury pesticides for rice seed, laundry fabrics, and antifouling paints for boats, because of the cumulative danger of *Minamata Disease.* Discharges from a plastic-paint factory into Minamata Bay, Japan caused 121 cases of the disease including 46 deaths between 1953 and 1970. Symptoms are progressive blindness, deafness, uncoordination, and intellectual deterioration. The disease passes easily from the mother to the unborn fetus and results in a disability somewhat like cerebral palsy in children.

Environments within the city can also become unbalanced. We now know that the widespread use of antibiotics has created new strains of pathogenic microorganisms immune to every antibiotic so far devised. In many health facilities, the use of disinfectants has altered the natural balance of microorganisms and has created in its place a dangerous mix of streptococcal bacteria and viral strains; hospitals are no longer always safe places (even if doctors find it convenient to put us there).[2]

Since much of man's pollution ends in the oceans that occupy 70 percent of the earth's surface, many ecologists are concerned about its effect on the phytoplankton. These microscopic plants, which float in the ocean, convert carbon dioxide by photosynthesis to oxygen and are themselves an organic product that forms part of the food chain.

Maintaining a balanced life cycle requires that plants take from the earth and the air certain quantities of inorganic matter such as gases and minerals in proper balance for growth. These inorganic products thus enter into plant and animal food chains. Eventually, as part of the chain, bacteria and fungi decompose dead protoplasm into substances which are usable by soil organisms and by the phytoplankton of the ocean. In all of these processes the amount of light that living organisms receive from the sun also must be maintained within narrow limits.

There may now be a serious threat to the balance of life that has been maintained over hundreds of millions of years. Some scientists argue that man's technology adds carbon dioxide to the atmosphere and that increasing amounts of carbon dioxide in the air could act as a *trap,* allowing sunlight to enter but preventing radiated heat from the earth from escaping. This could lead to a rise in the earth's temperature, which would result eventually in the melting of the polar ice caps and a 60-foot rise in the level of the oceans. Even if life were to survive, such an oceanic rise would mean the inundation of coastal cities.

But other scientists maintain that an increase in particulates in the air would *reflect* incoming sunlight, causing a decrease in the earth's average temperature (.2 degrees centigrade is believed to be enough to create another ice age).

By means of photosynthesis nearly 80 billion tons of carbon is drawn from the atmosphere and changed into organic form each year, nearly half of it in the form of forest growth and the remainder about equally divided between ocean life and grass and crop lands. However, there appears to be no evidence of change in the carbon dioxide level in the atmosphere as a result of man's increased burning of fossil fuels and his denuding of forests which absorb carbon dioxide.[3] So far the calcium ions in the huge volume of ocean water have been able to combine with and to precipitate from it about half the increase in the carbon dioxide level and plant life has been able to "fix" the rest.

Only a foolish person would argue that since some scientists predict one kind of disaster and other scientists, another contradictory kind, man should forget it until they make up their minds. On the contrary, possibilities of ecological ruin are so serious that the construction of quantitative mathematical models of the biosphere must be given top priority.

While the scientists are busy finding out what the score is, all of us can get busy and stop pollution by redesigning our urban environments so that man's disruptions of earth life cycles can be minimized. If it turns out that the various scientific predictions are false, we can always go back to our old ways—if we must. The same reasoning applies to the world population explosion. Paul Ehrlich and others predict a decreased quality of life and mass starvation. If society takes their warnings seriously and does succeed in curtailing world population growth and then it turns out that their predictions were only a false alarm, we can always go back to raising large families.

But more than just curtailing world population appears to be required. Consumption rates on a per capita basis have grown even faster. Population *doubled* in the United States from 1918 to 1970 but food production has doubled since 1940; the volume of manufactured products has doubled since 1953; Gross National Product has doubled since 1958; the use of electric power and fertilizers have doubled, since 1960; and the use of pesticides has doubled since 1963.[4]

9.2 Environmental Effects of Man's Use of Energy

Fossil Fuels

Even though world reserves of gas, oil, and coal appear to be enormous there is no reason why man should use up this finite resource, and thus leave his children's children short of fuels in the event that new sources of energy do not develop as anticipated. In the authors' opinion man, in his planning, uses too high a discount rate on the

Table 9-1

129

Energy sources and uses (by percent).

Breakdown by source and use		Total percentages	
Primary Sources of Energy	Oil (44), Gas (33), Coal (21)	98	100
	Water power (1.7), Nuclear power (.2)	2	
Primary Uses of Energy	Household	20	100
	Commercial	14	
	Industrial	42	
	Autos & Trucks	18	
	Other Transport	6	

Source: "Reference Energy Systems and Resource Data," Associated Universities, Inc. (Upton, N.Y., 1972), Table II-3, page 12. Figures are adjusted for energy losses due to transmission and conversion to electricity. Data are for 1969.

future; this, for example, results in a current price per gallon for oil that does not properly reflect the true long-term value of keeping it in the ground. We feel that the correct policy is to keep it in the ground, i.e., to conserve fossil fuels.[5] See Table 9-1.

Energy Sources

The future, as far as energy sources are concerned, looks bright, and if fully exploited, these sources might in time enable man to resolve many of the problems connected with the world population explosion. Even assuming rates of consumption per capita ten times the average world levels in 1968, man still has truly enormous energy reserves, providing, of course, that scientific techniques can be discovered to tap these sources of energy.[6] See Table 9-2. It is hoped that in the future methods will be developed for obtaining energy efficiently from fusion and solar radiation.

Carbon Dioxide Balance

The burning of fossil fuels and forest products burdens the atmosphere with carbon dioxide. However, through photosynthesis the vegetation in the sea and on land uses this carbon dioxide in combination with sunlight to trap the sun's energy in the form of nutrients and cellulose and to produce oxygen. This sets up a cycle. The basic questions are: (1) whether there is enough vegetation to keep the carbon dioxide in the atmosphere at very low levels; (2) whether the form of vegetable growth can be useful to man. If levels of carbon dioxide rise above 0.4 percent, as noted earlier, this could affect the polar icecaps. If there are extensive growing forests, a good balance can be established: low concentrations of carbon dioxide, a flow of wood products by forest farming, and finally the burning of fossil fuels and discarded wood products to cycle carbon dioxide back to the forests and oceans.[7]

Table 9-2
*World supply of energy measured in years before
reserve sources are exhausted, assuming consumption rates
worldwide are ten times current per capita rates.*

Energy source	Reserve status	Years before exhaustion
Coal, Oil, Gas	Known reserves	13
	Potential reserves	270
Uranium (U_3O_8)	Accessible known reserves	6
	Accessible potential reserves	6
	Less accessible reserves	10^4
Fusion Power	Deuterium from the ocean	3×10^9
Solar Radiation	Life of the sun	10×10^9

The World Heat Cycle

Another consideration in choosing alternative sources of energy is the world heat cycle. Ultimately, all the energy we use is converted into heat, warming the earth and eventually radiating away into outer space. If we burn fossil fuels or use nuclear sources, we are increasing the amount of heat received on the earth's surface. The time will come when increased population, increased use of energy per capita, together with the use of energy from nuclear and fossil sources will influence the world heat levels enough to affect the climate and eco-systems noticeably.[8] Some say the temperature of the earth has already been measurably increased around cities.[9] Whether a slight warming up of the earth should be considered bad or good (for example, it might prevent an ice age) requires the development of mathematical models that properly simulate the world's climate, ecology, and energy resources and uses.

9.3 Solid Waste

Penny pinching. The chief difficulty with solid waste is that disposal is too easy. The cost of disposal is less than $25 per person per year. The average citizen, if he doesn't have to smell it or see it, couldn't care less where it is disposed. Actually the problem of waste collection and disposal in urban areas has as its source penny-pinching, rather than technological ineptitude. Man has produced vast institutions for production spurred on by his motive for profit. Historically, solid waste—industrial refuse and domestic refuse—was simply dumped into the public domain. Its removal became a municipal function which was achieved by dumping the gatherings into the nearest hole or stream. Thus it came about that the municipality and the public failed to see the need to develop, or even to motivate the development of, adequate systems for recycling wastes. Now it is evident that today's waste load is indeed something to be reckoned with. See Table 9-3.

Compacted, U.S. household waste alone in 1970 would have been enough to build a base for a new city 8000-by-8000 feet in ocean water 100 feet deep. The waste accumulation rate of five pounds per person per day in 1970 is increasing and is expected to rise to eight pounds by 1980. Collection costs have been found, in a survey of 166 cities, to run from $18 per ton to $24 per ton in large cities (1969 prices). Eighty percent of the costs are wages for the pickup crews.

Disposal is not the primary problem. A ten-by-ten mile area of ocean floor 1000 feet deep could hold the waste of the country for the next 400 years at present rates of accumulation. Alternatively, any unpopulated land area could be used to build up a mountain of trash (a "Mount Trashmore") which could make a nice ski slope in the winter.

The problem of waste disposal is primarily concerned with:

1. Finding acceptable sites close to the city.
2. Good pickup service.
3. Unobtrusive and inexpensive hauling.
4. Nonoffensive treatment at the dump.
5. Care that poisonous gases like methane are not released.
6. Care that there is no pollution of waterways or land areas.
7. The salvage of raw materials and the extraction of residual energy.

Perhaps as important as the cost of trash collection in densely populated areas is its unfortunate contribution to traffic congestion, litter, and noise. In 1966 in New York City there were 2700 private and 1800 municipal refuse trucks in operation. For the entire United States, it is estimated that there were at least 150,000 trash trucks in use in 1970. If the volume of solid waste continues to increase (as it will) and if handling methods remain the same (as is likely), about 275,000 collection trucks will be operating on roads and streets in the United States in 1980, each making its contribution to traffic congestion. We will probably witness foul-smelling pileups from time to time when our garbage collectors go on strike.

Table 9-3
Sources of solid waste (1969) in billions of tons*

Residential (.3), Commercial (.1)	.4
Industrial (nonrecyclable)	.1
Agricultural (mostly manure)	2.2
Mineral (mostly mine slag)	1.7
Total	4.4

*Figures in the literature vary depending on sources used and classification.

Instead of using trucks, the residents of some apartment complexes in Sweden drop the household refuse down a chute, where it is then moved through an underground tunnel by means of a high pressure system to a central point for processing (actually burning). A promising alternative that has been suggested is to grind up the refuse and to transport it as a slurry in underground pipelines.[10]

What are the alternatives to the open city dump? At the moment there is a trend in the United States towards converting the city dump into what is termed a controlled sanitary landfill. This is merely the systematic burial of compacted garbage. Open dumps are cheaper to operate and can handle, by burning, larger quantities of waste per unit area. But land is becoming scarce in big cities and the marginal land that has been created by sanitary landfill is very much in demand for building. Nevertheless 90 percent of the garbage disposal sites still take the form of unplanned open dumps. The reason is an administrative one. If all the land that can be used for dumping waste within the city is converted to other uses after completion of the sanitary landfill, the city must then find land outside the city for use as dumps. This is not always easy. Suburbia does not like to smell big-city garbage, and when new dump sites for garbage are found the costs of hauling it there are likely to be great.

An alternative to the open dump and to the sanitary landfill is the combustion of refuse in incinerators. These are designed so as not to contribute to the existing air pollution. The resulting heat energy (the refuse burned is 55 percent paper) can be used to generate power and to heat houses. This system is used in many apartment complexes in Europe, North America, and Japan. Incineration reduces the volume of waste to an ash that is biologically sterile, odorless, and hence easy and safe to bury or otherwise dispose of.

In some localities a traditional technique for handling solid waste is composting. It requires first the removal of metals, rocks, and glass. The organic material is then mixed with sewer sludge and allowed to rot. The mass is turned over occasionally for contact with air. Compost has little value as a fertilizer, but can be used to condition the soil as a humus. Mixed with manures as a "natural" fertilizer, compost produces (it is claimed) a more disease-resistant, better-tasting nutritional product. But, sad to say, the economics of agriculture is such that farmers seldom bother to rework even their own trimmings into soil conditioners; instead they pay someone to cart them away.

The end products of various disposal methods (some of which are still in an experimental stage) are listed in Table 9-4.[11]

Suggestions on Solid Waste Management

Metal recycling. Many of our basic metal resources are in limited supply and by the year 2000 will become scarce. This suggests that metals ought to be manufactured in forms that are more easily recy-

Table 9-4

133
Methods of recycling organic wastes.

Method		End products
Open dump + burning	→	Landfill, smoke, odor, health hazards
Dump + earth compacting	→	Sanitary landfill, slowly settling land, methane gas in atmosphere
Dump + high pressure compacting	→	Sanitary landfill with faster settling characteristics
High pressure compacting	→	Building blocks (experimental)
Composting	→	Soil conditioner, landfill (possibly odor and methane gas if open windrows used)
Incineration	→	Heating homes, smoke, disposable ash
Wet oxidation (slurry transport)	→	Energy source, chemicals, disposable ash (experimental)
Pyrolysis	→	Energy, methane, chemicals, disposable ash (experimental)
Anaerobic digestion (slurry transport)	→	Energy, methane, soil conditioner, biologically stable landfill
Microbial conversion of cellulose	→	Glucose, protein (experimental)

clable.[12] For example, if a bushing or a housing for a bearing is made of a special alloy (e.g., brass), then the replacement of that part ought to be accompanied by the relegation of the old part to a recycling system whereby old worn bushings are melted down and reprocessed. This means that a product would not be marketable unless its design were such that its repair and replacement would permit easy salvage. Under this plan, conceivably the quality of bushings might need to be down-graded in certain applications in order to facilitate the standard remelting of scrap bushings.

Paper recycling. About half the solid waste generated by households is paper.[13] In the early 1970s the annual paper and paperboard consumption in the United States exceeded 50 million tons and consumption appears to be increasing at the rate of 8 percent per year.[14] The rate of recycling waste paper has been below 20 percent. For each ton of paper recycled, 17 trees are saved. Newsprint from reclaimed newspapers conserved about 5.1 million trees in 1969.[15] Recently government, industry, and ecology groups have all expressed a desire to increase these rates. For example, the National Academy of Sciences has recommended that paper recycling be increased to 35 percent by 1985. If recycling of paper could be increased to 50 percent by 1980, about 500 million trees would be saved annually.[16]

This suggests that we should have a policy that is effective in preserving and extending the world's forests — a policy which would put a high value on (1) saving the forest as a wilderness area and recreational preserve for future generations, (2) maintaining the carbon dioxide-oxygen ratio in the atmosphere, (3) preserving the forest as a watershed, and (4) farming trees so that woodland remains after cutting and the possibility of forest fires is reduced. For example, the residents of future cities might decide to purchase wood products from only the companies that meet these standards of forest management. It would cost more, of course, but this is what is meant by paying our debt to the world and the future of mankind.

Overall city planning could ask such questions as: are newspaper advertisements the best way to educate the public on what products are available in stores? Can one copy of a newspaper be shared by several people? Can newspapers be published less often and still serve the public need for "gossip"? Can special TV circuits be used as an alternative?

In this connection, we remark that the automatic delivery system proposed for Compact City could play a useful role. Many people who read newspapers have specialized interests. Because of the ease of delivery through the automatic delivery system, it might turn out to be practical to order special sections of the paper for delivery. It may also be practical for more than one family to share the same paper. By such means and by continuous telecast on special television circuits of the latest news and other features such as classified advertising, it might be possible to reduce per capita newsprint consumption to a fraction of current levels.

Most paper (80 percent of it) is, however, manufactured for packaging. One idea is to replace paper-wrapped packages by a standard type of plastic, a plastic that could be recycled (perhaps one or two times) by heating it up until it turns into a liquid form that can be reconstituted to a plastic. (We will say more about this in a moment.) Once more, the automatic delivery system described in Chapter 6 could make this practical for it would mean that waste plastic could be conveniently dispatched from the home for recycling without first being mixed with other types of trash. Another idea is to use returnable packages for most delivered items. For example, standard items like canned soups, vegetables, and fruits could be ordered for immediate use via the delivery system. City demand could make it possible to use large-volume vats to fill glass jars which are then dispatched to the household. Glass jars would be returned empty and could be reused.

Thus the use of paper by one device or another could be sharply reduced. Recycled paper could be used in a variety of ways. For example, it is not always best to make newsprint out of old newspapers; they could be converted into tissue products or papers used for packaging. Such alternatives are desirable not only for maintaining fiber quality but also to conserve the water and power required for conversion.

Plastic recycling. Plastics could be made of a standardized composition enabling them to be recycled by turning them into liquids and then back into plastic. So-called thermo-plastics, such as polyvinyl chloride and polyethylene, can, in theory, be remelted (at temperatures well below 500°F) into liquid again and again. In practice, unfortunately, three or four sequential heating-cooling cycles will usually result in the loss of the desirable properties of the plastic at room temperature. This means that the recycling capabilities of plastics are limited. There are also problems connected with burning it as fuel; an exception is Monsanto's "Lopac," a plastic which is easy to oxidize completely. Researchers should be encouraged to develop plastics which would be easier to recycle. There is, in theory, practically no loss of energy if oil and gas are first processed into plastic and then later the waste plastic is burned for fuel.[17] In Japan waste plastics are shredded into a fine grain and pressed into sheets, boards, and containers.[18]

The operations research role. There are many alternative ways to recycle — some conserve the basic stock of material but require more energy. Operations research, in particular linear programming, provides natural techniques for deciding which combination of recycling processes would be best.[19]

Having outlined some of the broad environmental and natural resource considerations that are part of a total-system modelling, we are ready to turn, in the next chapter, to the specifics of selecting a plan for urban development.

Notes and References

1. For an excellent treatment of conservation, read Stewart L. Udall's *The Quiet Crisis*, Holt, Rinehart and Winston (New York, 1963), 209 pages. Read also Rachel Carson's *Silent Spring*, Houghton Mifflin (Boston, 1962), 368 pages. See also Gordon Young, "Pollution: Threat to Man's Only Home" *National Geographic*, December 1970, pages 738–780. Also "Fighting to Save the Earth from Man," *Time*, February 2, 1970, pages 56–63. And highly recommended for general reading: W. P. Lineberry (editor), *Priorities for Survival*, H. W. Wilson Co. (New York, 1973), 223 pages.

2. David S. Feingold, "Hospital Acquired Infections," *New England Journal of Medicine*, December 17, 1970, pages 1384–1391.

3. For an interesting discussion of the important role that forests play in carbon dioxide balance and heat balance by transpiration, see Frederick E. Smith, "Ecological Demand and Environmental Response," *Journal of Forestry*, December 1970, pages 752–755.

4. Statistics from *World Almanac 1970*, *FAO Statistical Yearbook 1968*, *U.S. Statistical Abstract 1968*.

5. H. H. Landsberg and S. H. Schurr, *Energy in the United States — Sources, Uses and Policy Issues*, Random House (New York, 1968).

6. "Energy and Power" Issue, *Scientific American*, September 1971. Reprinted as *Energy and Power: A Scientific American Book*, W. H. Freeman and Company (San Francisco, 1971), 144 pages.

7. Norman Brooks, "Energy and the Environment," *Engineering and Science*, January 1971, pages 20–23 and 30–33.

8. John R. Clark, "Thermal Pollution and Aquatic Life," *Scientific American*, March 1969, pages 18–27. (Offprint 1135, W. H. Freeman and Company, San Francisco.)

9. W. P. Lowry, "The Climate of Cities," *Scientific American*, August 1967, pages 15–23. (Offprint 1215, W. H. Freeman and Company, San Francisco.) A discussion of how cities are warmer than the countryside.

10. Iraj Zandi and John A. Hayden, "Are pipelines the answer to waste collection dilemma?" *Environmental Science and Technology*, Vol. 3, No. 9, September 1969, pages 812–819. Also see Iraj Zandi, "Pneumo-Slurry Pipeline Collection and Removal of Municipal Waste," The Towne School of Civil and Mechanical Engineering, University of Pennsylvania, Final Report 1971.

11. Some of the best work in recycling concepts using advanced scientific techniques (including operations research) is done in sanitary engineering laboratories. A good example of such research is *Comprehensive Studies of Solid Waste Management*, 3rd Annual Report, Sanitary Engineering Laboratory Report No. 70-2, University of California, Berkeley, June 1970.

12. *Recycling Resources*, National Association of Secondary Material Industries, Inc. (330 Madison Ave., New York 10017, August 1970). The report states that 30 percent of the aluminum, 45 percent of the copper and brass, 52 percent of the lead, 20 percent of the zinc, and 25 percent of the paper stock comes from scrap.

13. L. E. Williams, "Managing the Solid Waste Function," *American Paper Industry*, 1971, pages 40–45.

14. *American Almanac 1970*, "Statistical Abstract of U.S." (Grosset and Dunlap, 1970), Table 988, page 645.

15. Statement by C. R. Batton of the American Forest Institute.

16. Statement by J. L. Dietz at a Tappi-International Paper Meeting, February 23, 1971.

17. J. W. Sawyer, "Plastics and the Solid Waste Problem" (unpublished memo), University of Pennsylvania, 1971.

18. "Closing Plastics Cycle," *Chemical Engineering*, June 15, 1970, pages 88–90.

19. Norman Morse and Edwin W. Roth, "Systems Analysis of Regional Solid Waste Handling," Cornell Aeronautical Laboratory, Buffalo, N.Y., November 1968.

DETERMINING THE
GENERAL CITY PLAN

10.1 Setting Goals and Standards

In planning a city we need criteria which will help us to determine
its outward shape, its interior arrangement, and its total size. We will
select standards on the generous side deliberately in order to demon-
strate that even with generous standards the cost of Compact City is
low and therefore economically feasible.

How Many People?

The first consideration is the question of whether one size of population is to be preferred to another. In Chapter 2 we gave *convenience*
as the chief reason for deciding upon two million people as a good
upper bound for the population of a city. Beyond a certain size a city
no longer remains a convenient environment for its inhabitants.

In comparing various-sized predominantly two-dimensional
present-day cities there are some factors which favor large populations and some which favor small ones.[1] The most obvious one is
travel time — the smaller the city, the more accessible are its various
parts and the easier is the problem of transportation. (However, we
have already observed that a Compact City, even if large, would have
the same advantage of low travel time as a present-day small city.)

Good health facilities are something we consider to be important. It
has been observed that the ratio of physicians to population increases

with city size.[2] Larger cities apparently provide better opportunity for physicians to specialize. In spite of this, overall life expectancy is higher in the small city. This is probably because there is a different genetic mix of people in small cities and possibly because in small cities there is less tension and strife. Infant mortality rates are lower in larger cities—possibly because superior health services exist to treat acute cases. (The development of high sanitation standards in urban areas is, of course, an absolutely essential precondition for modern living. Their absence in past centuries was a major cause of high infant mortality.) A compact city design appears to have many of the advantageous conditions for promotion of health that exist in both the large and the small conventional city.

Public Safety is another factor to be considered. Automobile accidents and crime have been observed to increase with city size, but fire losses per capita are greater in cities under 50,000 than in cities over 1,000,000. Even the number of fires per capita has an inverse ratio to city size.

The probability that a nuclear attack will befall a small city is considerably less, for strategic reasons, than for a large city. A nation is less vulnerable if its cities are small and well separated. Compact City would be as vulnerable as any large city to a direct hit, but probably would be a better place to be in case of near hits.

Municipal service costs tend to decrease with the size of a present-day city until a minimum is reached after which it increases. A simple example is the cost of using electricity, which is lower in cities of around a million in population than in smaller or larger cities. In a compact city, costs for electric lighting would be higher; but garbage and sewage would require less extensive removal systems; there would be little need to use energy to heat individual units within the city in the winter. However, energy would be needed at all times to keep the city cool. As already noted, the cost for electricity for a household in Compact City would be about the same as for gas, oil, and electricity in a conventional city. But overall energy requirements for Compact City would be less, primarily due to the lower transportation needs.

Advanced education requires facilities mostly found in the larger cities today. A university or college with students drawn from a surrounding city needs a population base of at least 100,000. A population of nearly 500,000 is needed for professional schools in business, law, and medicine. Libraries meet minimum professional standards in cities as large as 50,000–75,000. In spite of these requirements, there is no substantial discrepancy between the educational levels of people living in cities of various sizes.

Other factors to consider are retail facilities (they require a 50,000-base for development), churches and associations (these require population of between 15,000 and 30,000 for a base). More people marry and own houses in smaller cities. However, dwellings are better equipped in larger cities.

The main reason for developing a city with a large population is to make it possible for inhabitants to have variety, innovation, special services, and a better opportunity for advanced education, research, and cultural pursuits. It seems to us that Boston, the Minneapolis-St. Paul area and the San Francisco–Oakland area provide evidence that an urban area of under two million people could meet these criteria for a cosmopolitan center. On the other hand there is much evidence to show that cities can develop all kinds of administrative headaches when they grow beyond a population of two million.[3]

From considerations of the effect of population size on city management, health, education, markets, manufacture, sports and cultural activities, our criterion for selecting city size becomes essentially this: The maximum population should be set at the smallest value consistent with the creation of a cosmopolitan center in which a high level of intellectual, commercial and special-service activity can be sustained.

Nothing, of course, would prevent the population from exceeding a planned maximum figure. For example, six people could live in a dwelling designed for the convenient habitation of only four people. The same applies to transportation, schools, and other facilities. We expect that social forces will continue to encourage families to have fewer children. If population growth is not stabilized, we anticipate that Compact City, like conventional cities, would become crowded and would no longer be a convenient place to live.

We envision that if the population of Compact City grows beyond the planned maximum, another "New Compact City" would emerge. It need not, of course, be a look-alike. The small amount of land needed to build a compact city means that many compact cities could be built near each other—each surrounded by open space (something that is no longer feasible when today's oversized cities expand). Cultural and leisure activities that give each city individual dignity and character could, of course, be emphasized, so that each additional Compact City could develop according to its special interests.

Can a City Limit Its Population?

Perhaps one of the most obvious of statements is that birth control is working. Among many groups, women are simply not having the large families that were so common two or three generations ago. It is also obvious that birth control needs to be pushed to the point of zero-population growth. There is evidence that "the pill" and other contraceptive devices, liberalized abortion laws, and social pressures in the 1970s are beginning to have a dramatic effect on the birth rate in the United States.

The age at which women have children is just as important as the number of those children.[4] For example, suppose there are two cities that start out with the same population, and that each woman during her lifetime has exactly two children. However, in the first city the women have their babies at an average age of eighteen and in the second city at an average age of thirty-six. It is easy to see from this oversimplified example that even though each city will eventually stabilize its population, the first city will do so at twice the size of the second.

How Close Should People Be to Each Other?

A second basic concept in city planning is that of the density of people per square mile. From our description of Compact City it is clear that the number of people per *cubic* mile might be a more meaningful criterion when the vertical dimension is effectively used. Historically, population density has been viewed as a kind of indirect measure of the average number of person-to-person encounters that a person makes while moving about the city. It is greatly altered by the presence or absence of the automobile. How dense a city ought to be is a matter of taste, available space, custom, psychological needs, socioeconomic necessity, and sometimes technological efficiency. (An example of the latter might be the construction of a city in Antarctica, where for easier heating a high density design would be more efficient.) Because of the wide separation between levels of Compact City, the density that people would be aware of would be the number of people per square mile on a level. We will refer to this definition of density as *equivalent* (standard) density.

When do people feel the pressure of density? When do they have a desire for greater or lesser density? The danger of mob pressure, which threatens people with ochlophobia, is said to increase rapidly with density. Urban planners realize that sufficient area should be provided so that an individual can escape at least from time to time from the pressure of crowds. In many crowded present-day cities the presence of parks and open spaces within high-density neighborhoods, very near places in which people live, has helped to satisfy this minimal need to escape.[5]

But just as people have a need to find escape from crowds, so also there appears to be the psychological need for people to gather closely together from time to time—to press against one another. This is evidenced by voluntary attendance at sports events where spectators can hardly see the players and at concerts where half a million young people gather in a field, but indoors too, at crowded night clubs and during intermission times at concerts and operas. The design proposed for Compact City may partially satisfy this need since people from all over the city would find it convenient to go to its gathering places in the centralized core area.

Let us turn now to the question of what population density standard should be selected for Compact City. In the heart of Paris, a million people occupy an area of about 15 square miles. The average density is 85,000 per square mile. New York City has an average density of 25,000. However, the average per square mile density at its center, Manhattan, is 77,000. Here are some comparative statistics:[6]

Urban area	Population per sq mi
Singapore (Central Area)	971,000
Hong Kong (Victoria Area)	650,000
Algiers (Casbah)	500,000
Calcutta (Average)	86,000
Paris (Central Area)	85,000
New York City	
(Manhattan Area)	77,000
(Brooklyn Area)	35,000
San Francisco–Oakland	16,000
Compact City (equivalent density)	14,000
Los Angeles	5,000

The equivalent standard density of people per square mile proposed for Compact City is 14,000. It is close to that found in the general San Francisco–Oakland area. Moreover, if Compact City were to make more effective use of the time dimension, it would have the effect of making the equivalent density seem even lower. We have cited *low density* as a "self-evident virtue" for a well-planned city. Like the concept that there should be lots of open space, it is open to question.[7] As noted earlier, we have purposely selected our standards to be on the generous side to test economic feasibility. (In Section 13.1 we discuss a somewhat higher-density plan that would result in a 35 percent saving for a moderate-income family in costs for superior transportation and comparable housing.)

How Much Park Land?

An acre of park land per 100 city residents is used as a desirable standard,[8] but large cities do not satisfy this requirement and only a small fraction of cities with populations of between 50,000 and 250,000 do. In addition, parks are more accessible in the smaller cities. For a maximum of two million people, the amount of park land needed is 31 square miles. In Compact City, because of the proximity of 8 square miles of major park on the roof of the city and presumably hundreds of square miles of countryside just outside the city, we have set up a very ample specification of 27 square miles (an area equivalent to three entire levels) of interior open space.

What About Travel Time?

Probably the most important yardstick in determining a conventional city's dimensions is transit time. For example, Hans Blumenfeld[9] points out that a city with a center-to-edge-travel radius of one hour (at a travel rate of 20 miles per hour) has a circular area of about 1,250 square miles. Ten million people can live in a part occupying 312 square miles with single-family houses on 30- to 100-foot lots. Combined with streets, schools, and other facilities, the residential area would be 500 square miles. Industry, commerce, and other nonresidential facilities require another 150 square miles—leaving 600 square miles (about half the total area) for parks, golf courses, forests, farms, and lakes. Blumenfeld next supposes that the travel speed from city center to edge is increased to 30 miles per hour—then the area within one hour's distance could accommodate 15 million people in single-family houses on 60-by-100-foot lots. Open land would increase to about 1,000 square miles. The density is different in the two examples. A million people could be assumed to occupy 125 square miles in the city where an hour of travel covers 20 miles, and 188 square miles in the city where a travel-hour covers 30 miles. In either city the space allocations are considered very generous. However, the commute time of between one and two hours a day seems to us to be unacceptable.

Short travel time is significant for a reason other than the usual one of providing more time for other activities. It also reduces the number of person-to-person encounters, and should have the psychological effect of making people less conscious of the density of the city.

10.2 Determining Space Needs

Area Standards in a Modern Metropolis

As we noted, Hans Blumenfeld cites the following land allocation figures for a large megalopolis.[10] His figures reflect generous use of land and good-sized family houses, and are based on 10 million population and a family lot size of 30-by-100 feet (average family size, 3.33 people):

Residential housing area (minus streets)	312 square miles
Residential area plus streets, schools, local shops, clinics	500 square miles
Commercial, industrial areas	150 square miles
Parks, golf courses, forests, farms and lakes	600 square miles

If we estimate 25 percent of the area is used for streets, we can deduce:

Roads in residential area and in local neighborhood—facilities area (25 percent of 500)	125 square miles
Local neighborhood facilities minus streets (500 minus 312 minus 125)	63 square miles

This can be summarized as follows:

Residential housing area and streets (312 multiplied by 4/3)	416 square miles
Local neighborhood facilities and streets (63 multiplied by 4/3)	84 square miles
Commercial, industrial areas	150 square miles
Parks, golf courses, forests, farms, and lakes	600 square miles
Total	1,250 square miles

Based on a reduction to a population of 2,000,000 we have:

Use of land	Square miles		
	Excluding Streets	Streets Only	Including Streets
Residential housing area	62	21	83
Local neighborhood facilities	13	4	17
Commercial neighborhoods	22	8	30
Parks	120	0	120
Total	217	33	250

Shape and Height of the City

Let us now consider what the dimensions of the city (its height, base area, and shape) should be in order to minimize transportation time to central facilities and at the same time provide excellent contact with nature.

From mathematics we know that the shortest fence that will surround an area is a fence taking the form of a circle. Thus, if one wishes to enclose the largest area within a fence of fixed length, one uses the circular shape. It is also known that if a given area is rearranged into an irregular shape (thin and long, or star-shaped) or is divided into disconnected parts, a fence many times longer will be required to encompass the total area.

Assuming that the city takes the form of several levels with a roof park on top, there are still a number of options open. Later in Section 10.2 we use as our criterion for determining the height of the city the minimization of the time to go from the Core at top level to the outer periphery of the city at ground level. This decision determines what the number of levels in the city should be and fixes for any given population the area (but not the shape) of the base of the city (or the Park-Roof). If next we wish the exposed vertical surface of the city to be minimal, then it is clear (from our discussion above) that for a city with a fixed base area, the shape of the base should be *circular*. This shape is also a good choice because it would make central facilities accessible to all, and it is a good choice because it would give the least exposure to outside elements and would thus reduce the amount of energy required in some seasons to heat the city and in other seasons to cool it. Moreover, a circular shape is also good if one's objective is to make a number of recreational spots that are scattered about the countryside readily accessible to everyone in the city by means of a special transit system. This shape, however, would not be best if our sole objective is to maximize the number of households with a view of the surrounding countryside. The circular-shaped base which we have selected for our discussion in Part One is not crucial: other shapes are possible and may in fact be preferable.

(In Chapter 13 we will discuss in greater detail alternative design possibilities).

In the design of Compact City, many people occupy a given area above the earth's surface. They are not necessarily crowded, however, since they would be distributed on levels separated in excess of 30 feet (i.e., with enough separation so that one is not aware of those living above or below). The density on any given level could be kept very low. Moreover, since houses on different levels are closer together than they would be if they were laid out in a flat city, the transit time throughout the city is radically less. As already noted, the shorter distances and the more even use of the 24-hour time cycle also means, on the average, fewer encounters per person. Thus, the three-dimensional design of a compact city does not imply what high density per square mile implies in present-day cities, namely a high frequency of personal encounters between people.

The desirability of fewer encounters per person, however, is open to question. In Compact City the sidewalks would be livelier because people would be walking more often. As pointed out by Jane Jacobs this may be important for the safety and well being of a neighborhood.[11]

Residential Space

How big should the houses and apartments be? Assuming that an average-sized family is 3.33 people, we select as a generous planning standard 1,400 square feet for an apartment unit and 2,400 square feet for a house unit. We also assume that half the families will want to live in houses and the other half in apartments. We emphasize that these are only averages; the lots, houses, and apartments would actually come in a variety of sizes and styles. See Figures 3-4 and 3-7.

We propose that the average-sized family lot have an area of 6,000 square feet (60 feet wide and 100 feet deep) occupied by a two-story house, each story of which would require 1,200 square feet. This leaves an area of 4,800 square feet for a front yard with a ceiling height in excess of 30 feet.

A complex consisting of two apartments and two houses would then occupy a space 100 feet deep by 150 feet wide. Walkway and ringway requirements can be conveniently added to the dimensions of the space for each residence, and they amount to one-half the road and walkway widths. Thus, another 15 feet of width should be added to take care of the walkway and ring allowances. Assuming that a 40-foot spoke road crosses a ring road on the average of once every 1,000 feet, the allowance is 5 feet of spoke width for every 150 feet of dwelling units along a ring. See Figure 10-1.

The average family dwelling base area requirement is therefore (115 feet × 155 feet)/4, which is approximately equal to 4500 square feet of 30-foot high space.

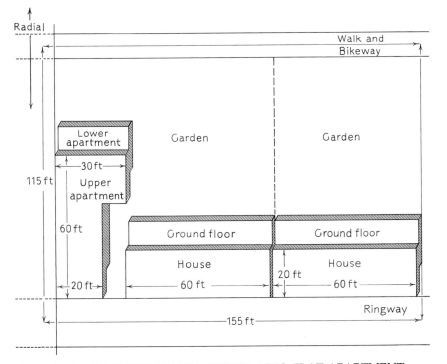

Figure 10-1 AN AVERAGE TWO-HOUSE, TWO-FLAT APARTMENT
COMPLEX
The average space requirement used for planning occupies 155 × 115
square feet of base area (including roadway allowances).

Commercial and other needs will be calculated in 30-foot height
units also so that the various areas can be added to determine total-
city size.

The area needed for 600,000 family units is, therefore,

$$\frac{4{,}500 \text{ square feet} \times 600{,}000 \text{ families}}{5{,}280^2 \text{ square feet per square mile}} \doteq 100 \text{ square miles,}$$

where we use the symbol = with a dot over it to mean "approximately
equal to."

Mid-Plaza Space

Frankly, we have found no good yardstick for estimating the area
needed for local neighborhood facilities. The space requirements we
use for local shopping, schools, small hospitals, and clinics are based
on Blumenfeld's estimates after adjusting them to a city population
of 2,000,000. Including roads, the space allotted by Blumenfeld would
be 17 square miles. If roads and parking areas are eliminated, one can
reduce this figure to 8 square miles. Assuming that the facilities are

in use around-the-clock in Compact City and that there is consolidation of facilities presently forced to spread out in conventional cities, the 8 square miles above could probably be further reduced to less than 4 square miles occupying between one and two floors of vertical space. For a first cut in the design of Compact City, we will assume "local neighborhood facilities" require 4 square miles of area occupying, vertically, two conventional floors. (This turns out to be half the Core area requirement.) For our calculations we have allotted 17 square miles for a total Mid-Plaza area, consisting of:

Local neighborhood facilities (30 feet high)	4 square miles
Interior parks in the Mid-Plaza (30 feet high)	13 square miles
Mid-Plaza total	17 square miles

We have purposely set the interior park figure high so as to help bring the total of all interior parks to the specified 27 square miles discussed earlier.

Core Space

The Core constitutes the main work area of the city. It includes universities, high schools, research facilities, hospitals, churches, as well as light manufacturing, shopping, hotels, exhibits, museums, auditoriums, and sports exhibitions.

Here again we have had difficulty finding a good yardstick for estimating this requirement. If we again start by reducing Blumenfeld's estimates to a city of 2,000,000 population, we have 30 square miles, including roads and areas of open space. Since the downtown of a major city contains many tall buildings, it is not correct to use this figure in calculating the base area of the Core of Compact City when other Compact City base areas assume a standard 30-foot height. This 30-square-mile figure can be reduced to roughly 15 square miles if we exclude roads and car parks but keep the open space. If we assume that half the remaining space is open space, and also assume that the buildings in the downtown area are six stories tall on the average, we obtain the equivalent of 23 square miles of 30-foot high facilities where we have placed two conventional stories in the 30-foot high space. Expanded to a 24-hour-use per day instead of the conventional 8, one might conceivably reduce 23 square miles down to 8 square miles of 30-foot high space required for Compact City's Core facilities.

The above estimate is admittedly very rough, so we cross-checked it by using another approach: namely, building up the figure by using *very* generous requirements. We might assume that space must be provided for up to one-half of 600,000 working adults at any instant of time. (We have used one-half rather than the actual one-third in order to overestimate rather than underestimate the requirements.)

We estimate that 80 percent of these people would work in regular offices and would require 500 square feet of space 15 feet high per worker, and that the remaining 20 percent of workers would require 2,000 square feet of factory-manufacturing, laboratory, exhibition, or warehouse space 30 feet high. This gives rise to an average of 600 square feet (of 30-foot high space) in use per worker at work. Multiplying by a maximum of 300,000 workers at work at any one time, we have

$$\frac{600 \text{ square feet} \times 300,000 \text{ workers}}{5,280^2 \text{ square feet per square mile}} \doteq 6.5 \text{ square miles}$$

of 30-foot high space. We have used the more generous allotment of 8 square miles (instead of 6.5) as the area required for facilities and have built up the total to 17 square miles by assuming that interior malls (and some access roads) would be a part of the Core:

Core facilities (30 feet high) = 8 square miles
Interior parks in the Core = 9 square miles
Core total = 17 square miles

Core Edge Space

The Core Edge is a ring intended as a major transfer area where people can either pick up or leave a car. The ring has roads, ramps, parking facilities for cars, and a promenade (or mall) to be used for exhibits and for viewing special interior gardens. It separates the Residential Area from the Core.

Core Edge facilities (roads) = 1 square mile
Interior parks in Core Edge = 5 square miles
Total = 6 square miles

The road requirement is small and actually can be arrived at only indirectly, since it depends on the circumference of the Core and the width of various roads. The circumference depends on the number of levels. Note, however, that so far we have not discussed *how* the number of levels can be determined. To calculate space for roads, we assume that there are (1) two 40-foot-wide two-way roads, (2) two 20-foot-wide-ramps within the Core Edge. When the Core Edge radius is 3000 feet and there are 16 levels, it turns out that about one square mile of roads is required.

The percentage of Compact City's total area devoted to roads is of interest. To estimate this, we measure the area on each level used for 32 spokes, each 8,840 feet long and 40 feet wide. For 16 levels the total area is $16 \times 32 \times 8,840 \times 40 \div (5,280)^2$, or 6.5 square miles. There are also 26 rings on each level, and each ring is 15 feet wide. The average ring radius is $8,840 \div 2 = 4,420$ feet. The area of all rings is $16 \times 26 \times 4,420 \times 2\pi \times 15 \div (5,280)^2$ or 6.0 square miles. Thus the total street area, excluding the relatively negligible area of walkways and bikeways, is 12.5 square miles or 8.6 percent of the total area. This percentage of the total 140-square-mile figure should be compared with 25 percent land area required for roads today—in fact, some present-day cities require 35 percent and more (Los Angeles, for example).

Summary of 30-foot-high Space Needs

Residential

Houses 2400 square feet × 300,000 units	
Apartments 1400 square feet × 300,000 units	100 square miles
House lot sizes 60 by 100 feet	

Mid-Plaza

Facilities, 4 square miles	
Interior parks, 13 square miles	17 square miles

Core

Facilities, 8 square miles	
Interior park, 9 square miles	17 square miles

Core Edge

Roads 1 square mile	
Interior park 5 square miles	6 square miles

Total 30-foot-high space needs in Compact City: 140 square miles

For comparison purposes, a present-day city built to the same standards would break down as follows: residential, 100 square miles; other local neighborhood facilities, 17 square miles; commercial, 30 square miles; interior parks, 31 square miles. Total: 178 square miles of land area for building a conventional city. The figure omits an additional requirement for large parks and recreational areas.

How High Should Compact City Be to Minimize Travel Time?

The ratio of height of a city (h) to its radius (r) might be determined so as to minimize the average time for travel from home to work when cars are used for horizontal travel and elevators are used for vertical travel. However, for short distances, walking and bicycling would be the preferred modes of travel. Instead of minimizing the average time, we have chosen to minimize the time to travel the longest distance from a point in the city to the outside at ground level, i.e., the vertical distance $AB = h$ plus the horizontal distance $BC = r$ in Figure 10-2.

The modern elevator takes about one minute to take passengers to the 500 foot level of the Washington Monument (555 feet tall). The elevator travels about six miles per hour without stops. Because express elevators in Compact City will have three or four stops from bottom to top, we assume three miles per hour as the average vertical speed. (In Section 4.3 we proposed a way to combine a local with an express elevator to attain an average of 4 miles per hour. To be conservative we have assumed here an average of 3 miles per hour. See Figure 4-8.)

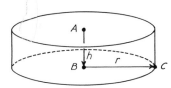

Figure 10-2 FINDING THE OPTIMAL
RATIO OF CITY HEIGHT TO RADIUS
The ratio of height to radius is selected
so as to minimize the travel time from
the center of the city at top level to the
outside of the city at ground level.

We expect that cars in the city will average 20 mph on short errands,
but for longer distances of travel over a length equal to the radius r,
we assume 27.5 miles per hour as the average horizontal speed. The
time to travel the height of the city is thus $h/3$ (where h here is measured using a mile as a unit) and the time to travel the horizontal
distance is $r/27.5$. We therefore wish to minimize

$$(h/3) + (r/27.5) = \text{Travel time (in hours)}$$

Earlier we fixed the volume of the city at 140 square miles of 30-
foot-high space. Calculated in cubic miles:

$$\text{Fixed volume of city} = \frac{140 \text{ square miles} \times 30 \text{ feet}}{5,280 \text{ feet per mile}} = .795 \text{ cubic miles}$$

This fixed volume is also given by $\pi r^2 h$. Thus

$$\pi r^2 h = .795 \text{ cubic miles}$$

There are, of course, different combinations of values of h and r that
result in the same fixed volume but give rise to different travel times.
It is an easy calculus problem to show that when the ratio of average
car speed to average elevator speed is (27.5)/3, or 9.16, then the ratio
of the radius to the height that minimizes travel time is twice 9.16,
or 18.32. Putting $h = r/18.32$ in the equation for fixed volume, we can
solve for the cube of the radius:

$$\text{Radius cubed } (r^3) = .795 \ (18.32/\pi) = 4.63$$
$$\text{Radius } (r) = 1.67 \text{ miles } (8,840 \text{ feet})$$
$$\text{Height } (h) = (1.67/18.32) \text{ miles} = 480 \text{ feet}$$
$$\text{Levels } (h/30) = 480/30 = 16$$

The Radii of Various Rings

Dividing 140 square miles by 16 (the number of levels) yields:

$$\text{Base area} = 8.75 \text{ square miles}$$

Assuming that the Mid-Plaza area is a band centrally located between the Inner and Outer Residential Areas, the areas of the various
rings and their radii are now easily determined. See Figure 3-6. The
results can be tabulated as follows:

Table 10-1

Size and location of principal parts of the city

City region	Area (square miles)		Distance from center		Radius or width of circular band (in feet)
	Total	Per level	In miles	In feet	
Core	17.0	1.06	.58	3,060	Radius, 3,060
Core Edge	6.0	.38	.67	3,540	Width, 480
Inner Residential	41.3	2.58	1.13	5,950	Width, 2,410
Mid-Plaza	17.0	1.06	1.27	6,700	Width, 750
Outer Residential	58.7	3.67	1.67	8,840	Width, 2,140
Total	140.0	8.75			Radius, 8,840

Notes and References

1. S. F. Singer, editor, *Is There an Optimum Level of Population?* McGraw-Hill (New York, 1971). See particularly the chapter by Manfred Kochen, "On Determining the Optimum Size of New Cities."

2. "Optimum Size of Cities" by Otis Dudley Duncan, in *Cities and Society,* edited by Paul K. Hatt and Albert J. Reiss, Jr., The Free Press (Glencoe, Ill., 1957), pages 759–772. Details of our discussions of public safety, municipal services, advanced education, and other factors are also based on this reference.

3. Gus Tyler, "Can Anyone Run a City?" *Saturday Review,* November 8, 1969, pages 22–25.

4. Ansley J. Coale and Edgar M. Hoover, *Population Growth and Economic Growth in Low Income Countries,* Princeton Univ. Press (Princeton, N.J., 1958).

5. Paul Ehrlich and Jonathan Freedman, "The Impact of Crowding on Human Behavior," *The New York Times,* September 11, 1971, page 27. See also Edward T. Hall, *The Silent Language,* Doubleday (Garden City, N.Y., 1959). And Edward T. Hall, *The Hidden Dimension,* Doubleday (Garden City, N.Y., 1966).

6. Peter G. Hall, *The World Cities,* World University Library, McGraw-Hill (New York, 1966).

7. Jane Jacobs, *The Death and Life of Great American Cities,* Vintage-Random House (New York, 1961). Ivor de Wolfe, *Civilia—A High Density City,* Architectural Press (London, 1970). The views of Jane Jacobs and de Wolfe regarding open space and density are presented in our Sections 2.4 and 13.3, respectively.

8. Hans Blumenfeld, "The Modern Metropolis," *Scientific American,* September 1965, pages 64–74. An excellent reference for general city standards. The entire September 1965 issue of *Scientific American* is devoted to the subject of cities.

9. *Ibid.*

10. *Ibid.*

11. Jane Jacobs, *op. cit.*

STRUCTURE
AND
SYSTEM
DESIGN

11.1 A Checklist of City Systems

A plan for a design for a Compact City is more than just a layout of
streets or ways to exploit the third and time dimensions. It also requires the analysis of various subsystems:

$$
\text{Subsystems} \begin{cases}
\text{Elevators} \\
\text{Transformer stations} \\
\text{Communication networks} \\
\text{Air ducts} \\
\text{Sewage-treatment plants} \\
\text{The multi-level base structure} \\
\text{The facilities for manufacturing}
\end{cases}
$$

and it requires analysis of how these can contribute to the fundamental functions (systems) of the city:

$$
\begin{matrix}
\text{Fundamental} \\
\text{Needs}
\end{matrix} \begin{cases}
\text{Air} \\
\text{Food} \\
\text{Water} \\
\text{Shelter} \\
\text{Movement} \\
\text{Communication} \\
\text{Work (effort, cost, convenience)} \\
\text{Leisure}
\end{cases}
$$

Table 11-1

*Relevance of subsystems of a Compact City to general city functions,
on a scale of 1–5.*

Subsystem	Effect on			
	Reducing delays	Controlling climate	Saving labor	Low city cost
City shape and size	5	5	5	5
Around-the-clock operations	5	–	3	4
Primary power sources	–	3	5	2
Secondary power sources	5	–	–	–
Vertical transport	5	–	–	1
Horizontal transport	5	–	–	1
Air conditioning	–	5	2	1

Table 11-1, above, is purely illustrative. It ranks subsystems with numbers from zero to five and helps in a qualitative way to indicate the relevance of various subsystems to the general functions. For example, as far as the goal of interior climate control is concerned, elevators rank 0 (low) but air conditioning ranks 5 (high). However, for transportation the elevator is very important (i.e., it ranks 5), but cost is not the overriding factor in making decisions about vertical transport since the elevator is one of the lifelines of the city, so in terms of its relevance to the low cost of the city, we assign "vertical transport" a low rank. The three-dimensional structural design and shape for a Compact City can greatly affect transportation, cost, climate, and labor savings (by eliminating delays). Organizing time so as to avoid congestion due to peak loads can contribute to the availability of transportation, save labor costs, and reduce dramatically the cost of facilities. Note that secondary power sources are highly relevant to reducing delays because vertical transport can be called upon for emergency evacuation. Evaluations similar to those above but on a more detailed quantitative basis can be used as part of a total-system model to develop (1) the best of various alternative plans and (2) a detailed schedule of the quantity and timing of activities necessary to build the city.

Outline of Physical Considerations

A plan must integrate two major types of systems: the first concerns the physical structure of the city and involves the talents of architects, geologists, sociologists, and construction engineers. The second concerns the operations of the city and involves various engineering specialists in electricity, heating, transportation, utilities, etc. A check list of physical considerations is provided on the next page.

1. Site work: excavation, grading, foundations
2. Structure: supporting slabs, structural frame, floors, and wall structures
3. Roofing: roofing deck and surface materials; park and terraces
4. Interior finishing: wall, floor, and ceiling composition, coverings, and decorations (one can anticipate all kinds of new ideas here)
5. Interior open space finishing: malls and fountains, indoor botanical gardens, shallow ponds (perhaps for ice skating).

Mechanical Systems

1. Heating, ventilating, air conditioning
2. Electrical installations
3. Lighting, including fixtures
4. Plumbing, including water and recycling systems
5. Special equipment for kitchens, laundries, fixtures, and appliances
6. Material conveyance: by hand (using stairs, escalators, elevators, mass transit, bikes, hand-drawn carts), by autos, trucks, moving belts, automatic lifts, and pneumatic tubes
7. Circulation and transportation: streets, walkways, bikeways, stairs, ramps, escalators, elevators, horizontal mass transit routes and vehicles, autos and buses, moving walkways (at locations like airports where there are many people in transit)
8. Streets, including street signs, benches, curbs, and landscaping
9. Electrical, nuclear, and other sources of energy for lighting, cooling, heating, and air conditioning
10. Communications: telephone, television, alarm systems, postal system, display signs, consoles remotely connected to computers

11.2 Structural Design

Foundations and Footings

One of the reasons for selecting a low-profile design, rather than a design having a greater height but smaller base area, is to spread the weight of the city more evenly. A city too large or too tall might concentrate too great a weight, which could exert unusual pressures on the soil beneath — perhaps causing uneven sinking and fracturing.

For example, suppose a city with a base of 3 miles by 3 miles (9 square miles) and height of 500 feet is compared with one that has a base of 2 miles by 2 miles (4 square miles) and compensating height of 1,250 feet. The pressure per square foot would be considerably more than 2.50 times greater beneath the taller city because heavier supporting columns and foundations would be required.

The purpose of footings is to spread the concentrated loads of building walls and columns over an area of soil so that the unit pressure will come within the allowable limits. The amount of footings required depends on the type of soil. A city built on a solid base of hard rock such as granite can have footings that exert 25 to 100 tons per square foot. A city built on soft clay, however, would require footings covering 25 to 100 times more area in order to spread the load because soft clay can only safely support one ton per square foot.[1]

Wood—or better—concrete piles would be needed if the soil is unstable. Structural steel "H" columns can be used in piles in land where corrosion is not a problem. Piles derive their support from the friction of the soil on their sides as well as from pressure upward from beneath them.

The Structure Support of Compact City

Structurally, the support design for Compact City may be likened to that of a typical high-rise apartment building. However, because of the large interior open areas it can also be likened to the support-design of a multiple-level car-park facility. The proposed spacing between levels of 30 feet or more was deliberately made part of the design in order to contribute to the feeling of openness. With such spacings it happens, because of the large open volumes, that the average weight per square foot on the foundations would be less than 1/3 of that for the same height found in conventional structures. Turning now to the spacing of vertical columns used to support the various levels in Compact City, it is, of course, desirable to have these spaced further apart than the 20 feet usually found in conventional construction in order to further increase the feeling of openness, but not so wide apart that structural costs become prohibitive.

The steps to be followed in planning, developing the site, and building Compact City are analogous to the steps pursued in the development of a new subdivision in conventional suburbia. The slab construction for a house and the open area around the house is comparable to conventional ground preparation and the laying of roads and foundations. This step includes not only the slabs (which support the houses, the open space, and the roads) but also the columns which support the slabs. It also includes the construction of the network of ducts for water, sewage, air conditioning, electricity, communication, and automatic deliveries. Thus, some of the costs usually included in conventional building (such as for foundations, walkways, patios, utility lines from streets to houses, etc.) are already covered in the platform support costs.

A possible support structure for residences is shown in Figure 11-1. Support of the platform of each level is provided horizontally

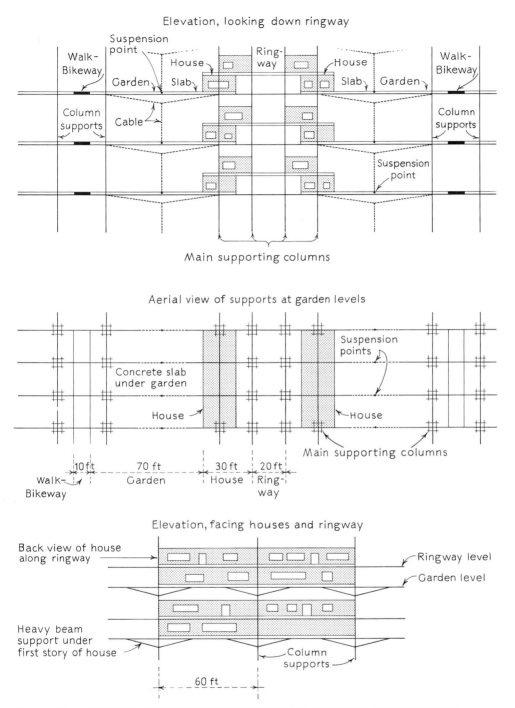

Figure 11-1 TYPICAL SUPPORT STRUCTURE FOR A HOUSE AND ITS YARD

by reinforced concrete, and vertically by columns, and also in some places by suspension cables. Note that part of the front yard (or garden) in the figure is shown suspended from above by 1/2-inch-diameter cables instead of being supported from below by columns. This has a number of advantages.

1. The cross section of the supporting cable need be only 1/300 of the cross section of a vertical beam of concrete supporting the same weight. Hence for all practical purposes the 1/2-inch-diameter vertical supports would be unnoticeable.
2. The vertical cable supports can be more numerous and would lead to an overall lighter construction.
3. The suspension cables might be conveniently incorporated into a construction procedure whereby a slab can be poured (or assembled) on the ground or on a previously constructed level and subsequently raised by its cables into position. This is called lift-slab construction.[2]
4. Suspension points can be shifted without too much effort after construction if they should interfere with the location of facilities.

Where Are the Ducts?

In the human body the main systems that relate the living cell to its external world are the blood circulatory system, the lymphatic system, and the nervous system. In a similar manner, there are ducts in Compact City that would carry good water to the home, remove waste water, bring in fresh air, take away stale air, automatically deliver small things, take away solid waste, and provide channels for electricity and communication. It is proposed that these ducts be built into the vertical support columns; that is, a column is made with a hollow space in the middle or along one of its sides.

Since the levels are 30 feet apart and a single duct could service two houses or two flats, each housing unit would require, on the average, only 15 feet of vertical duct for electricity or sewage, etc. In addition, there is a horizontal requirement since these ducts must eventually merge into a central distribution or receiving point. However, this turns out to be less than two feet of horizontal duct (as the shared part of each household). It should be evident that these requirements are considerably less than those for houses in conventional suburbia. Moreover, access to the duct system for servicing or augmentation would be much easier than the current method of digging trenches in streets and gardens.

Provision would have to be made for extra duct capacity, such as space for cables or wave guides, to be installed at some future time, which would transmit video displays of newspapers, pages of books, products for sale, etc.

In this section we outline an advanced water recycling system for Compact City. It would be applicable to a present-day city as well. The purpose of the system is to conserve water by reconditioning it.[3]

The withdrawal of water for municipal use in the United States is only a fraction (5 percent) of the total withdrawal for all uses; about 1/6 of this 5 percent is lost one way or another (e.g., through evaporation) and the rest is available for reconditioning and return either to the main source or for recycling. About 30 percent of U.S. cities in 1969, however, did little more than settle the sludge out of their own sewage and then dump it, and some chlorine, into the river for the next city downstream to upgrade for municipal use. Apparently people are less squeamish about recycling the sewage of the city upstream and drinking it than recycling their own. Properly treated, the waste water returned to the stream will not overload it "biologically"; by this is meant that the bacteria in the river will further decompose it and purify it without depressing the level of dissolved oxygen needed for fish life.

Compact City could collect rain water that falls on the Park-Roof and surrounding areas as one source of soft water. It could use separate storm drains that have no connection with the regular sewage system. In many conventional cities, a heavy rainstorm overloads a combined sewer–storm-drain system, resulting in the overflow of raw sewage directly into rivers, lakes, and oceans.

Because distances are short in Compact City, a trivially additional cost of $25 is added to that of a housing unit to have *two* separate systems of drains. One system, for example, would drain water from sinks, tubs, and showers; and the other would carry the heavier wastes from the kitchen disposal and the toilet facilities. This would simplify the treatment process since the bulk of the water—i.e., that from the sinks, tubs, and showers—would then bypass the primary sedimentation tank.

Primary Treatment would follow along present-day city lines: As depicted in Figure 11-2, the flow chart of the water recycling system, (1) a machine, called a comminutor, catches and then cuts (or shreds) the heavy solid material which is then returned to the main flow; (2) the main flow moves through two tanks, rather quickly through the first to allow just enough time for grit, small stones, and other high density objects to settle, and then next to the sedimentation tank, which allows time for the bulk of the heavy organic waste to settle out. The sludge is continuously removed from the bottom. This sludge plus the organic part of the solid waste (garden trimmings, big bones, soiled paper) is then treated in one of several ways discussed earlier. The sludge is mainly allowed to decompose naturally by means of bacterial "digestion" in heated tanks where odors can

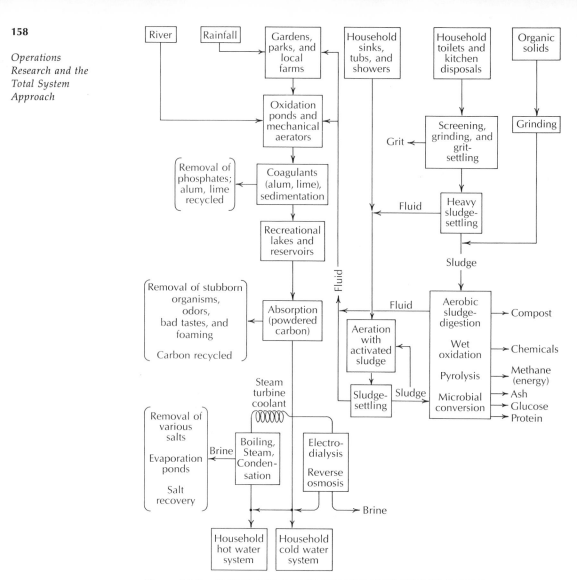

Figure 11-2 COMPACT CITY'S WATER RECYCLING SYSTEM
The system proposed is a complete three-stage primary, secondary, and
tertiary treatment system for recycling water.

be controlled. Since the digested sludge is 90 to 95 percent water, the
water is then removed by a rotating filter drum and by suction.

The digested sludge is inoffensive, biologically stable, and it can
be used as landfill, compost, or burned as an energy source. Using it
as compost may take a little more effort and may raise the costs
slightly, but it reconditions the soil, yields a more nutritious, tastier
food, and helps restore lands laid waste by strip mining and lumber-
ing. It is part of the price we pay for living in balance with—and
restoring—nature, and it is a very small price indeed.

Secondary Treatment (see Figure 11-2) requires combining the fluids from the household tubs, showers, and sinks with fluids withdrawn from the primary process. Suspended solids are biologically digested and precipitated by use of "activated" sludge. The latter is sludge recycled from the secondary process—it teems with bacteria. The fluid is agitated and aerated and organic substances are quickly decomposed. The sludge also serves as a flocculent that coagulates the wastes and helps them settle when the fluid is moved to a settling tank. After this treatment and possibly some addition of chlorine, the fluid is further purified by filtering through garden beds, parks, oxidation ponds, and mechanical aerators.

Tertiary Treatment is the step shown in Figure 11-2, at which recycling becomes part of the water input system. (The Santee Lakes Filter Pilot Project Plant, 15 miles northwest of San Diego, California is a good example of a tertiary treatment system.) Here the water from the input stream and the recycled water is upgraded to the highest drinking standards. Stubborn organic materials that cause odors, bad taste, or foaming are removed by using coagulants such as alum (or lime) and by absorption using carbon granules or powdered carbon. About 90 percent of the phosphates are removed by these processes. Recycling up to this point still leaves dissolved salts in solution. Household use of water increases the amounts of these ions and two or three recyclings would result in an accumulation of them to unacceptable levels unless various inorganic (metallic) ions are removed by a desalination process. Adding soft water (if available) to the system and draining off some of the recycled water can reduce the salt concentration—obviously this is the cheapest way. If input soft water, however, is scarce, then part of the water could be boiled and the steam condensed for use. The salts in the brine residue can be recovered in evaporation ponds. Reverse osmosis and electrodialysis are also used for desalination.[4] Nuclear power plants that also desalinate sea water are under development. These are promising alternatives. However, since hot water is required for homes, boiling and condensation would probably be the best process, and it might be efficient to combine water-recycling and electricity-production processes to achieve this. Much of our electric energy is presently generated by steam turbines using fossil fuels. (In the future, nuclear fuels will play a more important role.) Turbines are most efficient using steam at very high temperatures and pressures, with a maximum pressure difference between the two ends of the turbine. To achieve this, water is used as a coolant at one end. If recycled water is converted to steam, then its heat of condensation could be used (via heat exchangers) as part of steam production cycle of the turbine. The complex process could fulfill several needs: the need for a coolant, a water purifier, and for a source of hot water as well as power for the city.[5]

The water of Compact City, if treated as described above, would be extremely soft and would not build up deposits in the pipes. It would need to be aereated, "spiked" slightly with minerals to give a good taste, fluoridated, and disinfected (perhaps with ozone rather than chlorine). Extreme softness also lowers the basicity and increases the corrosion hazard in metallic pipes. Plastic pipes (and asbestos-cement pipes) could be used instead. The use of nonmetallic pipes raises special problems with respect to the grounding of electrical appliances.

Domestic consumption of water in conventional cities varies from day to day and from hour to hour. In order to meet this fluctuating demand, pumps and storage facilities (tanks and reservoirs) are built with extra reserve capacity. In Compact City, however, the use of water would be distributed evenly throughout the 24-hour day. The hourly variation in water consumption would be very small. Thus, pumping and storage facilities could be of lower capacity and could be used with greater efficiency.

One of the outputs of the water purification process (as we noted earlier) would be the generation of a brine solution. The various salts in this solution can be extracted by vaporizing the water in special ponds. Exposed directly to the sun's rays, these ponds trap the sun's energy and thus provide a potential source of heat. If not exposed to the sun, the evaporation itself acts as a cooling process and the brine solution could be used as a coolant.

Hot water, as noted earlier, can be obtained as a byproduct of the use of steam turbines to generate electricity. Alternatively, the lakes and reservoirs can serve as a coolant for the more efficient conversion of fuel into electric power. It is clear that a very careful total-system analysis is necessary to determine the optimal combination of the various processes for water conditioning, air conditioning, hot and cold water, general heating and cooling, cooling of turbines, etc. In this "game" the heat of the summer can be played off against the cold of the winter. The general idea is to use cooling towers and the large exposed surfaces of lakes to transfer excess heat generated by the air conditioning system of the city to the atmosphere with as little loss of water through evaporation as possible (for example by special treatment of the surface of lakes).

By altering the nature of the surface of a body (e.g., body of water) exposed to the sun, one can change the amount of heat absorbed. For example, a silvered louver surface will reflect the sun's rays when the louvers form a smooth surface and the body covered by the louvers will absorb more heat if the louvers are opened, as is shown in Figure 11-3.

To cite another example, during hot weather trees and other vegetation lose a great deal of moisture through their leaves by evaporation and this has a cooling effect. Thus the Park-Roof of Compact City would be naturally cool, and cooling can be enhanced by turning on the sprinkler system.

The system of lakes used to purify the water could be adjacent to the city. As noted, these lakes could serve as a source of heat or as a cooling source, depending on the time of the year. Their surface could be changed according to the weather, the time of day, and the season, for example, by covering them or exposing them or by floating

Figure 11-3 EXCHANGING HEAT WITH THE EXTERNAL
ENVIRONMENT
If louvres in the external surface of the city are closed, solar heat
is reflected. When the louvres are open, heat can radiate into,
or away from, the city.

a thin film of oil or thin foam plastic sheets on their surface. By doing
so, their evaporative and heat-conductive properties can be modi-
fied. An interesting question that requires further study is the effect
of the resulting more stable temperature of the lakes on the organisms
living in them.

11.4 Lighting Interior Open Space

Sunlight and Gardens

It would be a mistake, in the opinion of the authors, to develop the
interior open space around houses and apartment units the same way
we develop the open space around suburban homes in present-day
cities. Nature is more accessible in Compact City. The rural countryside would be only minutes away from any part of the city. Walking
to work in natural settings could be accomplished by taking a route
through the Park-Roof and this would add only a minute or two to
the journey. The open spaces around the houses, because they are
protected from the weather and from traffic danger, would probably
be put to more functional uses.

It is possible that people would regard the exterior of a house as
an extension of its interior, the chief differences being the degree of
privacy and the increased ability to run around actively. Some interior
rooms might be designed as four walls with an open ceiling and an
archway opening onto the interior open space. By way of contrast,
the open space in current suburbia is largely cosmetic. The landscaping is designed for easy upkeep and for making the neighborhood look nice. The sun, of course, makes things grow; but this
means that plants need to be trimmed, watered, and weeded; and in
the winter outdoor yards are bleak; at night and during hot summers
outdoor areas may not be hospitable.

In Compact City the interior open space would be artificially
lighted. This limits the kind of plants that can be used. Many arti-
ficially lighted lobbies of office buildings in conventional cities are
decorated with live plants. This is done by hiring a garden service
that "recycles" the plants every few months, bringing in replacements
that have been exposed to sunlight in the fields and greenhouses.
Rubber trees are popular because they do well in the shade. Other
favorites are orchids, *Philodendron, Aglaonema* (Chinese evergreen),

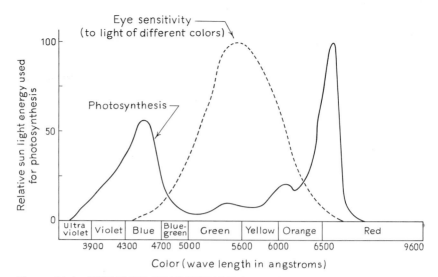

Figure 11-4 THE TYPE OF LIGHT NEEDED FOR PLANT GROWTH
For photosynthesis plants absorb the violet and red portions of the
color spectrum and reflect back the greens and yellows. This is why
leaves appear green in color. The eye is more sensitive to the colors
plants reflect.

Araucaria (Monkey puzzle or Norfolk Island pine), *Aspidistra, Cyperus,
Dieffenbachia, Dracaena* (Dragon tree), *Nephrolepis* (Boston or Sword
fern), *Sansevieria, Schefflera, Syngonium,* and palms (such as *Cham-
aedorea* and *Howea forsteriana*). They can be maintained with little
light for at least 12 months before recycling.[6]
  Very little artificial light is needed to maintain such plants in good
condition for long periods of time. Light bulb manufacturers make
special fluorescent tubes producing the light spectrum needed by
plants for photosynthesis.[7] See Figure 11-4. Some plants will even
grow in artificial light, but most of those which grow and bud indoors require too great an intensity of light to be practical (about 40
watts per square foot).[8] Therefore, it would be necessary also to use a
variety of other ways to decorate the open space—rock gardens,
plastic plants, fountains, decorative fences, and trims. Ground cover
using natural lawns would probably not be feasible.

Lighting the City

Streets and houses would be lit in the usual way. The lights on vehicles
would be used only in case of power failure. The lighting of the interior open space would, of course, be similar to that found in high-
ceilinged lobbies, banquet halls, convention centers, theaters,
airports, and railroad terminals. Flood lights could be positioned to
reflect light off the ceilings. The undersides of levels could be sprayed
with a material that reflects light and also absorbs sound. It would be

desirable for its reflective properties to give a skylike appearance of distance. (Recent studies of the reflective qualities of fish scales is of interest in this connection. They reflect the light but break up the reflection so that from a distance the fish blends into the background and is not visible as a surface. This helps to protect the fish from its predators.[9]) Lighting fixtures could be attached to the undersides of levels, to the column supports, and to the tops of houses, and special crews would be needed to replace worn bulbs on a routine basis (perhaps once a year), using special equipment.

Notes and References

1. L. S. Marks, *Mechanical Engineer's Handbook,* 4th Edition, McGraw-Hill (New York, 1941), pages 1583–1586.

2. R. M. Diamant, *Industrialized Building,* Iliffe Books (London, 1964), pages 3–6. See also pages 113–115, where an interesting application of catenary slab support by architects F. and D. Wynkoop and K. Imada is described.

3. U.S. Department of the Interior, *A Primer on Waste Water Treatment,* Federal Water Pollution Administration, U.S. Government Printing Office (Washington, D.C., October 1969). See also "Current Status of Advanced Waste Treatment Processes," U.S. Federal Water Quality Administration, July 1, 1970. Also see R. N. Rickles, "Conservation of Water by Reuse in the United States," *Chemical Engineering Progress Symposium, 63* (78), pages 74–87 (1967).

4. F. D. Dryden, "Mineral Removal by Ion Exchange, Reverse Osmosis, and Electrodialysis," and F. D. Dryden, "Wastes from Membrane Processes," both articles in *Environmental Science and Technology,* Vol. 3, No. 9 (September 1969) and Vol. 4, No. 6 (June 1970), respectively. According to Dryden, satisfactory techniques for treating or disposing of concentrated salt solutions do not exist unless the salt solutions are of the same mix as sea water.

5. Samuel E. Beall, Jr., "Agricultural and Urban Uses of Low-Temperature Heat," in *Beneficial Uses of Thermal Discharges,* New York State Department of Environmental Conservation (Albany, N.Y., 1970). (Conference held September 17–18, 1970). See also A. J. Miller et al., "Use of Steam-Electric Power Plants to Provide Low-Cost Thermal Energy to Urban Areas," Oak Ridge National Laboratory, January 1971 (U.S. Atomic Energy Commission Report ORNL-HUD-14). See also I. J. Spiewak, "Investigation of the Feasibility of Purifying Municipal Waste Water by Distillation," Oak Ridge National Laboratory, April 1969 (U.S. Atomic Energy Commission Report ORNL-TM-2547).

6. R. Van der Veen and G. Meijer, *Light and Plant Growth,* Philips Technical Library (Eindhoven, Holland, 1959). See also E. C. Cherry, *Fluorescent Light Gardening,* D. Van Nostrand-Reinhold (New York, 1965).

7. "Radiant Energy Sources for Plant Growth," Engineering Bulletin 0-278, Sylvania Corporation, Danvers, Mass.

8. Van der Veen and Meijer, *op. cit.*

9. Eric Denton, "Reflectors in Fish," *Scientific American,* January 1971, pages 64–72.

FINANCIAL
ANALYSIS

12.1 Cash Flows

The fact that Compact City will be continuously acquiring population and businesses during the period of its construction reduces the problem of its financing to moderate proportions, since during the construction period most of the direct construction and municipal services costs can be financed through internal cash flows.

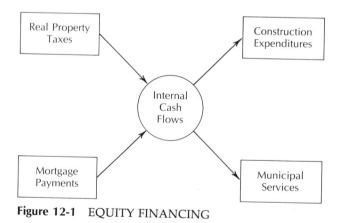

Figure 12-1   EQUITY FINANCING

We are grateful to Dr. Nelson Lipshutz of the Wharton School of Finance and Commerce, for providing us with this analysis of cash flows.

In order to have some quantitative idea of the magnitude of these flows, we make the following set of assumptions:

1. The total cost of construction of a maximum-sized city of two million people would be $36.5 billion.
2. The time for construction would be 16 years in 16 equal yearly increments (one level per year).
3. As soon as an increment is completed, it is occupied.
4. Residential property is financed by 5 percent 20-year mortgages. (The effect of inflation would be to increase the 5 percent rate.)
5. Residential property is taxed at an annual rate of 5 percent on assessed value, which is taken to be the construction cost of "land" and structures.
6. Forty percent of the nonresidential property is to be used for business purposes and is financed by 5 percent 20-year mortgages, and taxed at an annual rate of 5 percent on assessed value (equal to construction cost of "land" and structures).
7. The level of expenditure on municipal services on a per capita basis equals the national average.

The primary expenses and revenues resulting from these assumptions follow:

For a City of Two Million

Construction
Total cost: $36.5 billion
Construction period: 16 years
Resulting cash outlay: $2.281 billion per year for 16 years
Population increment per year: 125 thousand people

Municipal Services
Capita outlay per capita: $95 per year
  (Compact City's outlay is assumed
  to be the same as the U.S. per capita
  outlay. U.S. total outlay was $19 billion for
  municipal services and the population
  was 200 million in 1969.)
Outlay per occupied increment: $12 million per year

Residential Property Valuation
Total cost of structures: $11.4 billion
Total cost of "land": $ 8.4 billion
Total assessed value: $19.8 billion
Assessed value per increment: $ 1.24 billion

Nonresidential Property
Total cost of structures: $13.46 billion
Total cost of "land": $ 2.80 billion
Aggregate Cost: $16.26 billion
Fraction of private property: 40 percent
Assessed value per increment: $ .400 billion

Revenues
Mortgage payments per increment: $ .169 billion per year for 20 years
Tax payments per increment $ .085 billion per year
Average total per increment: $ .254 billion per year
(First year total, one half the above total, or
  $.127 billion)

Table 12-1

Fundamental cash flows by year for a Compact City of 2,000,000 people

End of year	Outlays (billions)	Revenues (billions)	Net cumulative (billions)	End of year	Revenues (billions)	Net cumulative (billions)
	Fundamental cash flows				**Fundamental cash flows**	
1	−2.281	+ .127	− 2.154	21	+3.980	+16.252
2	(per	.381	4.054	22	3.811	20.063
3	year	.635	5.700	23	3.642	23.705
4	for	.889	7.092	24	3.473	27.178
5	sixteen	1.143	8.230	25	3.304	30.482
6	years)	1.397	9.114	26	3.135	33.617
7		1.651	9.744	27	2.966	36.583
8		1.905	10.120	28	2.797	39.380
9		2.159	10.254	29	2.628	42.008
10		2.413	10.110	30	2.459	44.467
11		2.667	9.724	31	2.290	46.757
12		2.921	9.084	32	2.121	48.878
13		3.175	8.190	33	1.952	50.830
14		3.429	7.042	34	1.783	52.613
15		3.683	5.640	35	1.614	54.227
16		3.937	3.984	36	1.445	55.672
17	No outlays	4.064	+ .080	37	1.360	57.032
18	after year	4.064	4.144	38	1.360	58.392
19	sixteen	4.064	8.208	39	1.360	59.752
20		4.064	12.272	:	:	:
				49	+1.360	+73.352

Table 12-1 shows the fundamental cash flows for a 50-year period. Examining these results, we find that:

1. The maximum deficit that occurs is slightly more than $10 billion and it occurs at the start of the 10th year of construction.
2. The deficit would be reduced to zero by the end of the seventeenth year, only one year after construction of the last increment is completed.

We now turn to consideration of several possible financing mechanisms. We will consider equity capital and debt.

12.2 Equity Capital

In order to assess the attractiveness of Compact City as an investment, we have carried out a discounted cash-flow analysis of the fundamental cash-flow data. We present the results below in terms of the Net Present Value (NPV) of Compact City, evaluated over a 50-year period for various discount rates, in order to determine that rate of return which yields the "break-even value" of zero for the net present value of the cash flows. This is called the Internal Rate of Return

(IRR). Note below that this occurs for a discount rate somewhere between 10 and 11 percent:

If the percent discount rate is:	0	5	6	7	8	9	10	11	12
NPV (in billions of dollars) is:	73.3	15.0	10.5	7.1	4.5	2.4	.8	−.4	−1.3

The internal rate of return for Compact City is about 11 percent and this may be too low a value to attract private investment companies if the Compact City enterprise is subject to normal income taxes (i.e., investment companies are looking for investments that have a rate of return greater than 11 percent before taxes). It is, however, of the same order of magnitude as the expected after-tax profit rate of major corporations and so might be privately funded if special tax relief were to be granted to the entrepreneurs.

The large capital outlay ($10 billion) required and the long payback period (17 years) involved suggest, however, that equity financing would be difficult to obtain even in the presence of such tax relief.

An alternative source of equity, of course, is the federal government, which has large sums and reasonable patience at its disposal, and which is furthermore not subject to the profitability constraints affecting the private sector of the economy. A direct investment approach may also be attractive to the government in view of the fact that the "profits" from the operation of an initial Compact City could be used to finance the construction of an additional five or six Compact Cities, thus providing enormous leverage.

Although equity financing is possible, there are obvious social and political implications of centralization of the control of Compact City in the hands of a large private developer or of the central government, as evidenced by the experiences of residents of various "company towns." It is therefore of interest to consider another means of financing, one which is available to smaller developers and governmental units: debt financing through a bond issue.

12.3 Bond Financing

We have calculated the optimal schedule of bond sales for the financing of Compact City based on the cash flows, assuming the same taxation and mortgage conditions used earlier. See Figure 12-2. The assumptions are:

1. Bonds are issued with a 30 year maturity.
2. Bonds sell at par and carry a 4 percent coupon rate.
3. Solvency and liquidity are maintained at all times.

The condition of optimality is that interest payments be at a minimum over the projected 50-year life of the city. The schedule for bond sales is given in Table 12-2.

The entries suggest the feasibility of financing through debt, since the sizes of the yearly bond issues are comparable with those of

Table 12-2

*Financing Compact City by floating bonds (all quantities
are in billions of 1969 dollars)**

Year	Size of issue	Cumulative amount issued	Interest expense for year	Cumulative interest charge
1	2.376	2.376	.095	.095
2	2.223	4.599	.184	.279
3	2.063	6.662	.266	.545
4	1.897	8.559	.342	.887
5	1.724	10.283	.411	1.298
6	1.554	11.837	.473	1.771
7	1.356	13.193	.527	2.298
8	1.161	14.354	.574	2.872
9	.957	15.311	.612	3.484
10	.745	16.056	.642	4.126
11	.524	26.580	.663	4.789
12	.294	16.874	.675	5.464
13	.054	16.928	.677	6.141

*Total value of bonds issued: $16.93 billion. Total interest expense:
$20.32 billion.

large commercial bond flotations, so that the established capital
markets are large enough to provide the required funds; further, the
assumed coupon rate of 4 percent is comparable to that of present
municipal bond issues and could in fact be increased to any value up
to 11 percent, the internal rate of return of the Compact City project.
The total interest expense of $20.32 billion, entailed if 4 percent bonds
are issued, is about $45 billion less than the net income of $73.35
billion which Compact City would generate if financed through
equity. Thus, if debt financing of an initial Compact City were to be
undertaken, the enterprise would generate almost enough surplus
funds to make possible the construction of four additional Compact
Cities through use of equity financing.

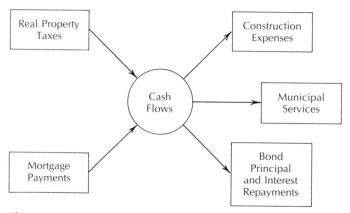

Figure 12-2 BOND FINANCING

13

ALTERNATIVES

13.1 A Design for Diversified Use of Open Space

In her book *The Death and Life of Great American Cities,*[1] Jane Jacobs emphasizes the importance of diversified use of "streets." As we have already noted, she feels that it is essential for the security and well being of a city. Streets, as she uses the word, refers to all public places where people walk with their two feet—i.e., not only sidewalks, but parks, lobbies or halls, elevators, and the stairwells of apartment buildings.

It is possible to develop neighborhoods in such a way as to enhance the diversified use of areas where people normally walk to and from their various activities and where children can have enough room to play safely. To illustrate the possibilities, we have chosen as the elemental unit a small group of houses and apartments around a commons or "local enclave" where young children can play. This is depicted in Figure 13-1.

In this arrangement the access roads in the back of the dwellings are seldom used. The normal flow of adults to and from their houses and apartments is *not* by car but by walking (or bicycling) around the common play areas. Thus all children (or strangers) in the open space around the houses, the apartment units, or the common area are constantly under the unstructured surveillance of the many adults who live in the enclave or in neighboring enclaves. Note again that the two-way roads shown in Figure 13-1 serve as back alleys which

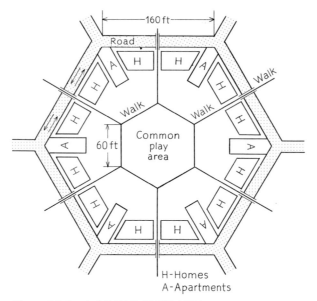

Figure 13-1 A LOCAL ENCLAVE
It is possible to develop an urban area in such a way
as to enhance the diversified use of areas where
people normally walk to and from their various
activities and where children can have enough
room to play safely under unstructured supervision.

are only occasionally used for transporting people by auto and are
mainly used for delivery of heavier objects to the home.

In a multilevel city such as Compact City these roads can be set 10
feet above the elevation of the open space (i.e., the same as described
in our earlier proposal). The walkway can thus pass under the roadway so that children are safe from traffic when they walk from one enclave to the next; i.e., there are no traffic barriers separating enclaves.

We now turn to a possible grouping of local enclaves to form a
"neighborhood." A neighborhood is usually a local community of
about 5000 people, large enough to support local shops, schools,
clinics, and larger recreational facilities. We can form such a neighborhood in a natural way from a cluster of enclaves that share a common
elevator and other local facilities and have a common transfer point
to the horizontal mass transit on the mid-level of the city. See
Figure 13-2.

To enhance the interaction of people living on a level, we have
placed near the elevator location a child nursery, a comfort station, a
refreshment stand, and some modest recreational facilities (e.g.,
ping-pong tables). In Figure 13-2 we have dotted the imaginary
boundaries of such a cluster of enclaves. Anyone living within the
area enclosed by the dotted line would find the elevator location
marked by the □ □ to be closer than any other. The average dis-

tance to an elevator is 320 feet (a little over a one-minute walk); the maximum distance is 480 feet (under two minutes). Such a cluster would encompass about 216 families.

A neighborhood would consist of eight such clusters—namely, those which are one above the other on eight levels and share the same elevator facility. It would comprise about $7 \times 216 = 1,512$ families or about 5,000 people (assuming 3.3 people on the average per family). See Figure 13-2. Note that Level 5 is used as the transfer point for mass transit. It is also the location of local shopping, elementary schools, clinics, and some apartment units as depicted in Figure 13-3. The larger recreational facilities located there are shared with other neighborhoods.

Compact City built along these lines would, at a population of 250,000, have about 50 such neighborhood centers on Level 5. At maximum size there could be 200 on this level and another 200 on Level 12.

The overall use of space is 30 percent more efficient than that proposed earlier because of the use of a "commons" within each enclave. As a result the residential part of the city would only occupy 70 square miles at maximum size (instead of 100 square miles). Note in Figure 13-3 that the entire arrangement of the local shopping level is de-

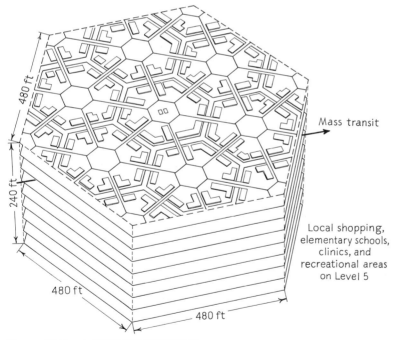

Figure 13-2 A NEIGHBORHOOD
Under the alternative compact city plan, a neighborhood would consist of a cluster of local enclaves on several levels around a common elevator facility indicated by ☐ ☐ in the figure.

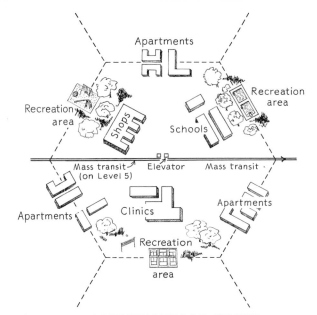

Figure 13-3 A NEIGHBORHOOD CENTER
Under the alternative compact city plan, local
neighborhood facilities and mass transit would
be located on the mid-level of a neighborhood.

signed so that workers who transfer there in going to and from the
Core should find it also convenient to do their local shopping and to
participate in neighborhood sports, recreation, and civic duties. It
appears to us that this design is conducive to lively, diversified
"streets" in the sense that Jane Jacobs has recommended; moreover,
the neighborhoods could serve as cohesive political units for making
their wants known at City Hall.[2]

Under this alternative the cost of the total city would be lower
(about 7 percent less) than the cost estimated in Table 5-2. Cost for a
moderate-income family for similar housing and superior transportation under this design would run 35 percent less in Compact City as
compared with that of a present-day city (see Table 5-3). As noted
there would be more diversified use of open space throughout the
neighborhood, all local facilities would be less than five minutes
walking from the homes, and neighborhoods would develop in a
natural way. The mass transit under this plan would be on two levels
instead of one when the city reaches maximum size. This would not
mean that the total number of mass-transit cars in service would be
greater. Indeed, since it would take a little less time to reach the mid-
level from a home one could increase slightly the average wait-time
between mass transit cars and still maintain the same portal-to-
portal time from home to office as was established before. This,
together with shorter horizontal routes, means that the number of

mass transit cars in service could be made about the same as (or a little less than) that proposed earlier for the city at maximum size (about 200 trams).

13.2 Variations in Shape and in Street Patterns

Ways to Increase the Surface-to-Volume Ratio

As a three dimensional object grows in size its surface-to-volume ratio decreases. For example, a $1 \times 1 \times 1$ cube has a surface-to-volume ratio of 6 to 1. A $2 \times 2 \times 2$ cube has a ratio of 24 to 8 or 3 to 1. It follows that if a high premium is placed on having dwellings with a view of the exterior landscape, then a smaller proportion of the dwellings would have such a view as the city grows. This is the reason why in our proposal additional apartment complexes were placed on the Park-Roof. There are two obvious ways to increase the surface-to-volume ratio (if this is felt to be desirable). The simplest is to "dimple" the outer periphery of the city structure. The other is to "swiss cheese" the volume by means of many open court yards as shown in Figure 13-4. Such modifications in the basic design could probably be done (within limits) without seriously affecting the efficiency of the transportation system. A third method that could be used would be to increase the height of the city and to reduce the size of its base. This would increase the exterior vertical surface. For example, stacking the four blocks shown in Figure 13-5, one on top of the other, would double the exposed *vertical* surface.

If our preliminary calculations are correct, the city built according to the earlier design would require energy to pump out the excess heat which would accumulate in the city during both summer and winter. If so, then it would make sense to change the proposed shape of the city so that the surface-to-volume ratio chosen would minimize the total energy needed for heating, cooling, and lighting during the year.

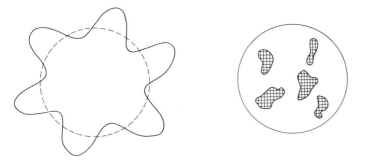

Figure 13-4 VARIOUS SHAPES FOR A COMPACT CITY
The surface-to-volume ratio of a city can be increased by giving the surface bulges, dimples, and holes exposed to the exterior atmosphere.

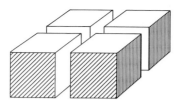

Figure 13-5 INCREASING SURFACE AREA
These blocks will have more vertical surface facing outward if they are stacked one on top of the other.

Growth through Replication

C. A. Doxiadis comments that human settlements often begin with a radial-ring pattern of streets. This is a workable form, he states, as long as the town is small, but the "centripetal forces in major settlements" make this form eventually unworkable. By way of contrast, urban areas built on "the grid-iron system can expand without difficulty."[3] See Figure 13-6.

Our approach to urban growth, however, is different. We think of a fully three-dimensional human settlement as similar to a child growing to adulthood. Cities should not grow indefinitely but their growth should level off when it reaches a certain "optimal" size. Growth beyond that, like people, should then take the form of new offspring. Because of the small amount of land needed for the base of a three-dimensional, or vertical city, compact cities could replicate themselves (in any local area in the United States) many times, for many generations, before any serious land shortage could arise. For example, the 4,000 square miles in San Diego County, California, has enough space to locate eventually 80 million people in the form of 40 Compact Cities spaced 10 miles apart (each surrounded by ample amounts of green space). As we have already shown in our proposal the spoke-ring pattern remains a highly convenient one even for a city of up to the maximum size of two million people.

13.3 Other Designs for a Compact City

There are, of course, more conventional ways to compact a city. There are designs that simply compress part of the downtown of present-day cities into one single structure and then place living quarters on top in the form of apartment dwellings. In these designs, no attempt is made to give families who desire it the opportunity to develop their own interior open space (as we proposed in Chapter 3) so as to be competitive with the best that present-day suburbia has to offer. Instead, such plans propose only to place windows in apartment towers so that by peeping out, one could see little ants (actually people) crawling on sidewalks below; one could tell night from day, winter from summer and, occasionally, real sky through the smog. Many people seem quite content with a home (apartment) without open space as long as the interior where they spend their time is nice and the location is convenient. Proposals currently advanced for making conventional cities more compact fall broadly into two classes:

1. The lower stories extend across the entire area of the city and would be used for working space only. On top of this platform a parkland would be laid out on which would rest many apartment towers connected to the lower structure by elevator shafts. The towers could be separated by wide distances with parkland between and could be constructed in a variety of shapes so as to minimize boredom and monotony.

2. A star-shaped configuration of high-rise apartments on the outer edges of the city is designed so that terraces open onto a parkland surrounding all sides of the city. Eventually aerial bridges could be provided at various levels for easy passage between the outer areas of the star and to a central core. (Alternative to a star-shaped configuration is a spiraling helix or a set of concentric rings interconnected by bridges. The latter might be viewed as a variant of our proposed design.)

The popular term for such proposals is *superblocks*. Here are some advantages as described in a recent newspaper article.[4]

> You'll be walking in the sky—above the traffic, stoplights, and screech of the traffic cop's whistle—in the city of the future. Aerial sidewalks that meander gracefully away from street hubbub are ways of the future. Why? The American Institute of Architects thinks so because:
>
> There is a marriage of private owners and city planners to jointly plan downtown renewal.
>
> The case of air rights over property is getting more popular.
>
> There has to be some way to ease the congestion on the street.
>
> There is a tendency to treat urban development as a superblock, district, or zone instead of a collection of individual buildings which may not relate to each other efficiently.

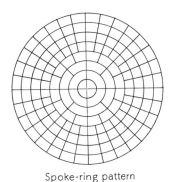

Spoke-ring pattern

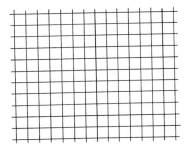

Gridiron pattern

Figure 13-6 VARIOUS ROAD PATTERNS
The spoke-ring pattern proposed for Compact City remains convenient even for a city that has grown to maximum size.

Among recent plans to build a superblock of high-rise buildings, shops, and parks that will function on an around-the-clock-basis is one proposed for downtown Houston. The projected cost of Houston's City of the Future is one billion dollars. Its planned residential population will be 10 to 12 thousand people occupying 5,000 units consisting of apartments and townhouses. It will also house offices and multilevel garages. In addition, another billion-dollar city-within-a-city project called Plaza del Oro is also being planned in the outskirts of Houston.

Fuller's Domed City

In 1971 R. Buckminster Fuller proposed building a pollution-free city in East St. Louis for 9,000 families.[5] They would live under a half-mile-diameter glazed glass dome designed to provide controlled weather, temperature, and sunlight. Outside the dome would be parks, open land, boat marinas, and small lakes. Under the dome a city would be built up along the inner and outer slopes of a hollow ring of terraces shaped like a moon crater. The steep outer slopes would be in the form of four decks each containing ten terraces so that those living in one of the terraced apartments would be able to look out over parks, river and sky. The steep inner slopes of the crater and the area under the center of the dome would contain shopping centers, malls, recreation centers, schools, churches, motels, night clubs, day-care centers and other facilities necessary for a community.

Civilia

As explained by Britain's Ivor de Wolfe, Civilia is the rebuttal to those who would argue in favor of dispersing people to new towns located out in the sticks. This proposed city would start by trying to pull people and jobs together again. The poor would not be left behind to live in cities deserted by the affluent but would be reunited with people of all income, age, race, and ethnic groups. To the protest that Civilia is much too dense — it has a density as high as two to three hundred persons per acre — Civilia's planners' response is "the higher the density, the more civilized is the place." Their idea is that higher density makes life easier. An example of their thinking is the following: "Sixty persons per acre can support a viable bus service. Two hundred people per acre can support a rapid transit system."[6]

It is proposed to locate Civilia in an abandoned quarry near the Birmingham — Coventry area. This means that there will be no need to steal more green space from the English countryside. Civilia would turn a quarry into an urban area which would be a bustling, exciting place to work and play.

Fashioned after Moshe Safdie's famous Habitat at Montreal's Expo 67, the purpose of Civilia is to prove that there is nothing to fear about high-density living. "It need no longer mean dreary glass-box apartment skyscrapers . . . Nor is it true that happiness can be found by merely getting into one's car and driving somewhere else. Civilia will bring a lake, public parks, outdoor recreation, and other ingredients of the good life close to everyone's doorstep.[7]

Doxiadis calls the belief that high density is bad a "myth."[8]

Sea Cities

There are a number of proposals to build cities that would float on the ocean or whose foundations would extend to the ocean floor.[9] Among the more current ideas along these lines is one due to Kiyonori Kikutake and John Craven. A Japanese architect, Kiyonori Kikutake has developed the concept of *Marine City*, a floating city without solid footing. He uses as his model the velella, a small sea creature with a sail-like membrane enabling it to move its lower parts. Craven, former chief scientist of the U.S. Navy's Special Projects Office, has been pursuing Kikutake's proposal to build floating cities in Hawaiian waters to relieve the pressures of increasing population. To implement this, he applies some of the concepts used by him to construct a naval vessel known as FLIP. A FLIP vessel is navigated in the normal way to its destination where it is then flipped over. When flipped, it assumes a vertical position with most of its body below sea level. The lower part is then used as an underwater research laboratory.

The floating city which Kikutake and Craven propose for Hawaii would ride on turbulence-stable platforms, resting on triangular clusters of pilons towed into position and then "flipped." Portions of the city would be at depths of 600 to 1000 feet below sea level. One of the activities of its citizens would be the domestication of marine mammals. The floating city could be reached from Oahu Island by hydrofoil and air-cushion vehicles.[10]

The British Pilkington Glass Age Development Committee has also proposed a stationary "Sea City".[11] It would be an offshore island made of glass and concrete, anchored on the bottom of shoal water. Its main structure would be a 16-story amphitheater resting on concrete pontoon islands supported by piles 20 to 30 feet apart and protected on the seaward side by an encircling breakwater. The city would extend 4,700 feet from north to south, and 3,300 feet across at its widest part. The terraced city wall would hold several 16 story air-conditioned apartments housing 21,000 residents. Other residents would live in individually designed houses. The city would make use of water buses; transportation to the mainland would be by hovercraft and helibuses. Schools would be built on floating islands; the lagoon where the city may be located features skindiving and water skiing. The city would manufacture boats, export fish from its fish-farming industry and fresh water from its large desalinization plant.

Buckminster Fuller has proposed two sea cities. "Triton City" is a neighborhood-sized floating community (adjacent to a land-based central city). It is constructed by the same technology as that used to build large ocean liners. The part of the structure built over the float-ing steel and concrete platform would be called the "megastructure," a single complete framework with optimum space and structural efficiency. Each community unit would house about 5,000 people. It would have an elementary school, a small supermarket, some local stores, and various services. It would also have about 300 dwelling units per acre, all facing the water. It would cost about $8,000 per person. Such community units could be combined to form towns. Triton is connected to the central city by a rapid transit highway; parking lots would be hidden. Fuller's second city, "Tetra," floats on hollow concrete boxes; it would have a million inhabitants all living in balcony apartments.[12]

The Non City

There is a school of planners and demographers which argues that the trends today, rather than favoring the high-rise metropolitan city, in fact tend towards decentralization to small towns scattered throughout the country.[13] They say that the reasons for a central city no longer exist. Their arguments run as follows. The need for a city as a transportation hub has been replaced by the automobile and the highway; labor has become mobile and is no longer dependent on heavy concentration of the population. Banking interests (whose loans help business) have now reached to the smallest community. Television (and the soon-to-be three-dimensional picture transmis-sion) make actual theatre and sports attendance obsolete; modern communication has made it increasingly unnecessary for people to travel in order to see one another. Small cities can be just as sufficient and satisfying as large cities, without the frustrations of large cities. Rapid inter-city transportation systems can move materials just as easily in and out of the small city. The presence in small towns of supermarkets and shopping centers, clinics, and local subdivisions of nation-wide businesses and industries mean that local jobs will be available, so that the need for living in the large city is considerably diminished. Advocates of decentralization point to the advantages of the small town's fresh air, sun, little or no crowding, easy access to nearby parks and recreation areas, and a more desirable social life with everybody acquainted with the people of the town.

The arguments against the non city run as follows: (1) the idea is basically inefficient, (2) it advocates a form of leapfrog suburbia, (3) it creates one dullville after another, (4) it limits the choice of working facilities, shopping, recreation, and cultural activities, and so limits the opportunity to interact with a variety of exciting people and activities, (5) it amplifies all the bad aspects of urban sprawl, and (6) the non city is born of defeat and is an attempt to see some good in urban sprawl by imagining it as something so dispersed that no one in his right mind would want to go somewhere else or do any-thing away from home.

Transportation in General

Compact City's dimensions were chosen to minimize transportation time while meeting certain standards.[14] See Section 10.2. The dynamics of the modern city can be characterized in terms of people and transportation systems. Without transportation, there could be no life in the city. Movement of goods, disposal of waste, and most other activities depend on physical transport—communication (in the form of wire or radio-wave transmission) being the important exception.

The same is true nationally. The United States goal of having a complete network of interconnected roadways linking the metropolitan centers of the country is planned to be reached in the early 1970s. This, together with excellent communication and airline links, has made every person more than ever accessible to everyone else. This is expected to promote economic opportunities. Good roads, to cite a city example, provide the fast transportation throughout the city. It can contribute to family stability by making it possible to transfer from one job to another job across town without having to sell one's house and move the family to a new one nearer the new job.

As a first approximation, it is possible to say that transportation demand arises out of three groups of needs:

1. The need for face-to-face contacts between individuals in order to carry out transactions.
2. The need to have access to facilities and resources which are spatially distributed.
3. The need to travel for recreational purposes.

Self-service supermarkets, coin-operated machines, ordering services or goods by mail and by telephone all contribute to reduced face-to-face contacts. In the future one can anticipate, in conventional cities as well as in new cities, a greater use of the new forms of communication technology: videophones, television, facsimile transmission, remote-access computers, computerized information systems, etc. Through use of such devices, direct contacts will be further reduced, particularly direct personal contacts now used to make routine purchases or to get routine information. In Compact City, improved communications could have the net effect of reducing the demand for transportation, because once a shopping order is placed for groceries over a videophone (for example), an automatic distribution system could inexpensively deliver the goods directly to the consumer's home.

Travel for routine everyday activities could also be appreciably reduced through the regular spacing of small shops, clinics, play areas, and elementary schools in the various local neighborhood centers. This would be particularly easy to do if the alternative design described in the first section of this chapter is used.

The task of a transportation system in Compact City would then be the efficient satisfaction of demand for those transportation services not eliminated by any of the measures described above. In considering a transportation system or systems for a compact city, it may be well to examine characteristics of some existing systems and accept or reject them according to their merits and defects.

A good transportation system is one that adheres closely to certain desired goals. In selecting a scheme for a compact city, we deemed the following three objectives relevant:

1. Rapid and efficient movement of people and goods.
2. Relatively cheap cost.
3. A system that promotes the planned development for the entire city.

We compared several transportation plans for Compact City, using the above as criteria. It turned out (much to our surprise and delight) that Compact City's internal transportation and delivery systems do not need to be elaborate.

In Chapters 3, 4, and at the beginning of this chapter we described the network of radials, rings, bikeways, and walkways proposed for Compact City. The general idea would be to keep the foot traffic separated from the bike traffic, separated from the auto traffic, and separated from the mass transit system. Walking and bicycling would take place along walkways and bikeways that run alongside the radials and along the interior open-space in front of homes. We now give a quick review of the proposed system.

The major arteries in and out of the Core of the city are the radials (spokes), located 20 feet above the garden (walkway) level to avoid intersection with traffic along any of the 26 one-way ring streets. The one-way ring streets are 10 feet above the garden level and are connected to the spokes above and below by ramps. The second floor of houses and apartment units have (back) doorways that open onto the ringways. Vertical movement within the three-dimensional structure is dependent on the multiple-cage elevators and escalators, on the downward ramps in the residential areas, and on the main ramps in the Mid-Plaza and the Core Edge. The latter allow cars to ascend as well as descend the height of the city. There is also a road system along the outside terraces. Allowing a four percent grade, one could ascend (using this system) from the bottom to the top of the city in a quarter turn about the city at maximum size. See Figure 17-2.

The Automobile as an Alternative for Mass Transit

After analyzing the various layouts and possible vehicles, it seems to us that an automobile might still turn out to be the most convenient when door-to-door travel is needed and that no special roads would be necessary other than the narrow ring roads used for access to the individual dwelling units.

A gasoline engine or any internal combustion engine would, how-ever, create major noise, heat, and pollution problems in an arti-ficially ventilated and air conditioned environment. (Nor did it seem desirable to have as an alternative transportation form a heavy rail transport in the interior of the city, for distances would be too short for acceleration to high speeds and there would be too much vibra-tion. And we rejected the idea of air cushion vehicles because they appear to be cumbersome and noisy to operate.) The best bet ap-peared to be the electrically powered automobile. The requirements to be met by such a conveyance within Compact City are not rigor-ous. Cars need a maximum speed of only 30 miles per hour along level roads and the capability to sustain such a speed for .5 to 1.5 miles.

Also there appeared to be little need for private automobiles in Compact City. They would occupy space, would seldom be used by the family, and would be a nuisance to park if a large number of them were left for long periods about the town. It seemed preferable to propose that residents simply call a taxi as needed or procure (on a rental or shared basis) a car parked in a lot conveniently close by.

We even looked into the possibility of having driverless cars which would be guided by electronic television camera eyes and automatic "robot"-like computer controls. Such cars are almost a reality because of the intense research going on at Stanford University in Artificial Intelligence (John McCarthy), at the University of Pennsylvania, and elsewhere. Such cars may become generally available in the early 1980s at a reasonable cost if used on a shared basis.

It is interesting to note that a family's shared investment in a con-ventional car (or equivalent rental) would be nominal. Assuming a cost of $3,000 per car, and the excessive requirement of 25,000 such cars, the capital investment would be only $125 per family. (For 10,000 cars, the cost per family would be $50.) By way of contrast, a fleet of 200 mass transit cars costing, say, $50,000 each would amount to less than $17 per family and would last several years before replacement.

The conventional lead-acid battery and D.C. motor electric cars available today (for two adults and weighing 1,100 pounds) can main-tain a constant 25 miles per hour cruising speed for 40 uninterrupted miles and can climb a four percent grade at 25 miles per hour for 7 miles. This demonstrated performance more than satisfies our needs.

Thus, the technology needed for a utility car in the City has already been developed. Besides meeting the primary objectives, these cars are silent, exhaust-free, smooth-running and maneuverable—all assets within the city.

Estimates for the cost of power used in electric cars stands today at about .81 cents per mile. The Federal Power Commission projects a cost of only .6 cents per mile in 1980. Unfortunately, lead-acid bat-teries have a short lifetime of about two years. The replacement of batteries drives the operating costs up to 4.0 cents per mile; if indus-trial ironclad lead-acid batteries and heavy duty automotive types are used, the costs go up to 11.0 cents per mile.[15]

To recharge these cars could be a problem. Conventional batteries can take from three to eight hours to recharge. With appropriate batteries, this time can be reduced with a rapid charger to only a few minutes, but such a device would cost more than the car, even though it could be used to charge a number of cars per day. The rate of recharge is limited to a maximum beyond which battery cell damage will occur. This whole problem of rapid charging can, of course, be side-stepped by removing the battery from the car and installing a recharged one.

The current search for a battery powered auto which can compete with Detroit's standard gasoline guzzlers has intensified research in the automotive field. It now seems clear that more efficient electric cars will be available soon. Thus, those now available and those on the drawing boards will be more than adequate for the short distances and level roads found in Compact City. Special electric cars as well as conventional autos could be used for travel between cities.

An Attractive Alternative: The Minibus Transit System

The ring-and-spoke pattern of streets, with elevators at every ring-and-spoke overpass, provides an efficient network for a minibus system. The minibus is a small jitney-vehicle, electrically powered and guided by an attendant or possibly by a wire embedded in the roadway. The small size, efficiency, and low cost of these vehicles would permit frequent bus service to ensure a system competitive with the automobile — whether publicly or privately owned — while exhibiting none of its familiar drawbacks.

Because there are separate walkways and bikeways that do not intersect the roadways, because trucks could be designed to load and unload without blocking the street, and because rings and spokes do not intersect directly but run through the city at different elevations, it may be practical to have minibus vehicles automatically guided and to have a simple sensing device detect and stop the vehicle if there is danger. Even if the vehicles are operated by drivers, the minibus alternative is attractive.

The routes for the minibuses would be along selected rings and spokes. For example, on each level three circular roads could be selected, one near the outer extremity of the city where most people live, one 2/3 of the way out from the center where local services are concentrated, and one 1/3 of the way out from the center where the remaining inhabitants reside. Every fourth spoke could have a minibus route. The rings and spokes selected would also be different on different levels.

Assuming an average speed of 20 miles per hour (including time for stops), a minibus along a spoke could reach the Core in less than 5 minutes, could traverse the city's diameter in 10 minutes and travel the three rings in 31, 21, and 10 minutes respectively.

A person desiring service and finding no route on the ring or spoke that is closest to him need only walk to the nearest spoke-ring lift (average distance about 575 feet, and a maximum distance of 850 feet) and take the elevator one or two levels up or down, depending on where the route is located. Transfers would be made at spoke-ring intersections and at the central core.

For service with a maximum waiting time of 5 minutes (average wait time would be 2.5 minutes), fewer than 288 minibuses would be needed throughout the entire city, or 18 minibuses per level, to service the eight spoke routes in both directions. (Eight routes, each 8,840 feet long × 2 directions, lead to a total of 141,440 feet which can be covered in 1 bus in 90 minutes. Hence 90/5 min = 18 buses.) One-way service at 5-minute intervals on the ring roads would require a total of 208 additional minibuses, or 13 additional vehicles per level. (Calculation: $2\pi(3,500 \text{ feet} + 6,500 \text{ feet} + 8,000 \text{ feet}) = 115,000$ route feet covered by 1 bus in about 65 minutes; hence 65/5 = 13 buses per level.) Adding to this figure a 20 percent contingency, the entire system would require 595 vehicles.

Trip time under this system consists of three components: walking time, waiting time, and vehicle travel time. The maximum walking distance is at the outer ring and is 850 feet, which can easily be walked in three minutes. Thus, the upper bound to walking time is six minutes. Waiting time occurs at the beginning of each trip and when transferring. A trip could be made by utilizing no more than two bus routes (the time spent in vertical travel is assumed to be insignificant) so the maximum waiting time would be 10 minutes. This can be reduced to 5 minutes by installing devices in each dwelling or office signalling the arrival of a vehicle. The longest vehicle portion of a trip is 10 minutes (two radii), so the maximum conceivable time (for the longest trip) is 26 minutes. On the other hand, an average trip can be expected to be less than 10 minutes, an inconsequential amount of time.

If the 288 mini-buses along spokes carry 11 people (8 seated and 3 standing), their capacity to deliver people to the Core area is about the same as a fleet of 200 trams of the kind proposed in Chapter 4. With the city-wide accessibility of the minibus fleet, there would be no need for either the trams or the 10,000 or so public autos. Instead a single fleet of 600 or so minibuses would suffice.

Other Possible Alternatives

In addition to such things as moving sidewalks, we considered two other basic transportation designs:

1. The first was a plan whereby the transportation routes would cut through the city levels, and would not need to operate on separate horizontal planes. To this end we examined several ideas proposed for rapid transit using guided vehicles in our present cities.[16] For example, G. Haikalis has proposed an electrically powered (by battery or fuel cell) car system which would travel on rubber tires along guideways. The idea seems to be well suited for Compact City purposes. Haikalis has designed his car so as to be convertible from horizontal to vertical trans-

port. To prevent substantial slowdown in average speeds due to abrupt changes in vertical or horizontal direction, the guide shafts could be made to slope down or up at an angle as they cut across the levels.[17]

The cars proposed to be used with this system are each four feet wide, six feet long, and six feet high, with facing pairs of folding seats. Each car would have a weight of, at most, 1,000 pounds, and would carry a comparable load. It would also accommodate most freight carried by truck today. The system could be designed to travel at speeds up to 60 miles per hour but there appears to be no need for such speeds because distances are so short in Compact City.

2. Since Compact City makes full use of the vertical dimension, our inclination, of course, was not to use a single level (or possibly two levels, as suggested in the first section of this chapter) of the city for the location of the rapid transit system. Nevertheless, we considered this conventional approach as well: an individual could take an elevator to the transport level where he could transfer to horizontal transport and finally to an elevator to take him to his destination level. For horizontal transportation, small individualized driverless electric cars on guide rails could be used, along with conventional battery-powered cars with drivers.

Another possibility would be to use town buses and trams instead of individualized transit.[18] The bus or trams system would, of course, in some ways be similar to the one used in cities today; it turns out to be also very effective for Compact City and by far the cheapest. In fact, we have proposed in Chapter 4 just such a system: we recommended there using on the mid-level an overhead supported tram carrying 32 people running along the radials and around the Mid-Plaza Ring; arrival time between trams would be once every two minutes. Only 200 such vehicles would be necessary for Compact City with a maximum population of two million people. Moreover, these could do a better job than the million or so autos that are being currently used in a conventional city with a population of comparable size.

Notes and References

1. Jane Jacobs, *The Death and Life of Great American Cities*, Vintage-Random House (New York, 1961).

2. John C. Weicher, "A Test of Jane Jacobs's Theory of 'Successful' Neighborhoods," Division of Economic Research, Department of Economics, Ohio State University, December 1971, 24 pages. Weicher claims that Chicago neighborhood data do not support her theory. He presents an interesting "mathematical model" which is worthy of further development.

3. C. A. Doxiadis, *Ekistics*, Oxford University Press (New York, 1968) pages 313, 249.

4. *San Francisco Chronicle*, June 27, 1970.

5. James Fitzgibbon, "The Notebooks, Old Man River Project," Washington University School of Architecture, September 1972. A description of R. Buckminster Fuller's Domed City for East St. Louis.

6. Ivor de Wolfe, *Civilia—A High Density City*, Architectural Press (London, 1971). See also Wolf von Eckardt, *The Washington Post*, Saturday, December 11, 1971, page A12.

7. *Ibid.*

8. Doxiadis, *op. cit.*

9. Shoji Sadao, "Buckminster Fuller's Floating City," *The Futurist*, February 1969, pages 14–16; Clifford J. Woerner, "Floating Cities," *American Oceanography*, April 1969, Newsletter, 2 pages.

10. John Lear, "Cities on the Sea," *Saturday Review*, December 4, 1971, pages 80–90.

11. "Building a City in the Ocean," *The Futurist*, June 1969, pages 66–69.

12. R. Buckminster Fuller, "Man with a Chronofile," *Saturday Review*, April 1, 1967, pages 14–18; see also Shoji Sadao, *op. cit.*; it is also described by Wolf von Eckardt in "Floating Cities," *The Washington Post*, March 2, 1969, page G3.

13. Irving Kristol, "An Urban Civilization without Cities," *Horizon*, Fall 1972, pages 36–41. Excerpts from his article can be found in *The Washington Post*, December 3, 1972, pages B1, B4.

14. See Peter Wolf, "The Structure of Motion in the City," *Art in America*, January-February 1969, pages 66–75. Reviews various proposals past and future in an interesting nontechnical way with beautiful drawings. Also see Stanford Research Institute, *Future Urban Transportation Systems*, Stanford Research Institute (Menlo Park, Calif., March 1968). Also see *Report of the Governor's Task Force on Transportation*, State of California, November 1968. Also see N. V. Petersen, *New Transportation Concepts for Urban Growth Control*, System Development Corp. (Santa Monica, Calif., October 1971).

15. "Electric Vehicles and Other Alternatives to the Internal Combustion Engine." U.S. Government Printing Office, publication 79-607 0 (Washington, D.C., 1967); see the statement there by M. F. Ference, a Ford Motor Company Vice President, before a Congressional subcommittee, on pages 211–238; see also V. K. Heyman's statement on comparative costs, on pages 168 and 169. Also see Leon Griffiths, "The Electric Car," *Automobile Engineer*, August 1967, pages 329–340; U.S. Bureau of Power, "Development of Electrically Powered Vehicles," Federal Power Commission, Doc. FP1.2; El 2/12, U.S. Government Printing Office (Washington, D.C., February 1967), pages 12–45; B. S. Hender, "Future of the Battery Electric Car," *Electronics and Power*, August 1964, pages 250–254.

16. W. F. Hamilton II and Dana K. Nance, "Systems Analysis of Urban Transportation," *Scientific American*, July 1969, pages 19–27.

17. George Haikalis, "Supra-Car," *Highway Research Record, No. 251*, pages 63–68, National Research Council Highway Research Board (Washington, D.C., 1968).

18. Another possibility is a continuous belt or continuous train of vehicles that stops periodically. See, for example, J. H. Day, C. W. Hamilton, and K. L. Nielsen, "Trends in Urban-Transportation Research," *Battelle Technical Review*, Vol. 17, Nos. 9 and 10, September–October 1968.

Part
Three

SOME
SOCIAL
IMPLICATIONS

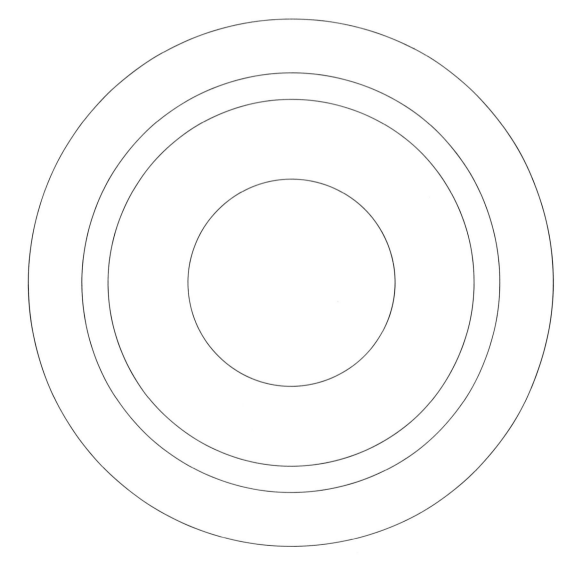

The reader is probably as qualified as the authors to speculate on the socioeconomic aspects of a city designed along Compact City lines. It is a fascinating subject requiring further study by experts. Accordingly in Part Three, many of the comments that we make are very general and reflect trends which are equally applicable to any city of the future—compact or not. About certain things, however, we will be quite specific. For example, in Chapter 14 we consider some of the possible effects of greater accessibility in terms of space and time than is available in present-day cities. In Chapter 15 some advantages of this accessibility are discussed in terms of a future health-care system.

We collect, in Chapter 16, some of the criticisms made against a compact-type city. For the most part these have been made by those with short acquaintance with the proposal. Some, however, reflect people's subconscious worry that our current cities are highly vulnerable. To allay this, we indicate how, by means of back-up systems, future cities could be made less vulnerable than present ones. In Chapter 17 we speculate on the effect of current technological trends on the culture of cities of the future.

Finally in the short finale we observe that this book is at best a feasibility study, not an implementation proposal—the difficult challenge remains to make Compact City happen.

ACCESSIBILITY:
ITS SOCIOECONOMIC
EFFECTS

14.1 More Available Time and Opportunity

The characteristic of Compact City which is expected to have an important effect on the life of its inhabitants is the accessibility of its parts both in time and space. Accessibility in space is due to the physical design of the city. Its accessibility in time is a consequence of spreading the life cycles of the inhabitants evenly around the clock.

Accessibility in space means that every location in the city is a vantage point from which any other location can be reached in, at most, a few minutes. In this respect Compact City would offer all the advantages of suburban living; yet its compactness enables all inhabitants to have the convenience and excitement of living in a downtown section of such cities as London, Paris, or New York.

Round-the-clock living has even more far-reaching and totally unexpected results. In a city of 2,000,000 almost one third of the population comprises the working force. Two times a day in conventional cities—once in the early morning hours and then again in the evening—the force of 600,000 people floods the streets of the city, going to and from work, creating a congestion phenomenon unparalleled in history. On a Sunday the streets are left relatively idle except for the emergency working force and for social visiting and sightseeing. (In countries where the siesta is popular there are four traffic jams a day. In 1971, the Mexican North American Cultural Institute blamed increased smog in Guadalajara, a city of 1,500,000, on increased traffic and declared that the traditional siesta must be eliminated so that the central city could breathe.)

In Compact City the work cycle of any individual could consist of work for several days followed by several days off, just as in present-day cities. Suppose, however, that work days, weekends, and holidays were staggered for the population so that sometime in an average 24-hour period about 22 percent—approximately 440,000 people— would be working. (This percentage is obtained by assuming there is only one wage earner per average family of 3.3 individuals, who works 5 out of every 7 days, plus some holidays.) Moreover, the time that people report to work would also be spread evenly around the clock. Assuming ten minutes were spent in travelling to work and ten minutes in returning, about 1/72 of the day would be used in transit. Thus, if schedules are fully staggered, 22 percent times 1/72, or 6,000 people will be on their way to work or returning at any instant of time. Less than 1/3 of the total transit time would be in the Core proper so the number of working people in transit in the Core area would be less than 2,000 at any one instant.

This is a negligible quantity of the order of a few thousand when compared with the several hundreds of thousands of people in transition through the Core area of a comparable conventional city during the rush hour. Roughly speaking, the principle of exploiting use of time reduces rush-hour congestion by a factor of 300 to 1.

Of course, many other people would be on the streets going to shops, recreation facilities, schools, and participating in numerous other activities. Assuming everyone (including workers) spends 20 minutes in transit during the course of a 24-hour period, approximately 28,000 people would be in transit at any instant. Of these, perhaps as many as 5,000 would be found in transit in the Core area at any one time. Even if each person were to go downtown several times a day, the number of people in transit in the work area would be 1/50 to 1/100 the peak congestion of conventional cities. Naturally, at some times, more people would be present in the Core area than at other times, but under normal conditions never would they number in the hundreds of thousands.

Moreover, because of staggered living patterns, there would be no sudden and excessive demand on the electrical power, water supply, or food facilities in the city, nor on the outside transportation system between cities. The even demand throughout the day for power, water, food, work facilities, and purchases means each facility has a similar reduction of its peak load. A good example is restaurant facilities, which we mentioned earlier. Let us take a restaurant whose principal business is noontime lunches. In a conventional city, during luncheon period, one table for four serves three or four customers. Occasionally it can be used twice. A restaurant with 24 tables might serve 75 customers during an hour. However, if people desiring lunches were to arrive throughout the day for an hour lunch, the restaurant could serve 75 people at each of the 24 tables throughout the day, or 1,800 customers. If there are only 75 customers, then the number of tables needed could be reduced from 24 to only 1. The reader will recall we illustrated this point in Section 2.6.

We have already seen in Chapter 4 the dramatic reduction in transportation facilities that could be affected. A present-day city of 2,000,000 might well have over 1,000,000 autos—Compact City could get by with 10,000. In fact, 200 trams, each with a seating capacity of 32, could do the whole mass transit job.

The capital investment needed in many types of physical facilities in a compact city would be but a fraction of the amount needed for conventional cities because the peak demand would be less. Even the man-hours needed to run a facility would be considerably less because personnel are constantly working and are not idle as they would be just before and after a peak period.

Reduction in capital facilities usually means that the smaller facility is used more intensively. For example, the restaurant table could be used 24 times as much in a 24-hour period. Consequently, it would wear out more rapidly and the entire facility could be modernized and updated in a shorter period of time.

It is likely that small specialized shops would flourish in Compact City. A small business whose service is to mend broken china, for example, does not survive easily in a conventional city because there is only enough potential business in the whole city to support one shop and most people would find the location of the shop too inconvenient to be worth the trip no matter where it were located. However, because distances within Compact City would be negligible, a china repair shop might be a feasible undertaking. Indeed, it could be located in one of the local neighborhood centers and still be accessible to everyone.

In a conventional city there might be three small specialty shops of the same type located in different areas, each barely making enough to survive and cover its rent. It would not be worthwhile for them to consolidate into one location if only customers located close to the store were to come to it. But shared facilities could work in Compact City by making use of the same facility around the clock. Some specialties require only a small amount of space and the success of the business depends primarily on the skill of the specialist. For example, a maker of fine jewelry might need only a small workbench and a portable toolbox. There is no reason why his facility could not share floor space with other specialties but at different times of day. Even the interior open space could be used for temporary-based businesses—particularly by artists, artisans, and people who are trying to start a new business on a shoe string. (Jane Jacobs's recommendation that there be a mix of old and new buildings in present-day cities was precisely for the purpose of giving new businesses a chance to start on a small scale in low-rent facilities. See Section 2.4.)

Schools as we know them in conventional cities are usually overcrowded part of the 24-hour day and empty from late afternoon until early the next morning. In Compact City school facilities could be consolidated and operated on a continuous 24-hour cycle. A high school course in elementary French, for example, could be given many times during a 24-hour period. This would make it easier for students to take almost any combination of subjects without conflicting class schedules.

The most evident socioeconomic effect of accessibility would be that many routine activities will take place more quickly. For example, housing facilities would normally be built with teams working around the clock. The lapsed time to have an extensive repair job done would run about one-third the time it takes now in a conventional city.

Facilities that are always open and easy to get to mean life is less complicated, congestion becomes negligible, the size of facilities is dramatically reduced, and facilities will be remodeled and modernized more frequently. Because in Compact City there would be no commuting in the strict sense of the word, the one to two hours a day that are currently spent by many people commuting are freed for people to use for other activities. Moreover, the elimination of long commutes would also result in less anxiety, for the current commute creates stresses in an individual which undoubtedly affect both his work and family life. Just as the Industrial Revolution eventually resulted in a shorter working week, so the proposed simple technological change in the design of the cities could also have a profound effect on people, their activities, and their leisure.

14.2 Adjusting to an Even 24-Hour Cycle

In this section we try to resolve some of the problems that may arise because of the proposal to use time more evenly throughout the 24-hour day. No claim is made that this use of the time dimension is perfect in all respects. What is claimed is that after all the pros and cons are considered, it will on the whole be far more convenient than current time cycles.

Perhaps the easiest problem to solve is the design of a sleeping chamber so that one can sleep in relative isolation from lights and sounds. As far as elimination of light is concerned, it is no more complicated than pulling the drapes, closing the door, and flipping the switch—everyone performs this routine all the time. For most people this may be sufficient also for keeping out unwanted sounds. Almost any degree of sound insulation is possible and people will probably vary in their requirements. The proper design of sleeping rooms so that one can get a good "night's" sleep is an interesting subject in its own right and deserves much study.

Most routine activities that employ large numbers of people doing similar activities (e.g., clerks in grocery stores) would probably have no difficulty arranging a continuous "shift" operation. Just as he does in present-day cities, a worker could wait until his replacement arrives to take over his duties. Supervisors could also spell each other in a similar manner. The fact that a person would be likely to have more than one supervisor during his shift should result in a fairer evaluation of his work performance.

Will there be people that one never meets simply because they are on a different schedule? The answer is probably yes, just as there are when people are on the same schedule in present-day cities. (Populations are large. so that no matter what time schedule prevailed it would be improbable that everyone would meet everyone else.) On a continuous-shift basis there would be fewer people around at any particular time and the chances would probably be better (than they are now) that one would get to know the people he encounters better. How do two people arrange to meet if their working hours do not overlap? The answer probably is that people will just have to be flexible and to arrange for mutually convenient meetings during their nonworking hours.

Arranging schedules so that the whole family could be together at eating time poses problems too. If there were only one wage earner in a family holding a steady job, there would be of course, no difficulty. If he were to change jobs in the city, then problems could arise. If his new job required working at a very different time of day, the family might be obliged to shift its schedule around. Another possibility is that once Compact City work customs evolve, it would be routine for an employee to work for a while, go home to have supper with his family, then return to work again, a concept roughly equivalent to the siesta style of life in warmer climates. One thing is certain, a change of jobs will not require the family to move to another part of the city or require a long commute.

Another interesting question is how does one arrange to clean a facility or repair a road that is in continuous use? Probably such work would be handled the way it is in conventional cities—there would be some inconvenience; round-the-clock work-crews could complete major jobs faster. While all this is happening citizens will just have to get out of the way, return at a later time, or use an alternative facility. Incidentally, offices need not be cleaned up at the same time each day. Offices could be cleaned once every 24 hours, or every 33 hours, or whatever time is appropriate.

Travelers between conventional cities on opposite sides of the country or ocean often become painfully aware that their internal biological clocks are out of phase with local time. Their sleep patterns and their digestive patterns are disrupted and it often takes several days to feel one's self again. However, future travelers between compact cities may find time differences less disturbing. Airplane passengers between cities at meal times could be given a choice of breakfast, lunch or dinner. Nonetheless, sleep after arrival at the destination may not be so easy to arrange, for if the traveler is on his way to a meeting, there is a 33 percent chance the meeting will be scheduled somewhere in the eight hours he is normally asleep. If so, he'll have to stay awake in the same way one presently does if he is invited to a late party. However, with some exceptions he should find it generally easier to keep to his customary eating patterns, and probably no more difficult than it is at present to adjust to his customary sleeping patterns.

14.3 Circadian Rhythm

Earlier we poked fun at *Cicadian Rhythm,* the custom of everybody doing things at the same time — getting up, eating breakfast, jamming the freeway, etc. The time principle suggests that arranging starting times of various activities more uniformly around the clock has many advantages. Nothing is proposed that in any way affects the basic 24-hour cycle of an individual. The time he awakes, eats, or goes to bed is, just as it is now, in some fixed pattern — the only difference is that patterns are different for different individuals.

In this section we examine an entirely different type of rhythm, *Circadian Rhythm,* which refers to our internal biological clocks. Both kinds of rhythm probably had their origins in the dim distant past in the rise and setting of the sun, but in recent times the availability of good clocks and artificial light has made the two types of rhythm independent of one another.

Circadian (from the Latin *circa*; around, and *dies*, day) rhythm — the daily rise and fall of the body's hormones and enzymes — is a phenomenon which has been scientifically confirmed to exist in humans and other living beings. Although there is no unanimity as to the causes of these rhythms, it is established that in many they occur in cycles varying somewhere between 23 and 28 hours. It may be possible to change the time the cycle starts up but not its length. Body temperature, which is affected by the hormones, fluctuates by about two degrees every day and serves as an effective index to the natural cycles we are aware of when we feel wide awake or lethargic and drowsy. If the duration of the cycle is precisely 24 hours, the temperature peak should occur at the same time each morning. Most people have not made a personal study of their circadian rhythm to find out whether or not their cycle is 24 hours in duration, nor do they know the times during their cycle when they are at their peak efficiency. However, some people have. One such person is Mr. Donald Erskine of Philadelphia. He has kept charts of his body temperature on a daily basis for 13 years. He has proved to his own satisfaction that his cycle has a 25-hour duration, and he lives by it. Each day he goes to sleep one hour later than the previous day and so he spends eight or nine days every month sleeping in the daytime.[1]

Body temperature is only one measure of circadian cycles. In the book *Body Time,* Gay Gaer Luce mentions example after example of experiments which show that some people feel fatigued and lethargic at times when custom says they should be wide awake.[2] It is believed that the basic cause is that these persons are forced to adhere to a 24-hour schedule that is out of phase with their natural body-rhythm. Some children perform badly at school in the morning (usually but erroneously attributed to lack of sleep) whereas if they could attend school in the afternoon they would excel; people who appear tired and nervous on the job might do better if they performed easy tasks early in their daily cycle and the more taxing ones later in the day.

The rhythmic patterns that regulate the cycles of people's lives are not well understood. Some conjecture that certain environmental phenomena such as the relation of the sun to the moon have impact on humans, an idea illustrated by the belief that a full moon has a romantic effect on young lovers. Others feel that changes in barometric pressure and the presence of positive or negative ions in the atmosphere can affect feelings of well-being. Certainly most people feel gloomy on a gloomy day. Gay Gaer Luce cites the evidence of Dr. Frank Brown, a biologist at Northwestern University, and that of Prof. Rocard, a Sorbonne physicist, which suggest that rhythmic circadian oscillations may be conditioned by cosmic radiation, light, electric and magnetic fields, and other regularly occurring environmental phenomena.

As already mentioned, light seems to play a useful role in glandular stimulation and secretion. Exposure to a moderate amount of natural light can result in remarkable health benefits. Rickets can be prevented by exposure to sunlight, artificial ultraviolet light, or by eating foods containing calciferol. Ergocalciferol ("Vitamin D_2"), formed by irradiation with ultraviolet light, is used as an antiricketic agent. Usually .01 milligrams is added to each quart of milk.[3] Excessive exposure to sunlight, however, could be damaging to the extent that some medical people think that when the full impact of natural light on our body is understood, it will be used in prescribed amounts like a drug. Most artificial light has wave lengths in the orange and red region of the spectrum, mainly because people like the appearance of skin tone under this light. But it is possible for artificial light to supply the same wave lengths found in natural light. It is not as pleasing to the eye, but by a proper mixing of wave lengths of artificial lights, the preferred appearance of skin tones can be maintained at the same time that enough ultraviolet light is provided for health purposes.

There is abundant evidence that light affects our sleeping patterns. People have been observed to develop behavioral cycles which are affected by the availability of light. This is certainly true in animals. (Egg production can be controlled by the way chicken hatcheries are lighted. In some vertebrates [e.g., ducks and sparrows] there are unidentified organs in the brain that respond to light passing through the skull, even when the animal is blind, that serve as pacemakers for circadian rhythm.[4])

It is interesting to note from experimental evidence that circadian rhythms do not depend on the awareness of the day-night cycle or even on exposure to light and to dark. Honey bees, plants, and humans all alternate between activity and rest and show a sense of time even when isolated from the outside world.[5]

Experiments with 48-hour cycles (36 working, 12 sleeping) have shown that man is not yet fully aware of the factors governing his adaptability to changes in his time cycle. Compact City facilities, being available for use more or less equally around the clock, might turn out to be a boon for individuals whose rhythm cycles vary from the "normal." For example, if the individual is what society describes as a "night person," he would not be faced with the problem of finding a place to get dinner at 4 a.m. A writer or any other person free to vary his work schedule to suit his own fancy could decide to make his "daily" cycle coincide with his circadian one (of 23 hours, or 25 hours, or whatever it happens to be).

Thus there is substantial evidence that there are many people whose body efficiency follows some fixed cycle whose length is different from 24 hours. If the duration of their cycle is not exactly 24 hours, then the time some individual cycle starts up will move up (or back) perhaps one or more hours per day. If these people should opt to live by their own natural rhythm instead of by a socially imposed rhythm, it would be far more convenient to do so in a compact city. It may turn out eventually that most people would prefer a cycle different from the currently prevalent one of 24 hours!

References

1. Patricia McBroom, *Philadelphia Inquirer*, December 26, 1971, page A1.

2. Gay Gaer Luce, *Body Time*, Pantheon Books-Random House (New York, 1971), page 53.

3. W. F. Loomis, "Rickets," *Scientific American*, December 1970, pages 77–91. (Offprint 1207, W. H. Freeman and Company, San Francisco).

4. Michael Menaker, "Nonvisual Light Reception," *Scientific American*, March 1972, pages 22–29.

5. *Ibid.*

HEALTH CARE
IN FUTURE CITIES

15.1 The Health-Care System

To illustrate how the accessibility of facilities in space and time can affect the quality of services we will spell out in some detail a health-care system which we believe would be greatly superior to anything available today.[1] The approach is to make the maximum effective use of health facilities for the city as a whole. These include such medical facilities as: (1) intensive care, (2) acute care, (3) extended care. (4) neighborhood health centers (the sector clinics), and (5) blood banks. Professional personnel include nurses (RN, LVN), physicians (MD), and the new kind of medics known as paramedics (PM). We will say more about a PM's training and responsibilities later.

In the future, health care may become a right rather than a privilege. Its goals: To make a high standard of health care equally accessible, available, and acceptable to all citizens.

Material in this chapter is based on informal conversations with well known health administrators and planners: in particular, Dr. Morris F. Collen and Dr. Sidney R. Garfield of the Kaiser Permanente Foundation Hospitals, Dr. John R. Goldsmith of the State of California Public Health Department, and Professor Charles Flagle of The Johns Hopkins University. The authors are grateful to Mr. Arlin Torbett of Stanford Research Institute who drafted this chapter.

We present first a somewhat exaggerated picture of what a rather run-down mother may go through to get medical help in the United States today. She begins by calling her doctor's office for an appointment. Since there is not an emergency, a date is established for a visit some three weeks later. The time selected is one that is convenient for the doctor. It is not in the evening when someone can take care of the mother's three children, not on Wednesday afternoons when doctors play golf (and discuss mutual investment plans), and definitely not on the weekend. Her doctor, in whom the mother has abundant confidence, happens to be a specialist in gastrointestinal disorders. His time is valuable, and, as we have noted, he is hard to see. In fact, she considers herself lucky to have arranged to see the doctor so soon. She next arranges for a baby sitter.

Unfortunately, on the day of the appointment, the baby sitter can't make it (boy-friend trouble) and so the mother has to take the children with her. The parking lot is full, and she has to park three blocks away and they all walk to the office. The waiting room is full (the doctor had started his day late), and the mother has to wait an hour before seeing him. All of this would not be so bad except that there is no place for the kids to sit. They wander around picking up the latest virus from the other patients. Finally the doctor sees her and tells her she is run down; he suggests she get more rest and take a high-potency vitamin. Mother and children go next to the pharmacy. The parking lot there is also full. She has to wait in line to get her prescription. The kids by this time are quarrelling; the evening traffic jam has started. Supper is late.

15.2 Routine Medical Service in Compact City

Each residence would be equipped with a viewphone. The citizen desiring medical advice would call his neighborhood health center. The sector clinic is always open with a full complement of personnel available around the clock. Usually a paramedic (PM), familiar with the patient's medical history, would discuss the illness with the patient whom he sees on the viewphone, in "living color." If the patient's medical record is needed, the PM could immediately have it retrieved from a central computer data bank and displayed on his CRT Console (a console equipped with a cathode ray tube) beside him. The medical record would contain a complete medical history of the patient: immunizations, allergies, illnesses, and medications. It would also contain a computer analysis of trends in the patient's medical history. If the patient's current illness appears to be routine, the PM would prescribe the necessary basic treatment, updating— with an "on-line" computer—the patient's medical record. If simple medication is required, he would enter the prescription into the computer, which would record the prescription and send it to the central pharmacy at the medical center for filling. A computer would type the prescription label. Within a half hour of the patient's call to the PM, the medication could arrive at the patient's residence via the automatic-delivery system described in Section 4.7.

The Paramedic

The PM requires more training than a registered nurse (RN) but less than a general practitioner. The PM works under the supervision of an MD but he has more latitude in decision-making than an RN. Nevertheless, there are specific restrictions on his functions. He knows at what point he is required to call for an MD to take over the diagnosis and treatment.

The Sector Health Center

If the patient's illness necessitates an in-person examination, an appointment would be made at the sector clinic, which is always open and is located in the neighborhood center (Mid-Plaza), within a five-minute walking time (on the average) from the patient's home. At the appointed time the patient would arrive, having left children at the child-care center adjacent to, but separated from, the clinic. The patient would be examined by a PM without delay; and if the illness were severe, then the more highly trained MD would take over and complete the examination, diagnosis, and plan of treatment. If laboratory tests are required, the nurse would draw the specimen and send samples by way of the automatic delivery system to the central medical laboratory located at the medical center. The central lab would be equipped with the latest rapid-test equipment and the results of the tests would be quickly processed into the patient's health record. At the same time the local clinic would be notified. The PM (or if necessary, the MD) would notify the patient of the results, usually by viewphone, and recommend the necessary treatment.

For a maximum sized city of two million people, there would be 32 sector clinics—one for each vertical sector. For emergency reasons the clinics would also be distributed two per level. Thus, on each level there could be two clinics located at opposite sides of the Core in the Mid-Plaza area. The clinic could contain dental offices as well as general medical facilities. Each could be equipped to service about 60,000 people.

15.3 The Once-a-Year Multiphasic

The sector clinic would also serve as the neighborhood center for health education and preventive medicine. One of its important activities would be its multiphasic function. At periodic intervals (usually once a year) each person in the sector would have a complete head-to-toe medical and dental checkup. There is growing statistical evidence that such tests, when properly administered, with competent medical personnel and careful follow-up, result in healthier people (e.g., lower mortality rates).

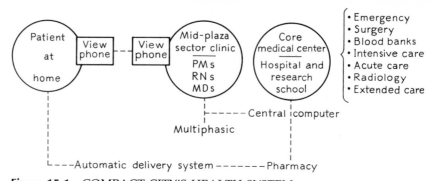

Figure 15-1 COMPACT CITY'S HEALTH SYSTEM
A diagram of the flow of information and medical supplies in the medical care delivery system.

The checkup would begin with a series of questions. These would appear on a console display tube under the control of the central computer. If the patient's medical history had already been recorded, then the purpose of some of the questions would be to obtain information about the results of various treatments previously prescribed while others would obtain information about the person's recent state of health. If the answer to any question were positive, then the computer would be programmed to question in depth. For example, if a patient had a respiratory complaint, then a series of related questions would be asked regarding the presence of fever, duration of fever, coughing of blood, aching in the joints, etc. Some questions would pertain to mental health.

Next a series of physical tests would be administered: blood pressure, temperature, weight, metabolism, and reflexes would be measured; blood samples, a cardiogram, and a chest x-ray would be made; checkups would reveal any glandular swellings, or lumps, or dental or ocular problems.

Before the patient leaves the clinic, the results of various tests would have been recorded, analysed by a computer, and reported to a doctor for review. If nothing alarming were noted, a PM would review the findings and set up a time for the next multiphasic exam with the patient. If a possibly serious problem were noted, then usually a medical doctor would discuss the results with the patient and arrange for special appointments, treatments, hospitalization, etc.

15.4 The Medical Center

The medical center located in the Core of Compact City would be a general medical and hospital facility consisting of surgery and emergency units, radiology and pathology laboratories, a pharmacy, specialized ambulatory clinics, a dietary department and kitchen facilities, a blood bank, the medical records data-bank and computer facility, a medical school and medical research facility, and a 100-bed intensive care unit (ICU). In the ICU the vital functions of patients would be monitored and any unexpected developments in the treatment of a patient would cause an automatic signal to alert the medical personnel on duty.

The Acute-Care Center

If the patient requires hospitalization or more extensive testing, arrangements for that care would be made through the neighborhood sector clinic. It would take five minutes by auto for the patient to arrive at the acute-care hospital located at the medical center in the Core. While he is en route to the hospital arrangements could be made so that he could be immediately tended to when he arrives: he would go without delay directly to a room or to a test facility as required.

Extended-Care Facility

As the patient recovers he would no longer require the level of care ordinarily furnished in a short-term acute-care hospital. However, he might still continue to need a professional level of medical supervision, skilled nursing care, and related services. Because residences would be located so close to medical facilities, extended care could usually be given in the home. Necessary equipment might be loaned, and delivered by the automatic delivery system. Medical advice in such cases would be transferred back to the sector facility.

In some cases however, the convalescing patient would be moved to an extended-care facility located "down the hall" from the acute-care hospital. The extended-care facility would have less expensive technical equipment and less medical staff per patient. In case of a relapse the patient could be moved back to the acute-care facility in a few minutes. It is obvious that the convenient spacial arrangements of the medical facilities and personnel and their around-the-clock use would result in great savings and better service.

For the most part, the patients who need an extended-care facility are those persons past middle age who suffer from heart trouble, strokes, or cancer. As the diseases of infancy, childhood, and the early adult years are conquered, more people will be kept alive and will eventually *by default* fall victim to these disabling diseases. In the two decades 1950–70, the number of such people in the United States over the age of 65 has increased from 9 million to 19.5 million, and is expected to reach 24.5 million by 1980. Thus, there is a growing need for more and more facilities that provide extended care.

15.5 Comparative Services

Generally speaking, the consolidation of medical facilities proposed for Compact City would result in more effective use of various specialities and less duplication of equipment. Around the clock, evenly distributed use of facilities would mean that in Compact City the best treatment would be available at all times; it is likely that beds would be scheduled by the hour rather than by the day. The proximity of the home to the health facilities, the use of viewphones, and the automatic delivery system would make home care an important part of the system. Finally the increasing use of paramedics would permit the MD to devote more of his talents and abilities to patients who are very sick.

As a rule of thumb, in determining the number of office visits needed by patients, medical administrators usually assume an average of four visits per person per year. In future cities the use of viewphones could reduce the number of ordinary office visits. However, since the objective is better health care, we can assume that each resident would, on the average, come in contact with the health-care system five times per year. Three of these visits could probably be handled at the sector clinic and the other two referred to the Medical Center. Hence, we see that the average patient load on a sector health center is: 60,000 people/sector × 3 visits/year, or 180,000 visits/year. This is about 20 visits per hour; a staff of ten PMs and two or three MDs, and the associated nursing, health-education, and administrative staff would be more than adequate to handle this load.

The number of general beds required in the acute-care facility can be reduced from two to one bed per 1,000 people because of the even use of time, the centralization of facilities, and the more effective health care system.

For a maximum sized city of two million, on each of the floors of the hospital (except the one for surgical operations), there would be 150 acute-care beds, 50 extended-care beds, and 50 convalescent beds.

The current need of one MD per 1,000 people could be reduced by increasing the number of paramedics. If this were done, a total of 1,500 MDs (one MD per 1,333 people) seems adequate. Since only about 100 of these would be located at the 32 neighborhood sector clinics, this leaves 1,400 to staff the medical center. Assuming an average of 14 referrals per hour from the 32 sector clinics, each MD at the medical center need see (on the average) only one patient every 2 hours.

Note that the 25 percent savings in the number of medical doctors would also yield a much higher quality of medical service; medical specialities would not be spread thinly over suburbia; instead, in a compact city, facilities would be concentrated; they would utilize the best equipment, and be conveniently close to a person's home and work.

Reference

1. Sidney R. Garfield, "The Delivery of Medical Care," *Scientific American*, April 1970, pages 15–23.

CRITICISMS

16.1 Some Apprehensions

Most apprehensions people have about Compact City stem from their own fears about present-day cities and what the future holds in store for them. Many people have watched the inner cities deteriorate and have decided that nothing can (or ever will) be done about them. They view Compact City as a dream. Others fear that our proposal means that Orwell's *1984* is becoming a reality. They see, in any attempt to build a city for better living (or any proposal which appears to involve a change), just another step towards regimentation. Still others think they already know what is in this book without having read it, and their objections to Compact City therefore have no relation to what we have actually proposed. Here are some criticisms we have heard voiced.

Crowding

"The city would have too many people per unit area." "With so many people crowding in narrow corridors, it would be like living in a prison." "I wouldn't like people living above me and under me." The plan we propose bears no relation to these criticisms. Indeed, a great deal of effort went into creating an environment which would rank among the least dense large cities in the world. We know of no one actually living in a compact city environment at present. The closest approximation to its interior open space that we have actually seen are certain enclosed shopping malls, and hotel and airport lobbies with ceilings 30 feet or more high. We suggest readers look around them for buildings with large interior open areas and judge for themselves what the spacing between levels should be in order to achieve a feeling of spaciousness.

Lack of Sunlight

A common misconception about Compact City is that the interior open space about the homes would be used in exactly the same way as gardens around homes in suburbia. Actually we do *not* propose this. We feel the Park-Roof and the rural surroundings are readily accessible to all who claim they love nature, being respectively one minute and five minutes away from any part of the city. Moreover, if one insists on sunshine through every window, nearly half of all the housing units in Compact City would have exterior views and exterior patios. In a very real sense the "outside" is the real outside of the city and it is only a step away. Where we live and spend most of our lives, however, should be remade convenient and attractive. There are many ways to make the interior open space attractive and useful—not merely cosmetic, as so much open space is in suburbia today.

"The City Does Nothing for the Poor"

The purpose of this book is not to show how to cure all social evils. Our objective is to make cities better places to live. We believe, however, that our proposed design has a certain flexibility not found in conventional cities that will work for the advantage of the poor. For example, low-cost prefabricated homes and apartments could be built which would be fully protected from the weather. The units could be economically disassembled and rearranged in more functional patterns as needed. The city layout would provide a better opportunity for "shoe-string" enterprises to start. (We elaborated on this point in an earlier chapter.) The compactness of the city would help make it easy for everyone, rich or poor, to take advantage of the facilities of the city. A poor man would not have to travel long hours and pay high transportation costs to reach his job. His children would not need to be bussed in order to attend a good school. Moreover, building the city itself would provide lots of poor people with good jobs for a long time and therefore a new start in new surroundings. In short, Compact City may not be the cure for the ghetto, but it will help.

"All the Houses Look Alike"

Actually houses can vary in appearance, the same as they do (or could) now in suburbia. "Lots" are provided in the usual way for building homes from designs of one's own choosing.

In the final analysis, the list of seventeen advantages cited earlier can be the only reply to criticism of specific differences between Compact City and present-day cities. One should make a list of *all* the advantages and disadvantages of the proposed and the present system before deciding which is the best.

16.2 Vulnerability

All of us are more than ever aware that modern technology is completely dependent upon the flow of electricity, water, natural gas, and petroleum products. Moreover, the pumps that move the water, gas, and petroleum from the reservoirs and storage tanks are, for the most part, dependent on electricity. Communication systems as well as various control devices (such as thermostats) are also for the most part dependent on electricity. What happens to a city if suddenly the electricity is shut off?

What happens? There is the well documented observation that nine months later there is a noticeable increase in the number of babies. But, of course, this is the frivolous answer.

There are other questions everyone worries about in regard to conventional cities, which we naturally transfer to the context of Compact City, such as: What might an earthquake do? Will Compact City be more vulnerable to blackmail? Can it be held hostage through acts of sabotage or threats of perilous attacks? Would more people be killed by fire inside Compact City than in a conventional city? Would the communication systems of Compact City, and particularly television, be more likely to be used to regiment the people into a "1984," Orwellian world?

As we pointed out earlier, modern technology — based on power, water, communication, and air transport — is highly vulnerable. In every large city there are many individuals who are mentally unstable. The tactics of political violence — particularly its publicity — sets a pattern which can and does trigger some of these unbalanced individuals, particularly when two or three such individuals manage to act in accord. It may be only a matter of time before some grave premeditated acts with catastrophic consequences will turn all advanced nations into police states in order for society to protect itself.

In the design of Compact City such matters must receive careful attention. For example, would it be possible for someone to place sufficient explosives in key positions at the lowest level to collapse the entire structure of the city? Is it possible to design the lower structures so that they would be difficult to sabotage? Would a small, carefully placed nuclear bomb decimate the city? Could a small gang gain control of the air conditioning, ventilation, or the water supply systems and successfully terrorize the inhabitants? Could it be possible for someone to place sufficient poison in the water or to insert bacteria clandestinely in the air pumps so that the entire population would be annihilated? Could a demagogue hypnotize the masses while they are watching television and then incite them to riot and devastate city life. If an epidemic were to start somewhere in the city, would it be difficult to stop it from spreading quickly to the entire population, or could means be provided to seal off parts of the city?

We could go on and on listing possible dangers to a future city and to its residents. We will instead point out how certain of these dangers can be avoided or minimized. To begin with we do not advocate building Compact City (or any other city, for that matter) over any areas subject to strong earthquakes, such as along California's San Andreas Fault.

Some outstanding investigators of city life (e.g., Jane Jacobs) have pointed out that a neighborhood where many people move about at all times serves as a deterrent to criminals because their activities would be likely to be witnessed by a large number of people. The continuous life in Compact City, with overlapping day and night cycles, leaves few areas deserted and open to unnoticed intrusion for criminal purposes.

The mechanical systems for maintaining the city could be under decentralized control and special emergency units could be dispersed about the city on a standby basis. These units could be equipped with a number of detection and rapid-warning devices for foul play.

In particular, in Compact City there could be a number of built-in safeguards to guard against the possibility of electrical failure. Like conventional cities, Compact City would be largely dependent on the flow of electricity. To reduce the possibility of loss of major sources of supply, several power lines could enter the city from several directions. Loss of one, two, or even three of these lines would not call for any special measures. The separate lines would supply different sectors directly, but this supply could be switched to other sectors as required.

Close to the city there could be a standby power plant to be used only if there is a failure of major sources. Within the city itself there could be a special emergency power grid. The emergency generators would be powered by petroleum. Each sector on each floor would have its own emergency generator. In all 16 times 32, or 512 separate generators would be needed.

It is true that the air supply of Compact City would be entirely controlled by mechanical means; however, the ventilation could be operated from a large number of external centers and be so compartmentalized that it would be practically impossible for contaminants to spread from one part of the city to another through the air ducts. In this manner dangers to the entire population could be reduced. Throughout the air duct system there could be a variety of filters to insure the purity and adequate oxygenation of the air feeding into the city. A major requirement of the ventilation system is that it have the capacity to exhaust the air rapidly from any quarter of the City and to replace it with fresh, well-oxygenated, cool air.

Over 40 percent of the housing units would be constructed on the periphery of the city. Many more also would have direct contact with outside air. In case of emergency, evacuation of the city by walking out would be feasible and rapid. It would also be possible to crowd people, on a temporary basis, into the housing units with outside exposure.

In conventional cities, thousands of large buildings—both office and residential—have mechanical systems for cooling and ventilation. No case is known of a successful attempt to poison the air and thereby kill all the people living or working there. These systems are practically unprotected against possible overt or covert attempts. In Compact City, air conditioning, air purification, and circulation would be maintained on a much larger scale and could be a closely watched operation carefully monitored by controls and supervisory personnel.

Similar precautions could be built into the water supply and the filtering and sterilization units. Water could be stored at a number of independent reservoirs. More than one pipeline could bring water to the city. The pipelines within the city would have many crossovers. Water would be methodically sampled at various parts of the city before direct use. The Park-Roof could contain a small lake that would serve as a reservoir (also for maintaining water pressure). Thus the water system could be designed to be in less danger from tampering than are the water systems of conventional cities.

We have already indicated that the transportation system—walking, bicycling, autos, and mass transit—would, in case of an emergency, permit rapid evacuation of the population into the terrain surrounding the city, or to homes located on the exterior surface of the city, or possibly to an underground level which could be carefully designed and secured as a shelter area.

Strict health codes could be set up to control the spread of disease. As described in Chapter 15, clinics and hospitals would be organized so that patients could receive excellent medical advice by means of videophones in their homes and could receive their medical supplies there by means of the automatic delivery system. Thus patients with mild infections could be quarantined in their homes and treated there. If a serious emergency developed they could be quickly admitted to the hospital only a few minutes away from their homes.

In general Compact City could be designed so that its various facilities are less vulnerable than those of present-day cities.

CULTURE
IN FUTURE CITIES

17.1 Predicting the Effect of Technological Change

It is precisely because individuals have multiple goals and because
these goals differ from one individual to another and can change with
time that the task of forecasting social consequences of technological
change is so difficult. For example, take the impact of the Industrial
Revolution on the lives of the poor. Few would have been able to
predict its short-run negative aspects—namely, that the Industrial
Revolution would bring about a massive movement of people from a
rural to an urban environment, degraded working conditions, con-
tinued ignorance and poverty, and the barbaric use of child labor.
Few would have been able to predict the fundamental democratiza-
tion of society that would be the longer-term result—namely, that
the Industrial Revolution would enable the urban citizenry to identify
their needs and make gradual demands to improve their conditions
with a cohesiveness unfamiliar to and impossible in a rural society.
Finally, no one could have predicted the extent to which collective,
urban living would cause needs above and beyond those of individuals living in a rural environment—needs, for example, for schools,
well-stocked shops, modern homes, paved streets, traffic regulations,
sewer facilities, and so on.

Nor could one have predicted the long-term positive benefits of
the Industrial Revolution which we enjoy today in the way of material goods and services. To a large extent a scientific or technological
innovation may frequently have greater influence (sometimes good,

sometimes bad) on society through side effects than through direct effects. The automobile and the highway, which were supposed to pull communities together, in reality created sprawling suburbia and have tended to destroy community and family life. (We wave to each other as we pass each other in our automobiles and that's about it.)

When one views the bewildering variety, the delicate web of interconnected human activity, one wonders how it all is held together. Is it just the profit motive? The simplistic view is that money is the main motivation and that talent, training, and personal interest play only minor roles. We feel this is an oversimplification. In our opinion the richness of human activity derives from the great freedom of initiative of millions of people, and it is essential this freedom be protected. People are naturally creative; they are bored by idleness; they like to be helpful (particularly if they feel their help is needed or that some prestige, status, or power may be gained). But individual initiative can be easily suppressed by the organization of society. It becomes evident that initiative is being suppressed when a few rich families can effectively control politics and the economy; when a one party political system can effectively keep the same clique at the top; when a heavy-handed bureaucracy requires an involved approval procedure for every action (until finally initiative is no longer worth the effort); and when fear of job loss, economic insecurity, or physical fear of openly expressing one's opinion keeps one from undertaking some constructive action.

Society has begun to realize that machines are doing more and more of the work and that people are becoming merely button pushers. Moreover there is intense research on automation underway that will eventually eliminate even the button. There is a possibility that today's youth movement will result in a reduced emphasis on materialistic pursuits and acquisition of income as measures of success. If these ideas should become popular, then the decrease in materialism and the increase in automation will free more time than ever for other activities.

Unfortunately our society has a vast superstructure which has the effect of forcing people to work in order to exist—people have to have jobs and some one has to give it to them. Since most of our basic simple needs for food, clothing, and shelter are being produced automatically by machines operated by fewer and fewer people, this means that the rest of us have to be busy selling each other services or fancy gadgets. In the final analysis our needs for these services and gadgets are highly optional. This is why budget cuts anywhere—in government or industry or schools—can induce an unstable condition that can sweep the country causing the elaborate superstructure to fall apart. A future society, in order to maintain a stable structure, will probably, by one device or another, encourage people to keep busy, and what they do, short of doing harm to others or to themselves (e.g., through drug addiction, hence becoming a burden to others) will probably be tolerated.

We can anticipate therefore that in the future there will be more time for people to pursue alternative activities as industry, agriculture, and administration become more and more automated and society possibly becomes less materialistic. How man spends his newly acquired time will soon determine how he spends his life. Surplus time does not have to connote doing nothing. Rather, it allows one the time to participate in a variety of endeavors ranging from art or high achievement (e.g., in sports) to group problem-solving. When society has surplus time, the quality of life is dependent on the use of that time and how richly it contributes to the growth of man's total personality.

A new meaning for life could develop from this drastic reorientation of an old dictum that "all men must work hard to make a living" to a new one, "all men must work hard for the sake of mental and physical fitness." *The alternative is boredom.*[1] Work and leisure for many in present-day society are often indistinguishable. Often the only distinction is that one receives pay for work and has to pay to participate in leisure.[2]

To relieve population pressure and to satisfy increasing expectations, man modifies, extends, and redesigns his urban areas. But he is not the complete master of the city. The city also shapes the habits and thoughts of its people. It is not a formal stage on which the people are the actors. Rather, like a moving vehicle, it shakes and jerks them, confines their freedom, frustrates them, fills their lives with tensions and anxieties, and spoils them with its conveniences and goodies. It sets bounds on their functions and molds their personalities and ideas. The city is not passive.

Because cities do mold the people who live in them, so it follows that the physical or spatial dimensions and the time dimensions of Compact City would help remove many of the pressures which inhibit urban citizens today. Life in such a city (because of the accessibility of one part to another) could stimulate new opportunities for growth and change. At the same time it would be more stable because changes in living patterns brought about by changes in employment within the city or leisure interests would not necessitate a concomitant uprooting of entire families in order for an adjustment to be made. Because the facilities that make up Compact City's social institutions would always be open and easy to get to, more people should find it convenient to contribute to the social life of the city, to the politics of organizing it, to the mechanics of running its institutions, and to the continuous effort required to improve its quality, an involvement that is reminiscent, in a way, of the Greek city-state.

Unfortunately, man's capacity for adapting to physical change far outpaces his ability to accept and adapt to social change. In the space of a lifetime men have witnessed the transformation from horse and buggy travel to space flight. In spite of his physical adaptability to change and despite his higher level of education, man's social relationships continue to be about the same, or perhaps they are worse than they have ever been. The decade of the 1970s is full of violent conflict and profound subtleties of social interaction. And so it may turn out that the movement of people into compact cities (another form of collectivization) will have an effect analogous to the Industrial Revolution. It may lead to unimagined social benefits for mankind. But then again it may make life so easy that we become bored stiff and get into all kinds of mischief.

17.2 Schools, Arts, and Crafts

Knowledge has by now become a central economic resource of modern society. In the Post-Industrial Age of the future, the city will become one vast flow system for the communication of knowledge as well as the movement of material goods.

Today we regard learning as a bridge between relaxation and motivated work. In Compact City it would be easier for young (as well as the old) people to work part-time while they continue their education. This would permit someone whose working week is—let us say—nominally 20 hours, to acquire broad interest in a number of different areas. His life need not be completely given to work. In the environment provided by Compact City, it might be feasible for greater numbers of individuals to acquire skill for creativity in the arts than at present, for many more citizens to develop early training in the value of social action, and thus, for Compact City to produce a society in which many individuals will have interests that reflect a cross section of the interests of the community as a whole.

With the possibility of increased leisure time and less interest in material acquisition, latent artistic capabilities of the citizens of the city should gradually unfold. If this comes about, then mass-produced furnishings in homes might in time be replaced by individually designed articles.

Schools in the future will probably make more use of newly developed learning devices. Many of the lectures delivered to advanced classes could be given on closed-circuit television. To be completely successful, however, a closed-circuit educational television system would require improved screens and teachers who are better trained in the use of the medium than at present. Classes in which students use remote consoles connected to computers also will be commonplace. In the Compact City school system, the higher grades would be consolidated in a central location and operated around the clock.

Many special subjects taught in the school will probably be presented in the form of "canned" lectures. Thus standard courses in analytic geometry could be divided into a series of videotaped presentations by famous lecturers who would supplement their lectures with carefully prepared illustrations. A class instructor could then follow each video presentation with a class discussion, making use of video playbacks where necessary, and with the assignment of exercises. Students would be able to do their studying by rerunning the lecture on individual video consoles and could do rote learning by using a console connected to a computer source which would provide them with specially prepared programmed exercises. If so then it is probable that a new type of curriculum for universities will also emerge in which a sequence of courses will be replaced by a series of canned special topics tailored to the students' interests. For example, the general topics in mathematics could be differently illustrated for business students, biology students, statisticians, engineers, computer scientists, operations researchers, or historians.

17.3 New Emphasis in Research

Health Research

In speculating about new job opportunities that would exist in Compact City, we have selected three research areas as examples. The first is the ongoing revolution in biological research, and the consequences of this research, ranging from a better understanding of life processes—their preservation and prolongation—to the research and development of artificial organs and possibly to a deeper understanding of genetic structure and its manipulation. Related to these developments is a better understanding of the brain's thinking processes and the development of methods for alleviating—possibly curing—organic and deep psychotic problems associated with the nervous system. Biological research will also relate to problems of improved communications and learning, and to constructive, healthful use of leisure.

From biology and chemistry men may learn to synthesize foods which are more healthy, tasty, and abundant than at present. And food resources of the seas will have to be scientifically farmed if the world population cannot be stabilized.

Conservation

Another area of research that will be increasingly emphasized will be conservation, i.e., research directed towards a deeper understanding of the effect of man's activities on the future of his world. Today man has grown wary and fears every ecological change because he does not know enough to foresee its consequences. Man's inclination is to disapprove of nuclear power plants that warm the waters of the ocean, because of the effect thermal discharge has on fish populations and the long chain of life dependent on them. But perhaps warming the coastal waters could (as in the Gulf Stream) have beneficial results![3]

Environmental research will concentrate on developing large-scale computer models simulating ecosystems. In time it will be possible to predict accurately the effects of human population increases, of changes in the composition of the atmosphere, of pollution in streams and oceans, of man-induced biological mutations, of contamination by chemical and biological agents. With better methods of prediction, better decisions affecting ecosystems will be possible.

One can anticipate that the citizens of future cities will do everything to conserve scarce resources for future generations. For example, they may decide that the use of electric-powered cars (as well as those which are gasoline-powered) ought to be discouraged in order to conserve lead and other metals, and that petroleum ought to be used only in emergencies. Water will be recycled, waste reclaimed, excessive use of paper products discouraged, and the planting of new forests lands encouraged.

Helping the Handicapped

We hope that much new research will center on ways to help the handicapped to lead "normal" lives, and that gadgets that can help the handicapped will be developed and made available increasingly in the future. Today, although many such devices have been developed, they never actually reach the majority of those who need it. Blind people, for example, have to use the cane for walking in much the same way that the blind did two thousand years ago.

In present-day profit hungry society, there is very little in the way of profit to be made by making mechanical aids for the handicapped. Even though disabilities affect several million people in the total United States population, as a group the handicapped are mostly poor and do not constitute a political power base for getting substantial government subsidies. A crippled or paralyzed man currently is almost completely dependent on others to move him about in a wheelchair even when it is powered by an electric battery. He cannot climb steps or get into an auto without help. And yet this is the twentieth century, where technology could be used to increase the independence of the disabled. Prosthetic equipment can be designed that would be powered and have special controls. Obviously, if an amputee can paint a beautiful picture by holding a brush in his mouth, research and development of prosthetic equipment could make it possible for him to manipulate and control such equipment without the help of other people.

17.4 Automation

In future cities, financial transactions, vital statistics, transportation schedules, and the storage of information in general and its retrieval, all will undoubtedly be handled by the computer. There will be computer-automated, universal credit, audit, and banking systems so that payments for goods within the City and transfer of funds can take place without physically exchanging currency. In future cities, a person will walk into a shop and, upon presentation of his card, bracelet identifier, or his thumbprint or his face for scanning, will activate a computer to transfer funds for purchases made from his bank account to that of the shop. We will now review some of these possibilities.[4.]

Today even routine business is made complex by record keeping and paper work. We hope that most of the red tape and paper work that is now necessary before an endeavor is undertaken will diminish in the future. Salaries, taxes, rent, and accounting are, for the most part, already handled by the computer. Instead of weekly or monthly salaries, or yearly taxes, periodic transactions could be paid out on a continuous basis. (Banks probably would not like this idea because they would not be able to make money on the "float" as they do now.) An individual would be able to query the computer at any time regarding the status of his account.

Most routine purchases would probably also be handled automatically in the future. A housewife, for example, might be able to reorder supplies by using a "product identification tag" provided as part of the packaging on an item which could be detached from it and used for reordering. Several such tags could be accumulated and then inserted into a special electronic device in the home. The effect would be the same as ordering by telephone. In Compact City, deliveries could be made efficiently with the automatic delivery system. Viewphones might also be a means by which goods could be ordered and transactions could be made. All costs of purchases and transfers of money could then be automatically processed by computers, which would debit the purchaser's bank account.

In present-day cities people have only just begun to be dependent on the computer for handling information, and already the computer industries are among the giants of the economy. However, there is still a lot more developmental work required before computers will be used by the average individual in the way telephones are currently used. Learning methods for communicating with computers is a little like learning a new language in mechanical form — one that can be sophisticated and cumbersome. It would be desirable to develop direct and more natural ways for individuals to "talk" to computers without special training. Research on pattern recognition whereby computers could recognize patterns of human speech, is currently under intensive development and should have an impact on computer operations within another generation.[5]

Stock control — the decision as to what quantities of various standard items should be maintained in stores and factories — will someday be left entirely to the computer. The computer can be programmed to simulate variable future demands for items and possible delays in their production and delivery; this information together with certain formulae supplied to the computer can be used to determine the optimal amounts of stocks to carry in inventory. Grocery and department stores in the city would probably become fully automated. Removal of an item from stock could be recorded by computers and automatic reorders could be prepared. As noted earlier, orders made by customers by means of devices in the home would be handled by computers. The entire system of orders and deliveries could be viewed as one very elaborate vending machine.

Computers could also be used to provide custom services, such as guiding the automated production of a one-of-a-kind object or the detailed designing of a home to specifications provided by the potential owner.

Eventually we may even see the emergence of highly "intelligent," very compact, independently powered and controlled robot-like machines. These may be developed in the not too distant future, because it is now possible to make transistor circuits so small that they can only be seen under magnification.[6] Perhaps soon memory units will be miniaturized down to the molecular level.

17.5 Women's Liberation

We want to think also about what the effect of Compact City would be on a housewife who is a mother with small children. The need for chauffeuring the children would not exist. The housewife would thus have many hours released from such tasks which could be devoted to other activities. Moreover, a child would become more independent at an earlier age. A mother and a very young child might walk together to the neighborhood center or playground. The child would be able to run about freely without the mother fearing that an automobile will run over him. Thus, constant vigilance to protect a child from accidents would no longer be necessary. See Figure 4-4.

Because of viewphones (videophones), automatic reordering, automatic deliveries to the home, computers keeping track of deliveries and bank accounts, etc., most routine shopping by housewives as we know it could be eliminated. Even home-catered meals on a routine basis would become practical.

Because the mother would only be a few minutes away from her children, no matter where they are in the city, it would be easy for each to find the other in case of trouble. This would probably mean that the housewife-mother would be less inclined to worry and more inclined (than she is now) to place her children in kindergartens and nurseries. With greater free time the housewife mother would probably take on a part- or full-time job. In brief, the occupation of housewife-mother might disappear, in time.

17.6 Dining Out and Other Metropolitan Recreations

Restaurants and Catering Services

In Compact City, because peak loads would be replaced by round-the-clock activities, the size of restaurants could be smaller and yet these would never be crowded; they could be conveniently close and always open. Small restaurants with differing decor, entertainment, and specialities could dot the city and become favorite meeting places. When planning to dine out, before going to the restaurant, one could place an order over the viewphone. The menu could be displayed and the diner could make his selections with a light-pen.

Because of the compactness of the city, it would be practical to have several speciality kitchens where food would be cooked and then dispatched for "assembly" into a complete meal at the restaurant. Thus an order for roast beef would be dispatched from a centrally located roast beef kitchen, to arrive in a few minutes at a Core restaurant. Speciality chefs could prepare the roasts. The high volume of patronage at restaurants would make it practical to use fresh foods instead of canned and frozen foods. In the specialized kitchens, foods could be cooked continuously in small batches; hence, loss would be minimal and waste products could be recycled more efficiently because they could be treated in larger, more homogeneous quantities.

Recreation, Parks, Sports

The interior open space could be lined with benches and cafes where people could sit and watch the passing parade. See Figure 17-1. Those interested in parlor games, chess, bridge, or poker would find it easy to get to various clubs interspersed throughout the city. Alternatively, one could go to a concert to a theater, or to a sporting event.

In the parks surrounding Compact City and in the park above it, the usual types of outdoor activities would be possible: picnicking, bird-watching, rowing, sports. Access to outside parks would take only a few minutes. See Figures 3-2 and 17-2.

Many of the trends in life styles which we have just outlined are changes that might take place in any future city whether compact or not. It is interesting to interpret these trends in terms of their effect on human culture.

17.7 The Effect of Compact City on Human Culture

Culture is a combination of factors rooted in man's biological origin which drive him to communicate. Conversely, communication, which to some extent characterizes the totality of human group activities, can be used to define culture. There are aspects of culture that can enhance man's creative activity and his ability to communicate with others; it can increase his satisfaction and fulfillment. Culture also can and does have aspects which tend to diminish man. The deleterious effects that ghetto life can have on people reminds one of a saying by Albert Schweitzer: "The tragedy of life is what dies inside a man while he lives."

In his book, *The Silent Language,* the anthropologist Edward T. Hall has focused on the ten primary message systems (of which only the first is linguistic) that characterize culture.[7] These are listed below.

Our objective now is to evaluate formally how these ten aspects of culture might be affected by a Compact City environment.

1. *Interaction through language.* In general, interaction with the environment and with other forms of life is the first moving force of all living organisms. It is hard to imagine that life could exist without some form of dynamic behavior that produces interaction between organisms and creates irritation or stimulation. For man, his ability to communicate through abstract linguistic symbols (words) with others provides a powerful form of interaction.

   Improved means of verbal and visual communication has proved to be both a blessing and a curse. On the one hand it has brought information about the whole world to one's door. On the other, it has created the additional problem (at least for some of us) of making it necessary to reduce the flow of information and to screen out that which is unwanted.

   Communication with many people simultaneously through writing, pictures, and motion pictures, or more quickly with radio or television is a reality. In future cities, however, people will also interact with various automatic machines (rather than with other people), by using language suitable for such devices. This will probably profoundly affect the social structure. For example, the connection of videophones to computers can create new information sources, and these can be expected to change the way we do routine shopping. The role of secretaries in offices will change since letters will be composed on consoles, displayed, edited, and reproduced without delay. Today many business undertakings must first go through a "paper world" phase in which such things as writing out an order, obtaining approval to write a check, filing an application, and so on, are all done on paper. It is probable that most of this will be bypassed in the future or will at least be steps delegated to computers, which will communicate with mechanized data files without directly involving people.

2. *Association* is the bringing together of units of life to form higher and more complex units. By this process groups, organizations, even countries, are formed in which patterns of association develop, which encompass everyone, from leader to follower. Walking instead of driving in Compact City will foster more local community association. The compactness of the city will make it possible for people to participate in a wider variety of activities that interest them.

3. *Subsistence* is the elaborate process, ranging from the economic life of a nation to the job of an individual, by which people obtain food and other basic needs. Different cultural habits have evolved around the purpose that we ascribe to life and the associated idea of having to work hard to earn a living.

Figure 17-1 THE CORE EDGE SHOPPING MALL
The Core Edge would have roads, ramps, parking facilities, fountains, gardens, and special exhibits.

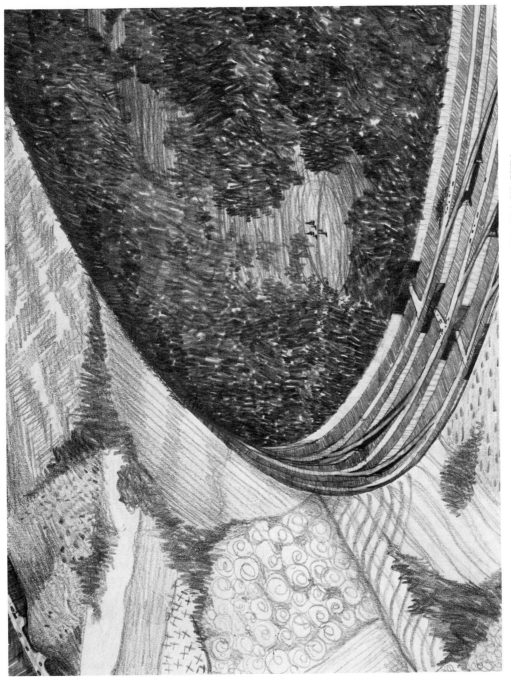

Figure 17-2 IN ONE MINUTE YOU COULD BE ON THE PARK-ROOF OF COMPACT CITY
In five minutes, you could be in the country.

Perhaps soon it will become evident to all that being made to grub for the basic necessities belongs to the past. Machines are already doing most of the work and people are merely button pushers. Certain fundamental jobs will remain, of course, but the concept of having to work hard to earn a basic living will become less and less true. Hence, the whole purpose of work could undergo radical change.

4. *Sexuality* describes the process of communication in which sexual roles and physical contact are the media of expression. Strong cultural differences have grown around sexual reproduction and sexual communication as a means of pleasure.

  Many of the customs of society with regard to family life and sex life have their origin historically in the need to protect children until they are old enough to be independent. The continuous sexual receptivity of the human female, as contrasted with the cyclical sexual receptiveness of other female animals, according to one theory of evolution, arose because it had the effect of keeping the old boy around to help protect, and therefore to raise, the children. In a compact urban environment it would be easier for parents to work and yet never be far from their children. This, coupled with the availability of birth control devices and the trend towards "women's liberation," could greatly affect traditional family structure.

5. *Territoriality* is the assertion of possessiveness for a certain space, for certain objects, and even for life (to the degree that one is possessive about one's family). Pride in development of the city could become an important manifestation of territoriality in a new city's culture.

6. *Temporality* is the dependence of man in all cultures upon time as it manifests itself in the cycles of the seasons, the phases of the moon, the heartbeat, the performance of tasks, etc. Obviously if Compact City establishes a continuous time cycle, temporality as we know it today will be changed profoundly.

7. *Learning* plays a vital role as an agent of culture. It is an instrument by means of which experience and abstractions of experience are passed on between the generations. With machines doing more and more of the essential work, it is clear that in the future our population will turn to other pursuits. Of these education and research could play a dominant role not only for children but for adults as well. Computers— programmed learning—will probably be extensively used in the future for education.

8. *Play* is used as a technique for seeking diversity, simulated experience, competition and sport, laughter, or even as a method of hiding vulnerabilities. The decreased need to do essential work will also bring about a greater emphasis on

sports, various other forms of competition (of which chess is one example), as well as exhibits, theater, parties, etc.

9. *Defense* is a means of protection against both external hostile forces and against possible threats from society and even from the self. Medicine is a form of defense, law enforcement is another, and military force is yet another. Undoubtedly the high vulnerability of modern society would be reflected in the way Compact City would seek to protect itself. Protection of facilities would of necessity take the form of back-up systems. Special repair units would be organized. The use of noninflammable or nontoxic materials would be encouraged. Evacuation and emergency procedures would be made part of the educational process.

10. *Exploitation* of available resources and of other people to enhance the fulfillment of individual and group needs is characteristic of man in his effort to optimize the use of his energy and the natural resources available to him. However, a culture should not be totally judged by its ability to exploit man and matter. Some of the cultural elements mentioned above require the pursuit of other things to obtain satisfaction — such as the exploration of new ideas! Thus a decrease both in materialism and in the need to work to obtain necessities could have a profound effect on society. *Our present society forces people either to work or suffer a low economic status.* Companies have complicated rules about what happens to people who are late for "work" or don't keep "busy." Money is allocated to exploit people's time in various ways and to show people who is boss or who has the power. *Congress taxes the "surplus energy" of a people and channels the funds to dictate where people must redirect their energies. In the final analysis this is a form of exploitation, because, with machines doing more and more of the work, it does not matter much what new activities people choose to do as long as they do no harm to one another.* There is a possibility that exploitation in Compact City could be rechannelled into *exploiting new ideas.* For example, finding new uses for computers, hormones, and drugs, for propulsion and communication in space, for developing better techniques for miniaturization, for obtaining energy from the sun, for building new cities and finding ways to increase the standards of living everywhere in the world.

Notes and References

1. Dennis Gabor, *Inventing the Future,* Knopf (New York, 1964), 237 pages.
2. Erich Fromm, *The Sane Society,* Fawcett (Greenwich, Conn., 1955), 320 pages.

3. S. P. Mathur and R. Stewart (Editors), *Beneficial Uses of Thermal Discharges,* New York State Department of Environmental Conservation (Albany, N.Y., 1970). (Conference held September 17–18, 1970).

4. For a general survey of computers and information handling, read the September 1966 issue of *Scientific American,* devoted to the topic "Information." Reprinted in *Information: A Scientific American Book,* W. H. Freeman and Company (San Francisco, 1966), 218 pages. See also by John McCarthy, "The Thinking Computer," *Stanford Today,* Spring 1968, pages 13–17.

5. John McCarthy, *op. cit.*

6. John McCarthy, *op. cit.* Also F. G. Heath, "Large-Scale Integration in Electronics," *Scientific American,* February 1970, pages 22–31. A discussion of how thousands of circuit elements can now be simultaneously made on a single "chip" (160,000 per square inch).

7. Edward T. Hall, *The Silent Language,* Doubleday (Garden City, N.Y., 1959), 240 pages.

FINALE

This book will have achieved its objective if the reader begins to ask himself questions: Where should Compact City be located? How can society make the transition from present flat, predominantly two-dimensional cities to four-dimensional cities in which vertical space and time are exploited. Will building compact cities cause a business boom? Will people in all strata of society want to move to Compact City? What will happen to present suburbs if Compact City is built near an existing city? Can Compact City be built in the middle of Manhattan? Will it solve the problem of dying inner cities?

The design of Compact City originally began with a simple theme —namely that of arranging our urban areas vertically to reduce travel time. But soon it became a study in organized complexity. It began not so much as a study of how people actually *do* live, work, and die in our present cities, but a vision of how they *might* live, how they might work in a city of the future.

We have spoken of many things: how the construction of a new city in the 1970s is practical; how elimination of the day and night cycle can even out the use of facilities, avoid peaks and congestions, reduce the lapsed time to complete projects, and can result in efficient utilization of capital goods and facilities; how the use of the vertical dimension saves land and time and could, under certain arrangements, bring the community together again; and, how building the city might mean an escape to a new life and opportunity for the underprivileged.

Throughout the book we developed the theme of *total-system models* and pointed out how these can lead to a design of a city that can effectively recycle its wastes, conserve resources, and bring about a good balance with the ecosystem. The resulting city would cost less, be more spacious, and provide a better environment for children. Compact City would be safer and more convenient than conventional cities, and would enable the individual to become more involved with the activities of his fellow man and yet remain close to nature.

THE ULTIMATE GOAL IS A RICHER QUALITY OF LIFE

SUPPLEMENTARY
READING

The readings below, which have been selected to supplement the basic references at the end of each chapter, are arranged under the following topics, and each topical heading is followed with a reference to relevant discussions in *Compact City*: (1) Urban sprawl, (2) Conservation, (3) Predictions about the future, (4) Why we must plan the future, (5) Human behavior, (6) Man and his city, (7) Slums, (8) Objectives of urban planning, (9) Proposed new cities, (10) Urban planning: ideas and practices, (11) On optimum urban development, (12) Utopias, (13) Transportation in cities, (14) Energy, (15) Recycling, and (16) Health.

1. Urban Sprawl (Chapters 1, 7)

Beaujeu-Garnier, J., and G. Chabot, *Urban Geography*, John Wiley and Sons, New York, 1967, 470 pages.

Carrothers, Gerald A. P., "A Historical Review of the Gravity and Potential Concepts of Human Interaction," *Journal of the American Institute of Planners*, Vol. 22, 1956, pp. 94–102.

Chapin, Francis Stuart, Jr., "Selected Theories of Urban Growth and Structure," *Journal of the American Institute of Planners*, Vol. 30, 1964, pp. 51–58.

Coale, Ansley J., "Man and His Environment," *Science*, Vol. 170, No. 3954, 1970, pp. 132–136.

Davis, Kingsley, "The Urbanization of the Human Population," *Scientific American*, Vol. 213, No. 3, 1965, pp. 40–53. (Available as Offprint No. 659, W. H. Freeman and Company, San Francisco.)

Doxiadis, C. A., "Ekistics, The Science of Human Settlements," *Science*, Vol. 170, No. 3956, 1970, pp. 393–404.

Ehrlich, Paul R., *The Population Bomb*, Ballantine Books, New York, 1968. 223 pages.

Ehrlich, Paul R., and Anne H. Ehrlich, *Population, Resources, Environment*, Second edition, W. H. Freeman and Company, San Francisco, 1972. 383 pages.

Gottmann, Jean, *Megalopolis, The Urbanized Northeastern Seaboard of the United States*, The Twentieth Century Fund, New York, 1961, 810 pages.

Kirschenbaum, Alan B., "Patterns of Migration from Metropolitan to Non Metropolitan Areas: Changing Ecological Factors Affecting Family Mobility," *Rural Sociology*, Vol. 36, No. 3, 1971, pp. 315–325.

Murphy, Raymond E., *The American City, An Urban Geography*, McGraw-Hill, New York, 1966, 464 pages.

Singer, S. F., *Is There an Optimum Level of Population?*, McGraw-Hill, New York, 1971, 426 pages. See in particular the paper by Manfred Kochen: "On Determining the Optimum Size of New Cities."

Taylor, Gordon Rattray, *The Doomsday Book: Can the World Survive?*, Book Club Associates, London, 1972. 285 pages.

von Eckardt, Wolf, The Challenge of Megalopolis, The Macmillan Co., New York, 1964, 126 pages. A graphic presentation based on Jean Gottmann's *Megalopolis*.

"World Population Projections, 1965–2000." *Population Bulletin*, Vol. 21, No. 4, 1965.

2. Conservation (Chapter 9)

Carson, Rachel Louise, *The Silent Spring*, Hougton Mifflin, Boston, 1962. 368 pages.

McInnis, Noel F., and Richard L. Heiss, *Can Man Care for the Earth*, Abingdon Press, Nashville, 1971. 119 pages. A potpourri of essays, poems, fables, and scriptures that illustrate the religious questions raised by pollution. Robert Theobald, Stewart Udall, Buckminister Fuller are among those quoted.

Udall, Stewart L., *The Quiet Crisis*, Holt, Rinehart, and Winston, New York, 1963, 209 pages.

Whyte, William Hollingsworth, *The Last Landscape*, Doubleday, Garden City (N.Y.), 1968. 376 pages.

3. Predictions about the Future (Chapters 1, 7, 8, 9; Part Three)

Beckwith, Burnham Putman, *The Next 500 Years*, Exposition Press, New York, 1968.

Brown, Harrison, *The Challenge of Man's Future*, The Viking Press, New York, 1956.

Calder, Nigel, *The World in 1984*, Vols. I and II, Penguin Books, Baltimore, 1968. The study states there will be a vast growth in cities; Calcutta, for example, may possibly grow to a population of 30 million; furthermore, there will be much turmoil around cities. See Vol. 1, Table C, "Conflicts and Choices."

Drucker, Peter F., *The Age of Discontinuity: Guidelines to Our Changing Society*, Harper and Row, New York, 1969.

Eells, R., and C. Walton, eds., *Man in the City of the Future, A Symposium of Urban Philosophies*, Collier-Macmillan International, London, 1968.

Ewald, William R., Jr., ed., *Environment for Man; The Next Fifty Years*, Indiana University Press, Bloomington (Ind.), 1967. 308 pages.

Fuchs, Victor Robert, "The First Service Economy: The New Society—I," *The Public Interest*, Winter, 1966. The United States has become the first nation in which more than half of the employed population was not involved in production.

Hellman, Harold, *The City in the World of the Future*, M. Evans and Co., New York, 1970. 186 pages.

Helmer, Olaf, "Science," *Science Journal*, Vol. 3, No. 10, 1967, pp. 49–53. By the end of the century there may be 25 million scientists and technologists in the world. Their productivity may have at least doubled and their motto may be "science for society's sake." Among the major scientific breakthroughs that can be expected by then will be the creation of artifical life and limited forms of weather control.

"Une Image de la France en l'an 2000: scénario de l'inacceptable," Documentation Francaise, July 1971. (29–31 quai Voltaire 7e, Paris, France.)

Kahn, Herman, and A. J. Wiener, *The Year 2000*, The Macmillan Co., New York, 1967. A framework for speculation about the next 33 years.

Landsberg, Hans H., Leonard L. Fischman, and Joseph L. Fisher, *Resources in American's Future*, The Johns Hopkins University Press, Baltimore, 1963.

Mayer, Albert, *The Urgent Future: People, Housing, City, Region*, McGraw-Hill, New York, 1967. 184 pages.

McHale, John, *The Future of the Future*, George Braziller, Inc., New York, 1969. McHale foresees the development of a single world community.

Mumford, Lewis, *The Urban Prospect*, Harcourt, Brace and World, Inc., New York, 1968. 255 pages.

Perloff, Harvey S., ed., *The Quality of the Urban Environment*, The Johns Hopkins University Press, Baltimore, 1969. 332 pages. Essays on "new resources in an urban age." The paper "The Value of Urban Land" by Edwin S. Mille uses an analytical model.

Schurr, Sam H., ed., *Energy, Economic Growth, and the Environment*, published for Resources for the Future, Inc., by The Johns Hopkins University Press, Baltimore, 1971, 232 pages.

Simac, Clifford D., *City*, Ace Books, New York, 1952, 255 pages. This science fiction book predicts that by 1986 cities will have become anachronisms that have outlived their usefulness. Hydroponics, helicopters, compact atomic energy units, and good communications will cause the downfall of cities. See description of the "non city" in our Section 13.3.

Veblen, Thorstein, *The Theory of the Leisure Class*, The Macmillan Co., New York, 1908. New edition, Viking Press, New York, 1931, 404 pages.

4. Why We Must Plan the Future (Chapters 1, 8, 9)

Fuller, R. Buckminster, *Utopia or Oblivion: The Prospects for Humanity*, Bantam Matrix Editions, Bantam Books, New York, 1969.

Gabor, Dennis, *Inventing the Future*, Alfred A. Knopf, New York, 1964. 237 pages.

Lineberry, W. P. (ed.), *Priorities for Survival*, H. W. Wilson, New York, 1973. 223 pp.

Ramo, Simon, *Cure for Chaos*, David McKay Company, Inc., New York, 1969.

Supplementary
Readings

Fromm, Erich, *The Sane Society,* Holt, Rinehart, and Winston, New York, 1955. Reprinted by Fawcett, Greenwich (Conn.) 1969. 320 pages. Discusses the customs that we have dubbed "cicadian" rhythm.

Hall, Edward Twitchell, *The Silent Language,* Doubleday, Garden City (N.Y.), 1959. 240 pages.

Toffler, Alvin, *Future Shock,* Bantam Books, New York, 1971.

6. Man and His City (Chapters 1, 2, 17)

Abrams, Charles, *The City Is the Frontier,* Harper Colophon Books, Harper and Row, New York, 1967. 394 pages.

Anderson, Nels, *The Urban Community, A World Perspective,* Holt, Rinehart, and Winston, New York, 1959, 500 pages.

Blumenfeld, Hans, *The Modern Metropolis: Its Origins, Growth, Characteristics, and Planning,* M.I.T. Press, Cambridge (Mass.), 1967. 377 pages. Selected essays in this book are edited by Paul D. Spreiregen.

"Cities," a special topic issue, *Scientific American,* Vol. 213, No. 3, September, 1965.

Eldredge, H. Wentworth (ed.), *Taming Megalopolis,* Doubleday-Anchor, Garden City (N.Y.), 1967. Two volumes, 1166 pages.

Eliot, T. S., "The Rock" (1934). In *T. S. Eliot, Complete Poems and Plays, 1909–1950,* Harcourt, Brace, Inc., New York, 1952. Page 101.

Geddes, Patrick, *Cities in Evolution,* revised edition, Williams and Norgate, London, 1949. 241 pages.

Glazer, Nathan, *Cities in Trouble,* Quadrangle Books-The New York Times Co., Chicago, 1970, 276 pages.

Goodman, Paul, and Percival Goodman, *Communitas, Ways of Livelihood and Means of Life,* 2nd edition, Vintage Books, New York, 1960. 248 pages.

Gordon, Mitchell, *Sick Cities,* Penguin Books, Baltimore, 1966. 444 pages.

Gunther, John, *Twelve Cities,* Harper and Row, New York, 1969. 370 pages.

Gutkind, Erwin Anton, *International History of City Development,* Vol. VI; *Urban Development in Western Europe: The Netherlands and Great Britain,* Free Press, New York, 1971.

Jacobs, Jane, *The Death and Life of Great American Cities,* Random House, New York, 1961. 458 pages.

Keller, Suzanne Infeld, *The Urban Neighborhood: A Sociological Perspective,* Random House, New York, 1968.

Lynch, Kevin, "The City as an Environment," *Scientific American,* Vol. 213, No. 3, 1965, pp. 209–219.

Moholy-Nagy, Sibyl, *Matrix of Man: An Illustrative History of Urban Environment,* Praeger, New York, 1968. 317 pages.

Panel of Science and Technology, *Science and Technology and the Cities.* U.S. Govt. Printing Office, Washington, D.C. 1969, 126 pages. Papers prepared for the 10th Meeting of the Panel of Science and Technology, U.S. House of Representatives, by: C. A. Doxiadis, "Ekistics"; A. Spilhaus, "Technology, Living Cities, and Human Environment"; R. Llewelyn-Davies, "New Cities—A British Example: Milton Keynes"; M. M. Webber, and S. Angel, "The Social Context of Transportation Policy"; W. W. Seifert, "Transportation Development—A National Challenge."

Toynbee, Arnold, ed., *Cities of Destiny,* McGraw-Hill, New York, 1967. 376 pages.

Tunnard, Christopher, *The Modern American City*, D. Van Nostrand, New York, 1968.

Tzonis, Sergius J., and Alexander Tzonis, *Shape of Community*, Penguin Books, Baltimore, 1971. 247 pages.

Vernon, Raymond, *The Myth and Reality of Our Urban Problems*, Harvard University Press, Cambridge (Mass.) 1966. 90 pages. A publication of the Joint Center for Urban Studies of M.I.T. and Harvard Universities.

Warren, Roland L. (ed.), *Perspectives on the American Community*, Rand McNally, Chicago, 1966, 618 pages.

"What Makes a City Great," *Time Magazine*, Vol. 94, No. 20, 1969, pp. 47–48.

Wilson, James Q. (ed.), *The Metropolitan Enigma*, Harvard University Press, Cambridge (Mass.), 1968, 392 pages.

7. Slums (Chapter 6)

Anderson, Martin, *The Federal Bulldozer: A Critical Analysis of Urban Renewal, 1949–1962*, The M.I.T. Press, Cambridge (Mass.), 1964. 272 pages.

Grodzins, Morton, "Metropolitan Segregation," *Scientific American*, Vol. 197, No. 4, 1957, pp. 33–41.

Taeuber, Karl E., "Residential Segregation," *Scientific American*, Vol. 213, No. 2, 1965. pp. 12–19. Available as Offprint No. 626, W. H. Freeman and Co., San Francisco.

Taeuber, Karl E., and Alma F. Taeuber, *Negroes in Cities: Residential Segregation and Neighborhood Change*, Aldine Publishing Co., Chicago, 1965. 284 pages.

Weaver, Robert Clifton, "Non-white Population Movements and Urban Ghettos," *Phylon* (Atlanta University, Atlanta, Georgia), Vol. 20, No. 3, Fall 1969, pp. 235–241.

8. Objectives of Urban Development (Chapters 1, 2, 8, 9, 10)

Anderson, Stanford, ed., *Planning for Diversity and Choice: Possible Futures and Their Relations to the Man-Controlled Environment*, M.I.T. Press, Cambridge (Mass.), 1968. 340 pages.

Elias, Claude E., Jr., James Gillies, Svend Riemer, *Metropolis: Values in Conflict*, Wadsworth Pub. Co., Belmont, Calif., 1964.

Goldwin, Robert A., *A Nation of Cities*, Rand McNally, Chicago, 1968, 128 pages. Contains essays by J. Q. Wilson, A. J. Glass, I. Kristol, John T. Howard, D. J. Elazer, H. V. Jaffa, as well as President Johnson's Message to Congress on Demonstration Cities Program of 1966.

Jacobs, Jane, *The Economy of Cities*, Random House, New York, 1969. 268 pages.

9. Proposed New Cities (Chapter 2)

Breckenfeld, Vivian Gurney, *Columbia and the New Cities*, Ives Washburn Pub., New York, 1971. 332 pages.

Goodman, Paul, and Percival Goodman, *Communitas, Ways of Livelihood and Means of Life*, 2nd edition, Vintage Press, New York, 1960. 248 pages. The Goodmans discuss conurbation and greenbelt culture, and propose a compact core arrangement for downtowns of cities.

Gruen, Victor, *The Heart of Our Cities: The Urban Crisis—Diagnosis and Cure,* Simon and Schuster, New York, 1967. 368 pages. Gruen advances a proposal for satellite cities.

Gutnov, Alexei, A. Baburov, G. Djumenton, S. Kharitonova, I. Levava, and S. Sadovskij, Renée Neu Watkins (translator), *The Ideal Communist City,* (1971), George Braziller, Pub., New York, 166 pages. Translated from the Italian text, *Idee per la Città Communista.*

Howard, Ebenezer, *Garden Cities of Tomorrow.* Reprinted by M.I.T. Press, Cambridge (Mass.), 1965. Original edition published in 1898.

Safdie, Moshe, *Beyond Habitat,* M.I.T. Press, Cambridge (Mass.), 1970. 244 pages.

Soleri, Paolo, *Arcology, The City in the Image of Man,* M.I.T. Press, Cambridge (Mass.), 1969. 122 pages. The book presents a series of pictorial sketches illustrating basic principles as well as several ways to develop a fully three-dimensional urban environment.

Spilhaus, Athelstan, "The Experimental City." The Daedalus Library, Vol. 15, Fall 1967. In Roger Revelle and Hans H. Landsberg, eds., *America's Changing Environment.* Houghton-Mifflin, Boston, 1970, pp. 219–231. Three hundred thirty thousand dollars have been allocated for defining the project. The first-year work was carried out at the University of Minnesota. This project was the subject of a report in *Science,* Vol. 159, No. 3816, February 16, 1968, pages 710–715.

Sweet, David C., ed., *Models of Urban Structure,* Lexington Books, Lexington (Mass.), 1972. 252 pages.

Wright, Frank Lloyd, *The Living City,* Mentor, Horizon Press, New York, 1958. 222 pages. In this book Wright recommends decentralized cities as the solution to the problem of urban sprawl.

10. Urban Planning: Ideas and Practices (Chapter 8)

Journals:
Architectural Forum,
Town Planning Review,
Journal of the American Institute of Architects

Bacon, Edmund N., *Design of Cities,* Viking Press, New York, 1967. 296 pages.

Branch, Melville C., *Comprehensive Urban Planning: A Selective Annotated Bibiliography with Related Materials,* Sage Publications, Beverly Hills (Calif.), 1970. 477 pages.

Goodman, William I., and Eric C. Freund, eds., *Principles and Practice of Urban Planning,* 4th edition, International City Managers Association, Washington, D.C., 1966. 621 pages.

11. On Optimum Urban Development (see Chapters 8, 13)

Ben-Shahar, Haim, A. Mazor, and D. Pines, "Town-Planning the Welfare Maximation: A Methodological Approach," in *Regional Studies,* Vol. 3, pp. 105–113, Pergamon Press, London, 1969.

Chapin, Francis Stuart, Jr., *Urban Land Use Planning,* 2nd edition, University of Illinois Press, Urbana (Ill.), 1965.

Dantzig, George B., *Linear Programming and Extensions,* Princeton University Press, Princeton, (N.J.), 1963. 632 pages.

Doxiadis, C. A., Ekistics, *An Introduction to the Science of Human Settlements,* Oxford University Press, New York, 1968. 527 pages.

Forrester, Jay Wright, *Urban Dynamics,* M.I.T. Press, Cambridge (Mass.), 1969, 285 pages. Models like Forrester's — but more elaborate — are urgently needed to predict the future state of the world, nations, regions, and cities, and to predict the outcomes of various proposed plans on these states.

Forrester, Jay Wright, *World Dynamics,* Wright-Allen Press, Cambridge (Mass.), 1971. 142 pages.

Harris, Britton, "Plan or Projection: An Examination of the Use of Models in Planning," *Journal of the American Institute of Planners,* Vol. 26, No. 4, 1960, pp. 265–272.

House, Peter William, "City I: Urban Systems Simulations: Player's Manual," Washington Center for Metropolitan Studies, Washington, D.C., October 1968. 26 pages.

Isard, Walter, et al., *Methods of Regional Analysis,* Wiley, New York, 1960. 784 pages.

Mason, Edward Sagendorph, "The Planning of Development," *Scientific American,* Vol. 209, No. 3, 1963, p. 235–244.

McLoughlin, J. Brian, *Urban and Regional Planning,* Faber and Faber, London, 1969. 331 pages.

Moore, Gary T., *Emerging Methods of Environmental Design,* M.I.T. Press, Cambridge (Mass.), 1970.

Morse, Philip M., and Laura Bacon, eds., *Operations Research for Public Systems,* M.I.T. Press, Cambridge (Mass.), 1967. 212 pages.

Rogers, Andrei, *Matrix Methods in Urban and Regional Analysis,* Holden-Day, San Francisco, 1971. 508 pages.

Wheaton, William L. C., "Operations Research for Metropolitan Planning," *Journal of the American Institute of Planners,* Vol. 29, No. 4, 1963, pp. 250–259.

12. Utopias

Our book, *Compact City,* is a proposal to remodel urban settlements — what we call "man's house." Although this subject has been of some concern to those who have made various utopian proposals during the past 2,500 years to restructure society, it has not been central to the literature of utopias. The following are general references on utopian societies.

Andrews, Charles M. (intro. by), *Famous Utopias,* Tudor, New York, 1937.

Ferry, W. H., Michael Harrington, and F. L. Keegan, "Cacotopias and Utopias," paper published by the Center for the Study of Democratic Institutions, Santa Barbara (Calif.), February 1965.

Morley, Henry, ed., *Ideal Commonwealths,* George Routledge and Sons, Ltd., London, 1886.

Mumford, Lewis, *The Story of Utopias,* 1962 edition, Viking, New York. Original edition published 1922.

Skinner, Burrhus Frederic, *Walden II,* 1948. 1962 edition, Macmillan, New York, 320 pages.

We are grateful to Edith Balas for supplying the following list of classical utopian references and sources:

Plato, 428–348 B.C.: *Republic*

Aristotle, 383–322 B.C.: *Politica*

Plutarch: *Lycurgus* (100 A.D.)

Sir Thomas More: *Utopia* (1516)

Johann Valentin Andreae: *Christianopolis* (1619)

Pieter Breughel, the elder: painting "Eldorado" (1567)

Sir Francis Bacon: *New Atlantis* (1627)

Tommaso Campanella: *Civitas Solis* (City of the Sun), (1602)

Arouet Voltaire, 1694–1778: Paragraph on "Eldorado" in *Candide*

Thomas Spence: *Spensonia* (1795)

Robert Owen: *New View of Society; or, Essays on the Formation of Character* (1813–1814)

Charles Fourier, 1772–1837: *L'utopie phalansterienne*

Claude Henri Saint-Simon, 1760–1825: *L'industrie rende l'homme maître de la nature*

More recent utopias include Cabet's *Icarie* (1840), Hertzka's *Freeland* (1894), Thirion's *Neustria* (1901), and Herzl's *Altneuland* (1903).

13. Transportation in Cities (Chapter 4 and Section 13.4)

Burby, John, *The Great American Motion Sickness: Or Why You Can't Get There from Here*, Little, Brown and Co., Boston, 1971.

Doxiadis, C. A., "Man's Movement and His City," *Science*, Vol. 162, No. 3851, 1968, pp. 326–334.

Dyckman, John W., "Transportation in Cities," *Scientific American*, Vol. 213, No. 3, 1965, pp. 162–177.

Hamilton, W. F., II, and Dana K. Nance, "Systems Analysis of Urban Transportation," *Scientific American*, Vol. 221, No. 1, 1969, pp. 19–27.

Harris, Britton, *Transportation and Urban Goals, Goals for Urban Transportation*, Institute for Environmental Studies, University of Pennsylvania, 1967.

Meyer, John R., J. F. Kain, and M. Wohl, *The Urban Transportation Problem*, Harvard University Press, Cambridge (Mass.), 1965.

Oi, Walter Y., and Paul W. Shuldiner, *An Analysis of Urban Travel Demands*, Northwestern University Press, Evanston (Ill.), 1962. 281 pages.

Pell, Claiborne de B., *Megalopolis Unbound: The Supercity and the Transportation of Tomorrow*, Praeger, New York, 1966.

Pegrum, Dudley Frank, *Transportation; Economics and Public Policy*, Rev. edition, Richard D. Irwin, Inc., Homewood (Ill.), 1968. 680 pages.

Roggeveen, Vincent J., "Transportation Folklore Important to Systems Analysis," *Annals of Regional Science*, Vol. 1, No. 1, 1967, pp. 213–222.

U.K. Ministry of Transport, *Traffic in Towns*, Her Majesty's Stationery Office, London, 1963. 223 pages. A study of the long-term problems of traffic in urban areas.

U.S. Urban Transportation Administration, *Tomorrow's Transportation: New Systems for the Urban Future*, U.S. Government Printing Office, Washington, D. C., 1968. 100 pages.

Landsberg, H. H., and Sam H. Schurr, *Energy in the United States—Sources, Uses and Policy Issues,* Random House, New York, 1968.

"Energy and Power," a special topic issue, *Scientific American,* Vol. 224, No. 3, September 1971. Available as *Energy and Power,* W. H. Freeman and Co., San Francisco, 1971.

15. Recycling (Sections 4.7, 6.4, 6.5, 9.3, 11.3)

Buras, Nathan, *Scientific Allocation of Water Resources: Water Resource Development and Utilization—A Rational Approach,* American Elsevier, New York, 1972. 208 pages.

"Comprehensive Studies of Solid Waste Management," Sanitary Engineering Research Report No. 70-2, June 1970, University of California, Berkeley. Excellent review of research and the use of operations research methodology.

Kneese, Allen V., and Blair T. Bower, *Managing Water Quality: Economics, Technology, Institutions,* Published for Resources for the Future, Inc., by The John Hopkins University Press, Baltimore, 1968. 328 pages.

U.S. Department of Interior, Federal Water Pollution Administration, *A Primer on Waste Water Treatment,* U.S. Government Printing Office, Washington, D.C., 1969. (1969-0-335-309)

16. Health (Chapter 15)

Garfield, Sidney R., "The Delivery of Medical Care," *Scientific American,* Vol. 222, No. 4, 1970, pp. 15–23.

INDEX